HOUGHTON MIFFLIN

Science

 HOUGHTON MIFFLIN   BOSTON

Program Authors

William Badders
Director of the Cleveland Mathematics
and Science Partnership
Cleveland Municipal School District
Cleveland, Ohio

Douglas Carnine, Ph.D.
Professor of Education
University of Oregon
Eugene, Oregon

James Feliciani
Supervisor of Instructional
Media and Technology
Land O' Lakes, Florida

Bobby Jeanpierre, Ph.D.
Assistant Professor, Science Education
University of Central Florida
Orlando, Florida

Carolyn Sumners, Ph.D.
Director of Astronomy and Physical Sciences
Houston Museum of Natural Science
Houston, Texas

Catherine Valentino
Author-in-Residence
Houghton Mifflin
West Kingston, Rhode Island

Content Consultants

Dr. Robert Arnold
Professor of Biology
Colgate University
Hamilton, New York

Dr. Carl D. Barrentine
Associate Professor of Humanities
and Biology
University of North Dakota
Grand Forks, North Dakota

Dr. Steven L. Bernasek
Department of Chemistry
Princeton University
Princeton, New Jersey

Dennis W. Cheek
Senior Manager
Science Applications International
Corporation
Exton, Pennsylvania

Dr. Jung Choi
School of Biology
Georgia Tech
Atlanta, Georgia

Prof. John Conway
Department of Physics
University of California
Davis, California

Printed in the U.S.A.

ISBN 13: 978-0-618-49225-1

ISBN 10: 0-618-49225-9

4 5 6 7 8 9-DW-14 13 12 11 10 09 08 07

Content Consultants

Dr. Robert Dailey
Division of Animal and Veterinary Sciences
West Virginia University
Morgantown, West Virginia

Dr. Thomas Davies
IODP/USIO Science Services
Texas A & M University
College Station, Texas

Dr. Ron Dubreuil
Department of Biological Sciences
University of Illinois at Chicago
Chicago, Illinois

Dr. Orin G. Gelderloos
Professor of Biology
University of Michigan - Dearborn
Dearborn, Michigan

Dr. Michael R. Geller
Associate Professor, Department of Physics
University of Georgia
Athens, Georgia

Dr. Erika Gibb
Department of Physics
Notre Dame University
South Bend, Indiana

Dr. Fern Gotfried
Pediatrician
Hanover Township, New Jersey

Dr. Michael Haaf
Chemistry Department
Ithaca College
Ithaca, New York

Professor Melissa A. Hines
Department of Chemistry
Cornell University
Ithaca, New York

Dr. Jonathan M. Lincoln
Assistant Provost & Dean of Undergraduate Education
Bloomsburg University
Bloomsburg, Pennsylvania

Donald Lisowy
Wildlife Conservation Society
Bronx Zoo
Bronx, New York

Dr. Marc L. Mansfield
Department of Chemistry and Chemical Biology
Stevens Institute of Technology
Hoboken, New Jersey

Dr. Scott Nuismer
Department of Biological Sciences
University of Idaho
Moscow, Idaho

Dr. Suzanne O'Connell
Department of Earth and Environmental Sciences
Wesleyan University
Middletown, Connecticut

Dr. Kenneth Parsons
Assistant Professor of Meteorology
Embry-Riddle Aeronautical University
Prescott, Arizona

Betty Preece
Engineer and Physicist
Indialantic, Florida

Dr. Chantal Reid
Department of Biology
Duke University
Durham, North Carolina

Dr. Todd V. Royer
Department of Biological Sciences
Kent State University
Kent, Ohio

Dr. Kate Scholberg
Physics Department
Duke University
Durham, North Carolina

Dr. Jeffery Scott
Department of Earth, Atmospheric, and Planetary Sciences
Massachusetts Institute of Technology
Cambridge, Massachusetts

Dr. Ron Stoner
Professor Emeritus, Physics and Astronomy Department
Bowling Green State University
Bowling Green, Ohio

Dr. Dominic Valentino, Ph.D.
Professor, Department of Psychology
University of Rhode Island
Kingston, Rhode Island

Dr. Sidney White
Professor Emeritus of Geology
Ohio State University
Columbus, Ohio

Dr. Scott Wissink
Professor, Department of Physics
Indiana University
Bloomington, Indiana

Dr. David Wright
Department of Chemistry
Vanderbilt University
Nashville, Tennessee

Contents

How Living Things Function

UNIT B
Living Things in Their Environment

Contents

UNIT C Earth's Surface

UNIT D — The Earth in Space

Contents

UNIT E Matter

UNIT F — Energy and Change

Features

UNIT D

UNIT E

UNIT F

Using Your Textbook

The Nature of Science

In this section in the front of your book, you will be introduced to scientists and to ways of investigating science.

Units

The major sections of your book are units.

Unit Title is what the unit is about.

Chapters are part of a unit.

Independent Reading are books you can read on your own.

Discover! Information in this unit will help you answer this interesting question.

Chapters

Chapter Title tells what the chapter is about.

Lesson Preview gives information about each lesson.

Every lesson in your book has two parts.
Lesson Part 1: Investigate Activity

Why It Matters tells why the science you will learn in each lesson is important.

Inquiry Skill tells about the main inquiry skill for the Investigate activity.

Lesson 3

How Can Resources Be Conserved?

Why It Matters...
For most people, old milk containers are garbage. And they could be, if they are not reused. These boys used old milk containers to build a boat. Making new things from old materials saves resources.

PREPARE TO INVESTIGATE

Inquiry Skill
Compare When you compare two things, you observe how they are alike and different.

Materials
- 4 plastic bowls
- marking pen
- plastic-foam packing peanuts
- pieces of crumpled newspaper
- plastic bubble wrap
- cellulose packing peanuts
- water
- clock

Science and Math Toolbox
For steps 3 and 4, review **Measuring Elapsed Time** on page H13.

C58 • Chapter 7

Materials lists what you will need to conduct your investigation.

Science And Math Toolbox references additional information in your book to help with your investigation.

Procedure lists the steps you will follow to conduct your investigation.

Conclusion guides you in thinking about your investigation.

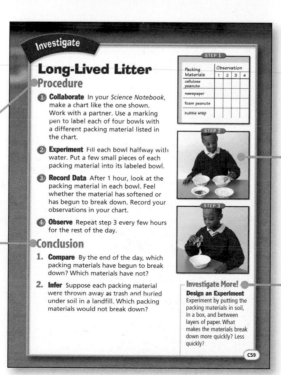

Investigate

Long-Lived Litter
Procedure

1. **Collaborate** In your *Science Notebook*, make a chart like the one shown. Work with a partner. Use a marking pen to label each of four bowls with a different packing material listed in the chart.

2. **Experiment** Fill each bowl halfway with water. Put a few small pieces of each packing material into its labeled bowl.

3. **Record Data** After 1 hour, look at the packing material in each bowl. Feel whether the material has softened or has begun to break down. Record your observations in your chart.

4. **Observe** Repeat step 3 every few hours for the rest of the day.

Conclusion

1. **Compare** By the end of the day, which packing materials have begun to break down? Which materials have not?

2. **Infer** Suppose each packing material were thrown away as trash and buried under soil in a landfill. Which packing materials would not break down?

STEP 1

Packing Materials	Observation			
	1	2	3	4
cellulose peanute				
newspaper				
foam peanute				
bubble wrap				

STEP 2

STEP 3

Investigate More!
Design an Experiment
Experiment by putting the packing materials in soil, in a box, and between layers of paper. What makes the materials break down more quickly? Less quickly?

C59

Visuals give more information about the investigation.

Investigate More! lets you take your investigation further.

Lesson Part 2: Learn by Reading

Vocabulary lists the new science words that you will learn.

Main Idea tells you what is important.

Visuals help you to understand the text.

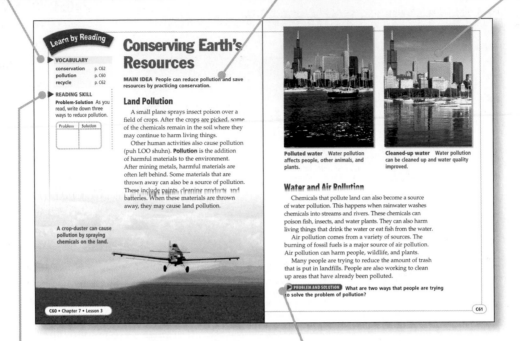

Reading Skill helps you understand and organize information as you read.

Reading Skill Check helps you check your understanding of the text.

Lesson Wrap-Up

Visual Summary shows you different ways to summarize what you've read.

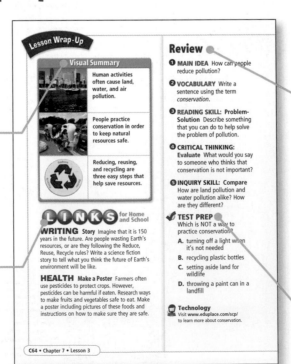

Links connects science to math and other subjects.

Review lets you check your understanding after you read.

Test Prep helps you meet standards. Standards are important goals for your learning.

Focus On

Focus On lets you learn more about a key concept in a chapter.

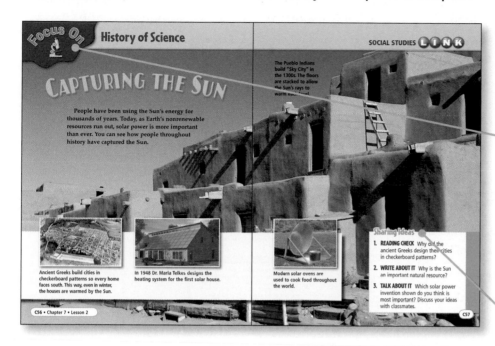

Focus On types include: Biography, History of Science, Technology, Primary Source, Literature, and Readers' Theater.

Sharing Ideas has you check your understanding and write and talk about what you have learned.

Extreme Science and Careers

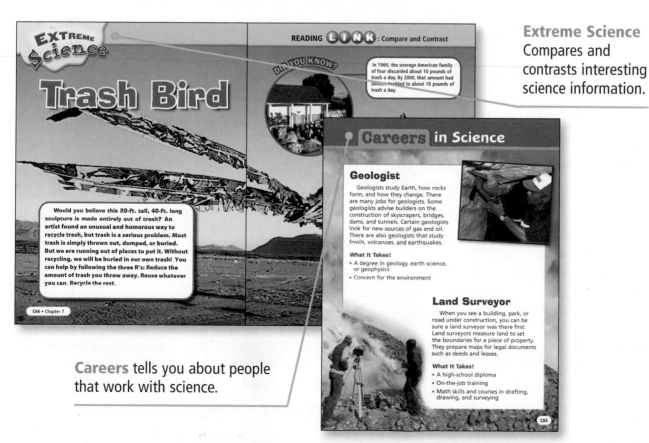

Extreme Science Compares and contrasts interesting science information.

Careers tells you about people that work with science.

Chapter and Unit Review and Test Prep

These reviews help you to know you are on track with learning science and reading standards.

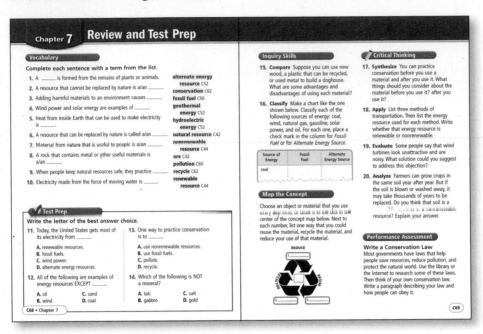

Chapter 7 Review and Test Prep

Vocabulary

Complete each sentence with a term from the list.

1. A _____ is formed from the remains of plants or animals.
2. A resource that cannot be replaced by nature is a/an _____.
3. Adding harmful materials to an environment causes _____.
4. Wind power and solar energy are examples of _____.
5. Heat from inside Earth that can be used to make electricity is _____.
6. A resource that can be replaced by nature is called a/an _____.
7. Material from nature that is useful to people is a/an _____.
8. A rock that contains metal or other useful materials is a/an _____.
9. When people keep natural resources safe, they practice _____.
10. Electricity made from the force of moving water is _____.

alternate energy
  resource C52
conservation C62
fossil fuel C50
geothermal
  energy C52
hydroelectric
  energy C52
natural resource C42
nonrenewable
  resource C44
ore C42
pollution C60
recycle C62
renewable
  resource C44

Test Prep

Write the letter of the best answer choice.

11. Today, the United States gets most of its electricity from _____.
   A. renewable resources.
   B. fossil fuels.
   C. wind power.
   D. alternate energy resources.

12. All of the following are examples of energy resources EXCEPT _____.
   A. oil   C. sand
   B. wind   D. coal

13. One way to practice conservation is to _____.
   A. use nonrenewable resources.
   B. use fossil fuels.
   C. pollute.
   D. recycle.

14. Which of the following is NOT a mineral?
   A. talc   C. salt
   B. gabbro   D. gold

C68 • Chapter 7

Inquiry Skills

15. **Compare** Suppose you can use new wood, a plastic that can be recycled, or used metal to build a doghouse. What are some advantages and disadvantages of using each material?

16. **Classify** Make a chart like the one shown below. Classify each of the following sources of energy: coal, wind, natural gas, gasoline, solar power, and oil. For each one, place a check mark in the column for *Fossil Fuel* or for *Alternate Energy Source*.

Source of Energy	Fossil Fuel	Alternate Energy Source
coal		

Map the Concept

Choose an object or material that you use every day. Print or draw it in the box in the center of the concept map below. Next to each number, list one way that you could reuse the material, recycle the material, and reduce your use of that material.

REDUCE

RECYCLE   REUSE

Critical Thinking

17. **Synthesize** You can practice conservation before you use a material and after you use it. What things should you consider about the material before you use it? after you use it?

18. **Apply** List three methods of transportation. Then list the energy resource used for each method. Write whether that energy resource is renewable or nonrenewable.

19. **Evaluate** Some people say that wind turbines look unattractive and are noisy. What solution could you suggest to address this objection?

20. **Analyze** Farmers can grow crops in the same soil year after year. But if the soil is blown or washed away, it may take thousands of years to be replaced. Do you think that soil is a _____ or a nonrenewable resource? Explain your answer.

Performance Assessment

Write a Conservation Law
Most governments have laws that help people save resources, reduce pollution, and protect the natural world. Use the library or the Internet to research some of these laws. Then think of your own conservation law. Write a paragraph describing your law and how people can obey it.

C69

Unit Wrap-Up

Learn more about the **Discover!** question that started the unit. Also find a link to a simulation on the EduPlace web site.

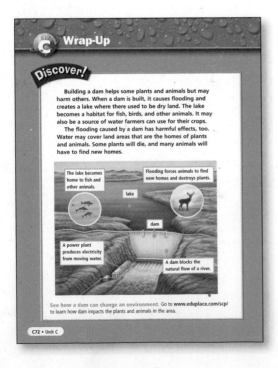

Wrap-Up

Discover!

Building a dam helps some plants and animals but may harm others. When a dam is built, it causes flooding and creates a lake where there used to be dry land. The lake becomes a habitat for fish, birds, and other animals. It may also be a source of water farmers can use for their crops.

The flooding caused by a dam has harmful effects, too. Water may cover land areas that are the homes of plants and animals. Some plants will die, and many animals will have to find new homes.

The lake becomes home to fish and other animals.

Flooding forces animals to find new homes and destroys plants.

lake

dam

A power plant produces electricity from moving water.

A dam blocks the natural flow of a river.

See how a dam can change an environment. Go to www.eduplace.com/scp/ to learn how dam impacts the plants and animals in the area.

C72 • Unit C

References

The back of your book includes sections you will refer to again and again.

Anteater, B36–B37
Ants, A48, B52
Index

A

ask questions (ask KWEHS chuhz) To state orally or in writing questions to find out how or why something happens, which can lead

Glossary

Health and Fitness Handbook

Science and Math Toolbox

Science and Math Toolbox

Using a Hand Lens H2
Making a Bar Graph H3
Using a Calculator H4
Making a Tally Chart H5
Using a Tape Measure or Ruler H6
Measuring Volume H7
Using a Thermometer H8
Using a Balance H9
Making a Chart to Organize Data H10
Reading a Circle Graph H11
Measuring Elapsed Time H12
Measurements H14

H1

The Nature of Science

Science is an adventure. People all over the world do science. You can do science, too. You probably already do.

National Science Education Standards

Science Content Standards

Grades K–4.A. ABILITIES NECESSARY TO DO SCIENTIFIC INQUIRY

- Ask a question about objects, organisms, and events in the environment.
- Plan and conduct a simple investigation.
- Employ simple equipment and tools to gather data and extend the senses.
- Use data to construct a reasonable explanation.
- Communicate investigations and explanations.

Grades K–4.A. UNDERSTANDINGS ABOUT SCIENTIFIC INQUIRY

- Scientific investigations involve asking and answering a question and comparing the answer with what scientists already know about the world.
- Scientists use different kinds of investigations depending on the questions they are trying to answer. Types of investigations include describing objects, events, and organisms; classifying them; and doing a fair test (experimenting).
- Simple instruments, such as magnifiers, thermometers, and rulers, provide more information than scientists obtain using only their senses.
- Scientists develop explanations using observations (evidence) and what they already know about the world (scientific knowledge). Good explanations are based on evidence from investigations.
- Scientists make the results of their investigations public; they describe the investigations in ways that enable others to repeat the investigations.
- Scientists review and ask questions about the results of other scientists' work.

Grades K–4.E. ABILITIES OF TECHNOLOGICAL DESIGN

- Identify a simple problem.
- Propose a solution.
- Implementing proposed solutions.
- Evaluate a product or design.
- Communicate a problem, design, and solution.

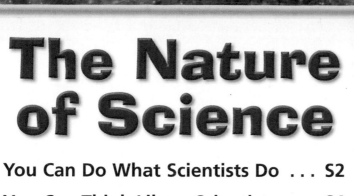

The Nature of Science

You Can...

Do What Scientists Do

Meet Dr. Paula Mikkelsen. She works at the American Museum of Natural History in New York City. She is In charge of the museum's collection of mollusks. The collection includes clamshells, snail shells, and the remains of slugs and squids. Dr. Mikkelsen helps other scientists find the mollusks they want to study.

Scientists ask questions. Then they answer them by investigating and experimenting.

In the Florida Keys, Dr. Mikkelsen has found 1,700 kinds of ocean mollusks. That number surprised her. It is three times the number other scientists predicted.

Dr. Mikkelsen has many questions about mollusks. For example, she wants to know how many kinds of mollusks live in the ocean around islands called the Florida Keys. To find out, she scuba dives to collect mollusks.

Back at the museum, Dr. Mikkelsen records the name of each new mollusk. Like all scientists, she keeps careful records of science information, or **data.**

Science investigations take many forms.

Dr. Mikkelsen collects animals to analyze. Other scientists make observations. Still others carry out experiments. Dr. Mikkelsen shares what she discovers with other scientists. They ask her questions about her data. Dr. Mikkelsen also shares her results with people in charge of protecting Florida wildlife. This helps them make decisions about how much scuba diving, boating, and fishing they can allow around the Keys.

Dr. Paula Mikkelsen uses tools such as these magnifying goggles to observe tiny mollusk shells.

Think Like a Scientist

The ways scientists ask and answer questions about the world around them is called **scientific inquiry.** Scientific inquiry requires certain attitudes, or ways of thinking. To think like a scientist you have to be:

- curious and ask a lot of questions.

- creative and think up new ways to do things.

- willing to listen to the ideas of others but reach your own conclusions.

- open to change what you think when your investigation results surprise you.

- willing to question what other people tell you.

What attracts the bee to the flower? Is it color, odor, or something else?

Use Critical Thinking

When you think critically you make decisions about what others tell you or what you read. Is what you heard or read fact or opinion? A *fact* can be checked to make sure it is true. An *opinion* is what you think about the facts.

Did anyone ever tell you a story that was hard to believe? When you think, "That just can't be true," you are thinking critically. Critical thinkers question what they hear or read in a book.

It looks like bees are attracted to certain flowers. I wonder if they use color, smell, or something else, to tell one flower from another?

I read that bees are attracted to flowers by their smell, but they identify different flowers by their color and shape.

Science Inquiry

Applying scientific inquiry helps you understand the world around you. Say you have decided to keep Triops, or tadpole shrimp.

Observe You watch the baby Triops swim around in their tank. You notice how they swim.

Ask a Question When you think about what you saw, heard, or read you may have questions.

Hypothesis Think about facts you already know. Do you have an idea about the answer? Write it down. That is your hypothesis.

Experiment Plan a test that will tell if the hypothesis is true or not. List the materials you will need. Write the steps you will follow. Make sure that you keep all conditions the same except the one you are testing. That condition is called the *variable.*

Conclusion Think about your results. What do they tell you? Did your results support your hypothesis or show it to be false?

Describe your experiment to others. Communicate your results and conclusion. You can use words, charts, or graphs.

My Triops Experiment

Observe Light appears to cause Triops to change how they move.

Ask a Question I wonder, do Triops like to swim more in the daytime or the nighttime?

Hypothesis If I watch the Triops in dim light and then in bright light they will move differently.

Experiment I'm going to observe how the Triops move in dim light. Then I'm going to turn on a light and observe any changes.

Conclusion When I turn on a bright light, the Triops speed up in the water. The results support my hypothesis. Triops are more active in bright light than in dim light.

Inquiry Process

Here is a process that some scientists follow to answer questions and make new discoveries.

```
Make Observations
        ↓
   Ask Questions
        ↓
    Hypothesize
        ↓
  Do an Experiment
        ↓
  Draw a Conclusion
       ↓        ↓
Hypothesis is   Hypothesis is
Supported       Not Supported
```

Science Inquiry Skills

You'll use many of these inquiry skills when you investigate and experiment.

- Ask Questions
- Observe
- Compare
- Classify
- Predict
- Measure

- Hypothesize
- Use Variables
- Experiment
- Use Models
- Communicate
- Use Numbers

- Record Data
- Analyze Data
- Infer
- Collaborate
- Research

Try It Yourself!

Experiment With a Matter Masher

To use the Matter Masher, put foam cubes or mini marshmallows in the bottle and screw on the cap. Then, push the top part of the cap up and down to pump air into the bottle.

1 Make a list of questions you have about the Matter Masher.

2 Think about how you could find out the answers.

3 Describe your experiment. If you did your experiment, what do you think the results would be?

You Can...

Be an Inventor

Jonathan Santos

His invention earned him his own trading card!

Jonathan Santos has been an inventor all his life. His first invention was a system of strings he used to switch off the lights without getting out of bed.

As a teenager, Jonathan invented a throwing toy called the J-Boom. He read about boomerangs. Then he planned his own toy with four arms instead of two. He built a sample, tried it out, and made improvements. Then he sold it in science museum gift shops.

Today, Jonathan works as a computer software engineer. He invents new ways to use computers. Jonathan is still inventing toys. His latest idea is a new kind of roller coaster!

"As a kid I quickly discovered that by using inventiveness you can design things and build things by using almost anything."

What Is Technology?

The tools people make and use and the things they build with tools are all **technology.** A wooden flying toy is technology. So is a space shuttle.

Scientists use technology, too. For example, a microscope makes it possible for them to see things that cannot be seen with just the eyes. They also use measurement tools to make their observations more exact.

Many technologies make the world a better place to live. But sometimes a technology that solves one problem can cause other problems. For example, riding in cars or buses makes it easier for people to travel long distances. But the fuel that powers cars and buses pollutes the air. Air pollution causes health problems for people and other living things.

A Better Idea

"I wish I had a better way to _____". How would you fill in the blank? Everyone wishes they could find a way to do their jobs more easily or have more fun. Inventors try to make those wishes come true. Inventing or improving an invention requires time and patience.

Many inventors have improved video game controllers. Maybe, someday, you will invent a new way to play video games.

Video Game Controller

joystick

buttons to choose actions

direction button

How to Be an Inventor

1. **Identify a problem.** It may be a problem at school, at home, or in your community.

2. **List ways to solve the problem.** Sometimes the solution is a new tool. Other times it may be a new way of doing an old job or activity.

3. **Choose the best solution.** Decide which idea will work best. Think about which one you can carry out.

4. **Make a sample.** A sample, called a *prototype*, is the first try. Your idea may need many materials or none at all. Choose measuring tools that will help your design work better.

5. **Try out your invention.** Use your prototype or ask some else to try it. Keep a record of how it works and what problems you find.

6. **Improve your invention.** Use what you learned to make your design work better. Draw or write about the changes you made and why you made them.

7. **Share your invention.** Show your invention to others. Explain how it works. Tell how it makes an activity easier or more fun. If it did not work as well as you wanted, tell why.

You Can...

Make Decisions

Troubles for Baby Turtles

Each spring adult female sea turtles come out of the ocean in the dark of night. They crawl onto sandy beaches and dig nest holes. They lay their eggs, cover them with sand, and slip back into the ocean.

A few weeks later, and all at once, the babies hatch and climb out of the nest. Attracted to nature's bright lights, the turtles should crawl toward the lights of the night sky shining on the ocean. But on many beaches, the lights from streetlights or houses are much brighter. The baby turtles crawl away from the ocean and toward the electric lights. Instead of finding their home in the sea, many of them die.

Deciding What to Do

How could you help save the most baby turtles?

Here's how to make your decision about the baby turtles. You can use the same steps to help solve problems in your home, in your school, and in your community.

Learn → Learn about the problem. Take the time needed to get the facts. You could talk to an expert, read a science book, or explore a web site.

List → Make a list of actions you could take. Add actions other people could take.

Decide → Think about each action on your list. Decide which choice is the best one for you or your community.

Share → Communicate your decision to others.

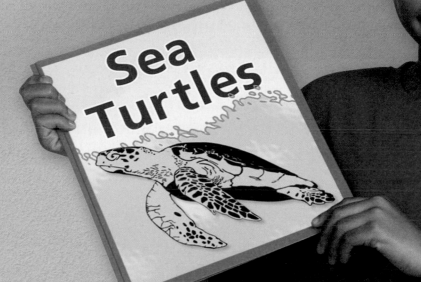

Sea Turtles

Science Safety

☑ Know the safety rules of your school and classroom and follow them.

☑ Read and follow the safety tips in each Investigation activity.

☑ When you plan your own investigations, write down how to keep safe.

☑ Know how to clean up and put away science materials. Keep your work area clean and tell your teacher about spills right away.

☑ Know how to safely plug in electrical devices.

☑ Wear safety goggles when your teacher tells you.

☑ Unless your teacher tells you to, never put any science materials in or near your ears, eyes, or mouth.

☑ Wear gloves when handling live animals.

☑ Wash your hands when your investigation is done.

Caring for Living Things

☑ Learn how to care for the plants and animals in your classroom so that they stay healthy and safe. Learn how to hold animals carefully.

LIFE SCIENCE

UNIT A

How Living Things Function

How Living Things Function

Independent Reading

Animals of the Past

The Animal Trackers

Follow Me, Be a Bee

Discover!

Dolphins and people differ in some ways. Dolphins have fins and flippers. People have arms and legs. But dolphins and people are alike in some ways. What traits do dolphins and people have in common? You will have the answer to this question by the end of the unit.

Chapter 1

Parts of Plants

Lesson Preview

LESSON 1

Carrots, radishes, turnips, and beets—what part of a plant are these vegetables?

Read about it in Lesson 1.

LESSON 2

Leaves, roots, and stems—how can these parts be used to identify plants?

Read about it in Lesson 2.

LESSON 3

From seeds in a tasty fruit to leaves shaped so they hold water—how do parts of plants help them survive in different environments?

Read about it in Lesson 3.

How Do Plants Use Their Parts?

Why It Matters...

Plants are living things that people use for many purposes. If you have ever enjoyed the shade of a tree on a warm day, then you have used plants. Plants provide people with food to eat, material for clothing and buildings, and many other items.

PREPARE TO INVESTIGATE

Inquiry Skill

Observe When you observe, you gather information about the environment using your senses of sight, hearing, smell, and touch.

Materials

- bean seed
- plastic bag with seal
- stapler
- paper towels
- water
- hand lens
- masking tape
- metric ruler

Science and Math Toolbox

For steps 2 and 3, review **Using a Hand Lens** on page H2.

Bean Bags

Procedure

STEP 1

1. **Collaborate** Work with a partner. Wet a paper towel until it is damp, but not dripping. Fold the paper towel and slide it into a plastic bag, as shown. Staple the bag about 2 cm from the bottom. Use a ruler to help you measure.

STEP 2

2. **Observe** Look closely at a bean seed with your hand lens. In your *Science Notebook*, draw a picture of the bean seed. Label the picture *Day 1.* Place the bean seed in the bag. Seal the bag.

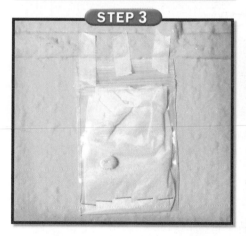

STEP 3

3. **Observe** Tape the bag so it hangs in a sunny spot. Use your hand lens to observe the bean seed each day. Draw and label a picture of the bean seed each day. Add water as needed to keep the paper towel damp.

4. **Research** After you have observed a change in the bean seed, use library books or the Internet to learn how to plant the bean seed in soil and care for it.

Conclusion

1. **Classify** Would you say that a bean seed is a living thing? Why or why not?

2. **Infer** Based on your observations, what does a bean seed need in order to sprout?

Investigate More!

Design an Experiment
Use scissors to cut off a small part of the bean plant. Use a hand lens to observe and draw the changes to the plant every day.

VOCABULARY

cell	p. A8
leaf	p. A8
nutrient	p. A7
plant	p. A6
root	p. A8
stem	p. A8

READING SKILL

Text Structure Read the headings at the top of each section. Write down an idea that you think you will read about in each section.

Plants Meet Their Needs

MAIN IDEA Plants use their parts to meet their basic needs.

Plants

Living things, or things that are alive, are found all over Earth. All of the living things on Earth can be separated into groups. Two groups of living things are plants and animals. A **plant** is a living thing that grows on land or in the water, cannot move from place to place, and usually has green leaves.

These sunflowers need sunlight and air to grow. They also need water and nutrients from soil.

The Needs of Plants

Humans and other animals need air to breathe, water to drink, and food to eat. Plants need certain things to live too. They need water, air, and sunlight. Most plants also need soil, which provides nutrients (NOO tree-uhnts). A **nutrient** is a substance that living things need to survive and grow.

▶ **TEXT STRUCTURE** What subheadings could have been used in the section called *The Needs of Plants*?

sunlight

water

air

soil

A7

Parts of Plants

Like animals and all other living things, plants are made of cells (sehlz). A **cell** is the smallest and most basic unit of a living thing. Plant cells have stiff walls that support the plant and give it shape.

Plants cannot move from place to place to find food and water like animals can. So how do plants meet their needs? They have parts that help them get the things they need to stay alive.

Almost all plants have three parts. Each part does a job that helps the plant live. A **root** takes in water and nutrients and provides support for the plant. A **stem** holds up the leaves and carries water and nutrients through the plant. A **leaf** collects sunlight and gases from the air. It uses them to make food for the plant.

The zebra plant is unusual because it has leaves patterned like zebra fur. What features does it have in common with other plants? ▶

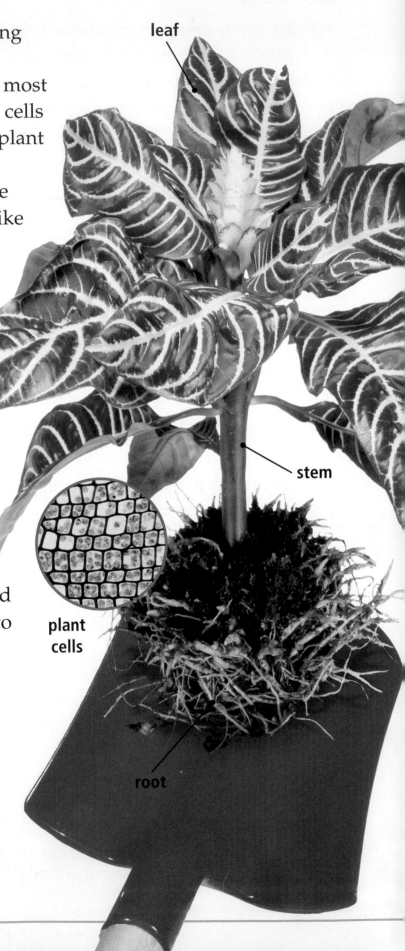

leaf

stem

plant cells

root

Roots

You usually don't see the roots of a plant. The roots of most plants grow underground. The most important job of roots is to take in water and nutrients from the soil. Roots have tiny hairlike parts that help them do this.

The roots of most plants also have another job. Roots are needed to hold the plant in place in the soil and to help it stand up. Tall trees have huge roots that help keep them from tipping over. Roots of grasses help hold them in place.

Sometimes, roots store food for the plant. The carrots you eat are actually roots. They contain many nutrients that they store for use by the whole carrot plant. Radishes, turnips, beets, and some other vegetables that people eat are also roots.

▶ **TEXT STRUCTURE** If page A8 ended after the first paragraph, what would be a better head for that page?

Root hairs viewed through a microscope ▶

Carrots are roots. They have tiny hairlike parts, called root hairs, that help take in water and nutrients from soil. ▶

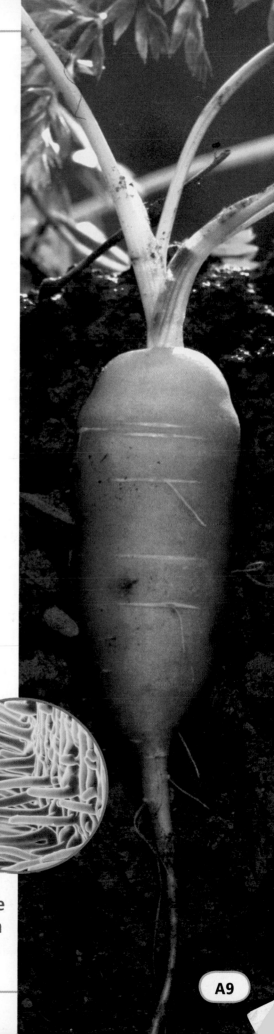

Stems

The stems of many plants are long and thin. They contain small tubes. These tubes carry water and nutrients throughout the plant. The stems hold up the leaves. This allows the leaves to collect sunlight.

Some stems, such as the stems of sugar cane, can store food. In a cactus plant, the stems store water. Tree trunks are also stems. Celery stalks and asparagus are examples of stems eaten by people.

▲ Stems help a plant grow tall. These bamboo plants have long, strong stems that grow very quickly.

This Japanese maple bonsai (bahn SY) is a tiny form of a full-size tree. It has roots, stems, and leaves, just like a large tree. ▶

Leaves

Leaves grow out of the stem of a plant. Most plants have many leaves. The leaf is the part of the plant that makes food. Leaves take in sunlight and air, and use them to make sugar. The sugar is food for the plant.

Leaves usually grow near the top of the plant so they can take in a lot of sunlight. Different types of plants usually have differently shaped leaves. The spines on a cactus are leaves. So are the needles of a pine tree. You might eat the leaves of some plants, such as lettuce, spinach, or cabbage.

▶ **TEXT STRUCTURE** **Look back at the last three heads in this lesson. What are the three parts of a plant?**

▲ This Japanese maple leaf is divided into sections called lobes.

This plant is called a ponytail palm. Its leaves are long and narrow. ▶

How Plants Meet Needs

The roots, stems, and leaves of a plant are all connected. They work together to help the plant meet its needs. To live and grow, a plant must meet its needs. Roots take in water and nutrients from soil. Stems carry the water and nutrients to the leaves and other parts of the plant. Leaves use sunlight, water, and air to make sugar.

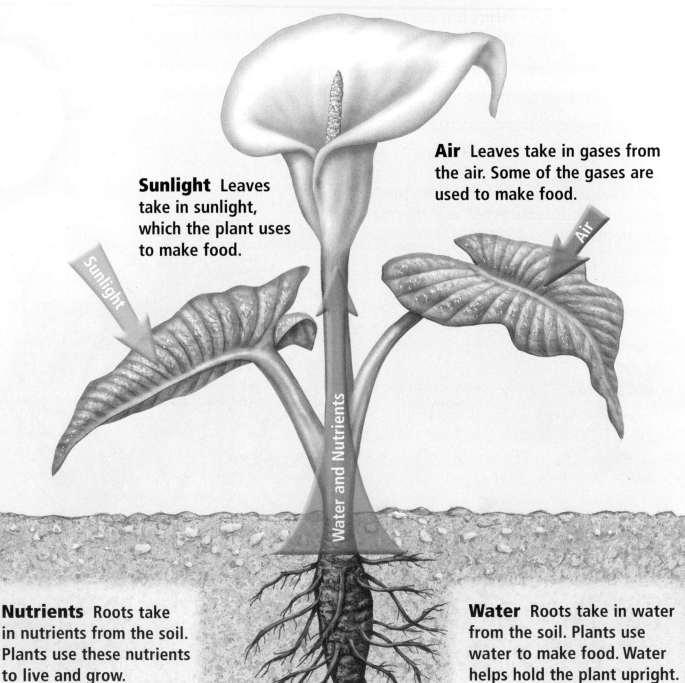

Sunlight Leaves take in sunlight, which the plant uses to make food.

Air Leaves take in gases from the air. Some of the gases are used to make food.

Sunlight

Air

Water and Nutrients

Nutrients Roots take in nutrients from the soil. Plants use these nutrients to live and grow.

Water Roots take in water from the soil. Plants use water to make food. Water helps hold the plant upright.

Visual Summary

 Plants need air, water, sunlight, and nutrients to live.

 Plants have roots, stems, and leaves and are made of cells.

 The roots, stems, and leaves of a plant work together to help the plant meet its needs.

LINKS for Home and School

MATH **Add It Up** A rabbit eats 2 celery stalks, 2 carrots, 3 radishes, 1 turnip, and 1 head of lettuce. How many vegetables does the rabbit eat in all? How many of the vegetables eaten are roots?

HEALTH **Make a Poster** Native Americans used the bark of willow trees as a pain medicine. Today, chemicals found in willow bark are used to make aspirin. Many modern medicines come from parts of plants. Make a poster listing some common modern medicines. Include drawings of the plants they are made from.

Review

❶ **MAIN IDEA** How does a plant meet its needs?

❷ **VOCABULARY** What is the job of roots?

❸ **READING SKILL: Text Structure** Which heading would most likely have information about root structure: *Parts of Plants* or *Needs of Plants*?

❹ **CRITICAL THINKING: Synthesize** Describe how stems and leaves of a plant work to help the plant live.

❺ **INQUIRY SKILL: Observe** Suppose a plant has plenty of light, soil, and air. Its leaves are turning brown and dry. Which of its needs is not being met?

✔ **TEST PREP**
The main job of leaves is to ___.

A. hold up the plant.

B. make food for the plant.

C. take in water and nutrients.

D. store food for the plant.

 Technology
Visit **www.eduplace.com/scp/** to find out more about the needs of plants.

How Do Parts Help Classify Plants?

Why It Matters...

There are over 300,000 kinds of plants! Plants vary greatly in how they look. You can use plant parts to tell one type of plant from another. It is helpful to be able to tell different types of plants apart. For example, you must be able to identify plants to use them safely for food and medicine.

PREPARE TO INVESTIGATE

Inquiry Skill

Communicate You can present science information using numbers, words, sketches, charts, and graphs.

Materials

- leaves
- hand lens

Science and Math Toolbox

For step 2, review **Using a Hand Lens** on page H2.

Leaf Detective

Procedure

1 **Communicate** In your *Science Notebook*, make a diagram like the one shown.

2 **Observe** Examine some leaves using a hand lens. Observe the size, shape, color, and texture of each leaf.

3 **Classify** First, group the leaves by size. Divide the leaves into two groups, small and large. Write these group names in your diagram. Write one group name in each box below the word *Leaves*.

4 **Classify** Work only with the small leaves. Classify the small leaves into two groups based on something other than size. Name each group. Write these group names in your diagram. Write one name in each box below the word *Small*.

5 **Classify** Repeat step 4 to further classify the large leaves.

Conclusion

1. **Collaborate** Compare your diagram with a classmate's diagram. How are they alike? How are they different?

2. **Analyze Data** What is one leaf trait that you used to group the leaves? Did your classmate also use that trait?

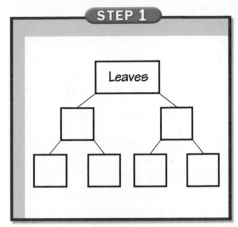

STEP 1

STEP 2

STEP 3

Investigate More!

Research Collect a few tree leaves. Ask a librarian for a field guide book to trees or use a guide on the Internet. Use the field guide to help you find the name of the tree each leaf came from.

Classifying Plants

VOCABULARY

netted veins   p. A16
parallel veins   p. A16
vein   p. A16

READING SKILL

Classify As you read, identify different traits of roots, stems, and leaves.

MAIN IDEA Plants can be classified by the different traits of their leaves, stems, and roots.

Classifying by Leaves

One way that scientists classify, or group, plants is by their leaves. Leaves can be classified by the shape of their outside edge, called the leaf margin. Leaves can also be classified by their texture or by the pattern of their veins (vaynz).

A **vein** is a tube that carries food, water, and nutrients throughout a leaf. Leaves can have parallel veins or netted veins. **Parallel veins** are veins that run in straight lines next to each other. **Netted veins** are veins that branch out from main veins.

Leaf Margin

pawpaw

elm

Smooth leaf margin
A pawpaw tree has large, long leaves with smooth edges.

Jagged leaf margin
A slippery elm tree has leaves with uneven, jagged edges.

Texture

jade

cucumber

sassafras

Waxy texture
Jade plants have leaves with a waxy surface. This helps keep the plant from drying out.

Rough texture
Cucumber plants have leaves with a rough texture.

Smooth texture
Sassafras (SAS uh fras) plants have smooth, shiny, green leaves.

Vein Pattern

corn

grape

Parallel veins
Corn leaves have long veins that run next to one another.

Netted veins
Grape leaves have a pattern of veins with many branches.

 **CLASSIFY** What are three ways to classify leaves?

Classifying by Stems and Roots

Plants can also be classified by their stem structures and root systems. Stems are either woody or soft. A root system is all of the roots of a single plant. Root systems are made up of either a taproot or fibrous (FY bruhs) roots. A taproot is a thick single root. Fibrous roots are small roots that spread out over a wide area.

Stem Structure

Woody stems
Bushes, such as this holly, and most trees, have hard, woody stems. Woody stems are protected by bark.

Soft stems
Some plants, such as tulips, have soft stems. These stems are held up by water inside their tubes.

Root Systems

Taproots
A dandelion has a single long, thick root. Carrots are also taproots.

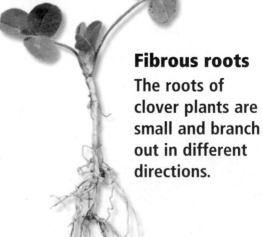

Fibrous roots
The roots of clover plants are small and branch out in different directions.

▶ **CLASSIFY** Name two kinds of root systems.

Visual Summary

Leaves are classified by leaf margin, texture, and vein pattern.

Stems can be classified as soft or woody.

Root systems can be classified as taproots or fibrous roots.

Review

❶ MAIN IDEA How are plants classified?

❷ VOCABULARY Write a definition for *veins* as it is used in this lesson.

❸ READING SKILL: Classify What are two kinds of roots? Give examples of plants that have each kind of root.

❹ CRITICAL THINKING: Evaluate If you found two leaves with the same leaf margin and vein pattern, could you conclude that they came from the same plant? Why or why not?

❺ INQUIRY SKILL: Communicate Draw a diagram that shows ways of classifying leaves.

 TEST PREP

Root systems are classified as either ___.

A. smooth or rough.

B. soft or woody.

C. parallel or netted.

D. taproots or fibrous.

 Technology

Visit **www.eduplace.com/scp/** to read more about classifying plants.

LINKS for Home and School

MATH Make Shapes Collect leaves from different trees and plants. Make imprints of the leaves by dipping them in paint and pressing them against a sheet of paper. What geometric figures do you see? Look for and label any parallel lines and lines of symmetry.

WRITING Persuasive Plants can be classified by their parts and in other ways. Write a paragraph to persuade other people that classifying plants is important.

It's So Corny!

You might not see it, but corn is all around you. You probably used corn today. It's hard to avoid eating, wearing, or using something made from corn! There's corn in soap, lotion, shampoo, and toothpaste.

Cornstarch is a type of flour that is made from corn. The paper, books, rulers, chalk, paint, crayons, and erasers that you use at school are likely made with cornstarch. You can't read, write, or draw without corn.

Even when you are riding in a car, you might be using corn. Ethanol, which is made from corn, is sometimes added to gasoline. When the gasoline that is burned in a car engine contains ethanol, less pollution is produced. Corn really is everywhere!

Corn is used to produce threads in pillows, comforters, and carpeting.

The paste in wallpaper is made from cornstarch. This paste dries slowly.

Cornstarch helps keep crayons from breaking.

Sharing Ideas

1. **READING CHECK** What are three things that are made from corn?

2. **WRITE ABOUT IT** What are some ways that you used things made from corn today?

3. **TALK ABOUT IT** Discuss why corn is an important plant.

A21

How Do Their Parts Help Plants Survive?

Why It Matters...

Have you ever blown on a puffy, white dandelion? If so, you have seen its small pieces of fluff drift around in the air. Some of those pieces land on soil and produce new dandelions. All plants have parts that help them survive and grow new plants.

PREPARE TO INVESTIGATE

Inquiry Skill

Infer When you infer, you use facts you know and observations you have made to draw a conclusion.

Materials

- cactus
- hand lens
- tweezers
- plastic spoon

Science and Math Toolbox

For steps 2 and 3, review **Using a Hand Lens** on page H2.

Cactus Spine

Procedure

STEP 1

① **Record Data** Work with a partner. In your *Science Notebook,* make a sketch of the cactus. Use tweezers to pull a spine off the cactus. **Safety:** Never touch a cactus. Cactus spines can be sharp.

② **Observe** Look at the spine with a hand lens. The spine is a leaf of the cactus. Record your observations.

STEP 2

③ **Observe** Use a plastic spoon to gently move some of the soil around the base of the cactus. Use the spoon to remove a small amount of soil. Place the soil on a sheet of paper. Observe the soil with a hand lens. Record your observations.

④ Continue to move soil around the base of the cactus until you can see some roots. Sketch them in your *Science Notebook*. Note whether the roots grew deeply or were close to the surface of the soil.

STEP 4

⑤ **Analyze Data** On your sketch of the cactus, label its roots, stem, and leaves.

Conclusion

1. **Infer** Based on your observations, where do you think a cactus lives?

2. **Infer** How do the parts of a cactus help it survive where it lives?

Investigate More!

Solve a Problem In some dry places, people use large amounts of water for lawns. Many communities are trying to reduce water use. How could these people help save water?

VOCABULARY

environment   p. A24
reproduce   p. A26

READING SKILL

Draw Conclusions
Identify some unusual features of a plant you read about. Draw a conclusion about that plant's environment.

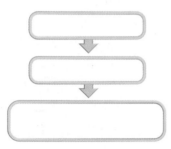

Ways to Meet Needs

MAIN IDEA Plants have parts that help them live in many different environments.

Getting and Storing Water

Plants grow in many kinds of environments (ehn VY ruhn muhnts). An **environment** is everything that surrounds and affects a living thing. Different plants have parts that help them survive in their environment.

Some plants in shady environments grow high on tree trunks. This allows the plants to reach sunlight. But their roots cannot reach the soil. The roots are able to take water from the air. Other plants, like cactuses, can store water to use at a later time.

◄ Orchids grow high on tree trunks. Their roots take in water from the air.

▲ A tank bromeliad stores up to 8 L (about 2 gal) of water between its leaves.

Root Support

Trees that live in warm, wet environments grow in soil that is often soft. Most of the nutrients in soil are near the surface. Trees that grow in such soil need wide, shallow roots for support and to take in nutrients.

Some types of trees have strong, woody roots called prop roots. Prop roots grow above the soil from the tree's trunk. They support the trunk in the wet ground.

Large trees need a lot of support. Some large trees have long, flattened roots called buttress roots. Buttress roots grow on the surface of the ground and widen the base of the tree. The widened base helps to hold up the tree.

▶ **DRAW CONCLUSIONS** **Draw a conclusion about what the air is like around plants that grow on tree trunks.**

▲ The buttress roots of a giant fig tree hold its huge trunk upright.

◀ Sturdy prop roots seem to hold these palm trees in midair.

Spreading Seeds

Most plants reproduce (ree pruh DOOS) using seeds. To **reproduce** means to make new living things of the same kind. A seed is the first stage of a new plant. To grow into a new plant, a seed must fall where there is enough sunlight, soil, and water. If it grows too close to the plant that produced it, a seed may not survive. The parent plant may take up most of the sunlight, soil, and water in the area.

Many seeds have parts that help them travel away from the parent plant. Some seeds travel on the wind, some float in water, and some hook onto the fur of animals. Some seeds are inside tasty fruit. Animals eat the fruit, leaving the seeds behind.

▶ **DRAW CONCLUSIONS** Draw conclusions about what may have prevented a seed from producing a healthy new plant.

▲ The shape of maple seeds causes them to twirl as they fall. The twirling helps the seeds travel farther away from the tree.

Burdock seeds hook onto the fur of passing animals. ▼

▲ Because coconut seeds float, they can drift on the ocean from island to island.

Lesson Wrap-Up

Visual Summary

Plants have parts that take in and store water in different ways.

Plants that grow in soft, wet soil have roots that help support them.

Plants spread seeds using wind, water, or animals.

LINKS for Home and School

MATH **Find the Number** There are coconut trees growing on an island. Use the following clues to find the number of fallen coconuts on the island. There is a 3 in the hundreds place. The digit in the tens place is less than 9 and greater than 7. The digit in the ones place is twice the digit in the hundreds place.

TECHNOLOGY **Make a List**
Sometimes inventors get their ideas from observing plants and animals. Make a list of machines that may have been invented when an inventor saw maple seeds falling from a tree.

Review

1 MAIN IDEA How are plants able to live in many different environments?

2 VOCABULARY What is an *environment*?

3 READING SKILL: Draw Conclusions You see a plant that has thick, waxy skin and a stem that stores water. What kind of environment might this plant live in?

4 CRITICAL THINKING: Evaluate A friend says that he cannot grow a garden because his area is too dry. Respond to this idea.

5 INQUIRY SKILL: Infer What can you infer about how a seed with a parachute-shaped structure moves away from its parent plant?

✔ TEST PREP
Prop roots help a plant ___.

A. stand upright on wet soil.

B. make extra food.

C. store water in a dry environment.

D. spread seeds.

Technology
Visit **www.eduplace.com/scp/** to research more about plants in their environments.

A27

Plants That Hunt

Gotcha! A fly smells some sweet sap. Looking for dinner, it crawls between two spiky leaves. Suddenly, the leaves snap shut. Instead of finding dinner, the bug becomes dinner. The Venus flytrap strikes again!

Most plants get enough nutrients from water and soil. The Venus flytrap, however, is a meat-eating, or carnivorous plant. Because it lives in places where the soil is poor, it adds to its diet by catching and digesting insects and other tiny creatures.

◀ **Sticky trap** A sundew leaf traps insects with sticky threads called tentacles. Then it folds up to digest its meal.

Danger! Keep out! Once inside this pitcher plant, insects slide down a slippery slope to a deadly pool. There the plant digests them, much as your stomach digests food.

Vocabulary

Complete each sentence with a term from the list.

1. The part of a plant that makes food is called a/an _____.

2. Corn leaves have _____ that run in lines next to each other.

3. Everything that surrounds and affects a living thing is a/an _____.

4. Some leaves have _____ that branch out from main veins.

5. A substance that living things need to survive is a/an _____.

6. To make more living things of the same kind is to _____.

7. The part of most plants that grow underground is the _____.

8. A living thing that cannot move from place to place and usually has green leaves is a/an _____.

9. A tube that carries water and nutrients throughout a leaf is a/an _____.

10. The basic unit that makes up all living things is a/an _____.

cell A8

environment A24

leaf A8

netted veins A16

nutrient A7

parallel veins A16

plant A6

reproduce A26

root A8

stem A8

vein A16

✓ Test Prep

Write the letter of the best answer choice.

11. The _____ of a plant holds up the leaves and carries water and nutrients to all parts of the plant.

   A. root system
   B. stem
   C. parallel vein
   D. leaf

12. Veins in a leaf can be _____.

   A. tap or fibrous.   **C.** smooth or rough.
   B. soft or woody.   **D.** parallel or netted.

13. Plants that grow on the trunks of trees have parts that help them get _____ from the air.

   A. water
   B. seeds
   C. roots
   D. food

14. Plants need water, soil, air, and _____.

   A. salt.   **C.** sunlight.
   B. seeds.   **D.** pots.

Inquiry Skills

15. **Communicate** Make a sketch of a leaf that has either a smooth or jagged leaf margin and parallel or netted veins. Write a brief description of this leaf to explain your drawing.

16. **Infer** Leaves need to collect enough sunlight to make food. Suppose you see two plants. One has large, broad leaves. The other has small, narrow leaves. What can you infer about the amount of sunlight in the environment in which each plant lives?

Map the Concept

Fill in the concept map with the parts of a plant. You may use each term more than once.

root system   **root**
leaf   **stem**

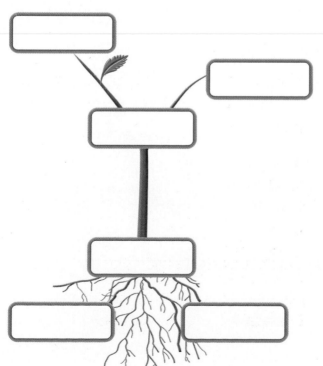

Critical Thinking

17. **Apply** Suppose you make a salad with the following vegetables: lettuce, celery, carrots, spinach and radishes. Classify each of these vegetables as a root, stem, or leaf.

18. **Synthesize** Imagine that you could change the parts of a cactus so that it could live in a wet, forest environment. What changes would you make to its roots, stems, and leaves?

19. **Analyze** If you cut off the roots of a plant, which of the plant's needs would no longer be met?

20. **Evaluate** Suppose you read an article that states that it is almost impossible to tell two particular plants apart. Their leaves and stems look exactly alike. How might you tell these plants apart?

Performance Assessment

Write Directions
Houseplants often come with cards that tell the buyer how to care for the plant. Write a set of directions telling someone how he or she could help a plant meet its needs.

Chapter 2

Classifying Animals

Lesson Preview

LESSON

1

From fish scales to bird feathers—how are animals with backbones classified?

Read about it in Lesson 1.

LESSON

2

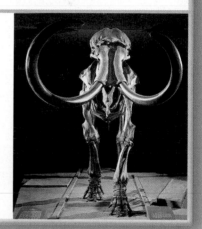

Spiders, worms, and clams—what do these animals have in common?

Read about it in Lesson 2.

LESSON

3

Woolly mammoths and saber-toothed cats— are these animals similar to animals living today?

Read about it in Lesson 3.

Which Animals Are Vertebrates?

Why It Matters...

When you pet a cat, you may feel hard bones along its back. What you are feeling is the cat's backbone. The backbone, and other bones, support the cat's body and give it shape. Most of the animals you know best have backbones. Your family and friends, dogs and cats, farm animals, fish, and even pigeons in the park have backbones.

PREPARE TO INVESTIGATE

Inquiry Skill

Use Models You can use a model of an object to better understand or describe how the real object works.

Materials

- pipe cleaner
- square beads
- plastic washers
- photo of snake
- photo of bird

Model a Backbone
Procedure

STEP 2

1. **Collaborate** Work with a partner to make a model of a backbone. A **backbone** is a series of bones that runs down the back of some animals.

2. **Use Models** Bend one end of a pipe cleaner so the beads will not slide off. Slide a bead, then a washer, onto the pipe cleaner.

STEP 3

3. **Use Models** String beads and washers until there is a small space left at the end of the pipe cleaner. Bend this end so the beads and washers do not slide off.

4. **Ask Questions** Examine pictures of a snake and a bird. Write one question in your *Science Notebook* about the shape of each animal's backbone.

STEP 4

5. **Communicate** Answer your question by bending your model to match each animal's backbone. Draw a picture of your model in your *Science Notebook*.

Conclusion

1. **Infer** How does a backbone that can bend help an animal to move?

2. **Predict** How might an animal's ability to move change if its backbone were rigid like a metal tube?

Investigate More!

Design an Experiment
Model another backbone. Place three small rubber bands between each bead. Bend the backbone to match the snake's backbone. How do the rubber bands change the way the backbone moves?

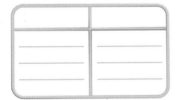
Classifying Vertebrates

MAIN IDEA Animals with backbones can be classified into groups according to their traits.

Traits of Vertebrates

You have learned that a plant is one type of living thing. An animal is another type. Like plants, animals are made of many cells. They can grow and change and they can reproduce. Unlike plants, animals eat food, and most animals can move from place to place.

Animals can be classified, or divided, into two groups depending on whether or not they have a backbone. A **backbone** is a series of bones that runs down the back of some animals. It helps to support the animal's body. An animal that has a backbone is called a **vertebrate** (VUR tuh briht). Most animals do not have a backbone.

▲ A vertebrate, such as this horse, has a skeleton inside its body.

Mammals

Vertebrates can be classified into several smaller groups. One of these groups is the mammal (MAM uhl) group. A **mammal** is an animal that has hair or fur and produces milk for its young.

Mammals, like all animals, need oxygen, a gas in air, to live. Mammals breathe air with their lungs. Even mammals that live in water, such as whales, sea lions, and dolphins have lungs and must breathe air. These animals swim to the water's surface when they need to take a breath.

Most mammals have a thick coat of hair or fur that traps air against the body for warmth. Mammals with little hair on their body keep warm in other ways.

▲ **Humans are mammals.**

 **CLASSIFY** **What are two traits of mammals?**

Sea lions are mammals that live both in water and on land.

Large wings, light feathers, and hollow bones help this owl to fly.

Birds

Another group of vertebrates is the bird group. A **bird** is a vertebrate that has feathers, lungs, wings, and two legs. Birds lay eggs that have hard shells. When the eggs hatch, most bird parents feed the young until they are strong enough to find their own food.

Most birds can fly. Strong muscles help a bird move its wings. Feathers keep a bird warm but are light so they do not weigh the bird down. Some of a bird's bones are hollow. Hollow bones make the bird lightweight so it can fly easily.

The strong beak of the puffin is used for catching and eating fish. ▼

▲ **The Victoria Crowned Pigeon has a feathered crest.**

sand tiger shark

parrot fish

Caribbean stingray

Fish

Fish are vertebrates that live in water. Many fish have long, narrow bodies that make it easy for them to move through water. Most fish are covered with scales—hard, thin, flat plates—that protect them and help them to swim. Scales are covered with a layer of slime which helps keep them waterproof. Fins keep the fish upright and help it steer through the water.

Like all animals, fish need oxygen to live. Fish do not have lungs. Instead, they have gills. Gills take oxygen gas from water. A fish breathes by taking water in through its mouth. The water is then pumped through the gills, which remove the oxygen.

▲ All fish have backbones. Sharks and rays have backbones made of cartilage (KAHR tih lihj), a material that is softer than bone.

 **CLASSIFY** What are two traits of fish?

Amphibians

An **amphibian** (am FIHB ee uhn) is a vertebrate that starts life in the water and then lives on land as an adult. Amphibians, such as frogs, toads, and salamanders, lay eggs in water. Young amphibians that hatch from the eggs look very different from adults. The young breathe with gills and have tails that help them swim.

As young amphibians grow, their bodies change. Lungs and legs develop, and their gills disappear. After the young amphibians' bodies change, they live on land and breathe air with their lungs.

▲ Toads, such as this Malagasy painted toad, have rough, dry, bumpy skin.

Frogs have wet, smooth skin. Wet skin prevents their bodies from drying out on land. ▼

Reptiles

A **reptile** (REHP tyl) is a vertebrate that has dry, scaly skin and lays eggs on land. Reptile eggs have tough, leathery shells. Reptiles can live in many different environments. The scales on their skin protect them from the hot Sun and from water. Reptiles can be found in hot, dry deserts or in wet rainforests. Some reptiles, such as turtles, use legs to move. Others, such as snakes, slither along the ground.

All reptiles breathe with lungs. Reptiles that spend a lot of time in water, such as crocodiles and alligators, must stick their noses out of the water to breathe.

▶ **CLASSIFY** What are two traits of reptiles?

Three-horned chameleons have scaly skin and three horns. ▶

▲ Snakes, such as these tree pythons, have no legs.

◀ Tortoises, such as the one shown, and turtles both have hard shells.

Comparing Vertebrates

Vertebrates can be classified in different ways. They can be grouped by their types of body structures, where they live, the way they reproduce, or the kind of coverings on their bodies. A body covering protects an animal and helps it live in its environment. For example, birds have feathers and fish have scales.

Body Coverings

Group	Covering and Function	Example
Mammals	**hair or fur** protects animal, keeps body warm	giraffe hair
Birds	**feathers** protects animal, keeps body warm, aids flying	parrot feathers
Fish	**scales** protects animal, aids swimming	Garibaldi fish scales
Amphibians	**moist, smooth skin** protects animal, prevents drying out, some air passes through skin	blue bullfrog skin
Reptiles	**dry, scaly skin** protects animal, prevents drying out	chameleon skin

▶ **CLASSIFY** What are four ways that vertebrates can be classified?

Visual Summary

Vertebrates

mammals	• hair or fur • produce milk for young
birds	• feathers • hard-shelled eggs • wings
fish	• scales • gills
amphibians	• breathe with gills, then lungs • lay eggs in water
reptiles	• dry, scaly skin • leathery-shelled eggs

LINKS for Home and School

MATH **Count it Up** Human backbones are made up of many small bones called vertebrae. Humans have 33 vertebrae at birth. Some vertebrae join together as humans age. Four vertebrae combine to form one bone, and five vertebrae combine to form another bone. How many vertebrae do adult humans have?

LITERATURE **Write a Journal Entry** Read *My Season with Penguins: An Antarctic Journal* by Sophie Webb. Use what you have learned to write a journal entry from a penguin's point of view. What are the difficulties you face? How do you meet your needs? How are you unlike other birds?

Review

1 MAIN IDEA Name one trait shared by humans and fish. Name one trait that is not shared by humans and fish.

2 VOCABULARY Write a sentence using the terms *backbone* and *vertebrate*.

3 READING SKILL: Classify What traits make a bear a mammal?

4 CRITICAL THINKING: Analyze How are young amphibians different from adult amphibians?

5 INQUIRY SKILL: Use Models A toy submarine could be used to model the way a fish moves. What could you use to model the way a bird moves?

 TEST PREP
Which of the following is true of reptiles?

A. They have fur.

B. They lay eggs.

C. They have gills.

D. They can fly.

 Technology
Visit **www.eduplace.com/scp/** to find out more about vertebrates.

Which Animals Are Invertebrates?

Why It Matters...

Dragonflies, like all other insects, do not have a backbone. In fact, most of the animals on Earth do not have a backbone. Every time you hear a buzzing mosquito, pick up a wriggling earthworm, or watch a snail slowly creep along, you are observing an animal that doesn't have a backbone.

PREPARE TO INVESTIGATE

Inquiry Skill

Experiment When you experiment, you collect data that either supports a hypothesis or shows that it is false.

Materials

- earthworm
- paper towels
- water
- hand lens
- shallow pan
- black construction paper
- flashlight
- clock
- disposable gloves

Science and Math Toolbox

For step 5, review **Measuring Elapsed Time** on pages H12–H13.

Worm Work

Procedure

1. **Observe** Work in a group. Place an earthworm on a moist paper towel. Use a hand lens to examine the earthworm. **Safety:** Wear gloves and handle the earthworm gently.

2. **Record Data** In your *Science Notebook*, describe and draw the earthworm. Then make a chart like the one shown.

3. **Experiment** Line the bottom of a shallow pan with moist paper towels. Place a sheet of black construction paper so it covers one half of the pan, as shown.

4. **Predict** Predict whether the earthworm will prefer the light or dark side of the pan. Record your prediction.

5. **Experiment** Place the earthworm in the center of the pan. Hold the flashlight about 30 cm above the uncovered side of the pan, as shown. Turn on the flashlight. Wait 3 minutes. Then observe which side of the pan the worm is in. Record your observations.

6. **Experiment** Repeat step 5 three times.

Conclusion

1. **Analyze Data** Was your prediction correct?

2. **Infer** Why do you think earthworms live in soil and not on top of soil?

STEP 2

Trial	Worm found in light or dark?
1	
2	
3	
4	

STEP 3

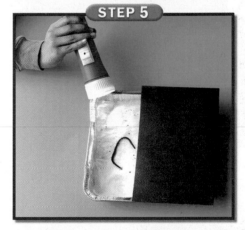

STEP 5

Investigate More!

Design an Experiment Find out if earthworms prefer smooth or rough surfaces. You can use sandpaper as a rough surface. Get permission from your teacher and carry out the experiment.

Invertebrates

MAIN IDEA The many kinds of invertebrates can be grouped according to their traits.

► **VOCABULARY**

arthropod   p. A48
invertebrate   p. A46

► **READING SKILL**

Draw Conclusions Fill in a chart to conclude which animals in the lesson are invertebrates.

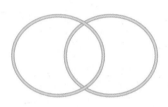

Traits of Invertebrates

Most of the animals on Earth are invertebrates (ihn VUR tuh brihts). An **invertebrate** is an animal that does not have a backbone. Some types of invertebrates live on land and some types live in water.

Sponges

Sponges are animals that move very little. Their bodies are full of holes. Sponges filter tiny bits of food from the water.

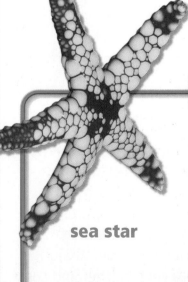

Sea Stars and Sea Urchins

Sea stars and sea urchins have spiny body coverings. Neither animal has a head, but they both have a mouth. They move and capture food using tiny suction cups called tube feet.

sea urchin

sea star

Worms

Worms have soft, tube-shaped bodies with no legs, eyes, or shells. Worms live in water, in soil, or even inside other animals.

earthworm

Corals and Jellies

Corals and jellies are underwater animals. They have soft bodies, but some corals have a hard outer skeleton. They both have mouths and armlike parts called tentacles (TEHN tuh kuhlz). When food floats by, these animals use their tentacles to grab it and put it into their mouth.

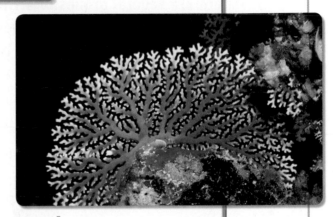

coral

Snails and Squids

Snails, squid, octopus, clams, oysters, and scallops all belong to the same group called mollusks. They have soft bodies. All of these animals, except for the octopus, have a shell.

snail

▶ DRAW CONCLUSIONS What can you conclude about an animal that has a mouth and tube feet, but no head?

Arthropods

The largest group of invertebrates is the arthropod (AHR thruh pahd) group. An **arthropod** is an invertebrate that has jointed legs, a body with two or more sections, and a hard outer covering. The hard outer covering is called an exoskeleton. An exoskeleton protects and supports the animal.

butterfly

butterflies and ants

There are several groups of arthropods. The largest group includes butterflies and ants. These insects have six legs and three body sections. They may or may not have wings.

centipede

centipedes and millipedes

Centipedes and millipedes have segmented bodies. Centipedes have one pair of legs on each segment. Millipedes have two pairs of legs on each segment.

spider

spiders

Spiders have eight jointed legs, two body sections, jaws, and fangs. Many spiders spin webs.

crabs, lobsters, and crayfish

Another group of arthropods includes crabs, lobsters, and crayfish. Many animals in this group have an exoskeleton that is very hard, like a shell.

lobster

▶ **DRAW CONCLUSIONS** Suppose you see an animal with an exoskeleton and one pair of legs on each of its body segments. Draw a conclusion about the kind of animal it is.

Visual Summary

Invertebrates

Sponges	• body with holes • move very little
Sea Stars and Sea Urchins	• hard, spiny covering • tube feet
Worms	• tube-shaped body • no legs, shells, or eyes
Jellies and Corals	• soft body • tentacles
Snails and Squids	• soft body • shell
Arthropods	• jointed legs • bodies divided into sections • hard exoskeleton

LINKS for Home and School

MATH **Use a Number Pattern** A certain centipede has 15 segments on its body. Each segment has 2 legs. Use a number pattern to find how many legs the centipede has in all.

WRITING Story In older times, sailors from Norway told of a sea creature called the Kraken. The Kraken was said to be more than a mile long and have tentacles strong enough to sink a ship! Today we know that these legends were probably based on a real animal, the giant squid. Choose an invertebrate and write a story about your own legendary creature.

Review

❶ MAIN IDEA Why are insects, lobsters, and spiders all classified as arthropods?

❷ VOCABULARY Write a sentence using the term *invertebrate*.

❸ READING SKILL: Draw Conclusions An invertebrate has a tube-like body. It does not have tentacles or legs. What can you conclude about the group it belongs to?

❹ CRITICAL THINKING: Analyze Lobsters and fish both have gills, but these two animals are not related. Why do you think they might both have the same body part?

❺ INQUIRY SKILL: Experiment Design an experiment to test this hypothesis: Ants like sugar more than they like salt.

✔ TEST PREP
One trait of the group containing sea stars is ___.

A. a head.

B. a body with many holes.

C. tube feet.

D. tentacles.

 Technology
Visit **www.eduplace.com/scp/** to learn more about invertebrates.

What's New at the Insect Zoo?

What's an insect and what's not? Students from the Liberty School think anything pesky that creeps, crawls, or flies is an insect. But on a visit to a nearby insectarium, they make some surprising discoveries.

Insect Zoo

Cast

Mrs. Spellman: teacher

Buzz: entomologist and insectarium guide

Carla

Raffi } students

Sam

Neisha

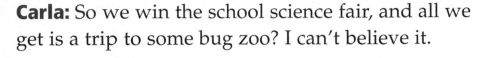

Carla: So we win the school science fair, and all we get is a trip to some bug zoo? I can't believe it.

Neisha: Shhh! Here comes Mrs. Spellman.

Mrs. Spellman: [*Enters.*] Okay, kids. First we'll see some amazing insects. Then we'll go outside for a bug hunt.

Buzz: [*Enters, carrying a small branch. Buzz is energetic and speaks quickly.*] Hi kids. My name is Buzz. It's a perfect name for a bug guy, right? I was a bug collector as a kid. Now I'm an entomologist, a scientist who studies insects. Let me introduce you to Twiggy. He's a stick bug. [*Buzz shows the branch to the group.*]

Sam: All I see is a branch.

Raffi: But the top of that branch just moved! I see Twiggy now. He looks like he's part of the branch.

Mrs. Spellman: Great camouflage!

Buzz: What makes Twiggy an insect? The 6-3-2 trick for identifying insects can help you with that answer.

Sam: What trick is that?

Buzz: Insects are arthropods with *six* legs, *three* body parts and *two* antennae. If an arthropod has any other number of legs, body parts, or antennae, it's not an insect. That's the 6-3-2 trick.

Carla: Wait a minute! Spiders have eight legs, don't they? Are you saying a spider isn't an insect?

Buzz: You've got it! Spiders are arthropods, but they aren't insects. They're arachnids. They have *eight* legs, *two* body parts, and *no* antennae.

Neisha: What about these guys—the millipedes? I can't even count all their legs! *[Points to a millipede exhibit.]*

Buzz: Same deal. They're anthropods, but not insects. Millipedes have anywhere from about 100 to 400 legs. I've even heard of one type that has 750 legs! *[He reaches into the exhibit and picks up a millipede.]* Anyone want to hold Millie? She tickles when she walks on you!

Raffi: Okay!

[Buzz puts the millipede in Raffi's outstretched hand.]

Raffi: He's right! She does tickle.

▲ stick bug

▲ praying mantis

▲ ladybug

▲ butterfly

Buzz: Let's look at the praying mantis next. *[Buzz helps Raffi put the millipede back.]* It's the only insect that can swivel its head all the way around. Swiveling makes it easier for the mantis to see all of its surroundings. When another insect wanders by, the mantis grabs it and gobbles it up.

Sam: Yuck!

Buzz: It may sound gross to you, but the truth is, gardeners love mantises. They keep other insects from destroying plants. Now, how about that bug hunt?

Mrs. Spellman: Sure. I'll pass out the equipment.

Buzz: Okay. Let's start with a few tips. Look for insects that crawl. The best places to look are on the ground, in the grass, around trees, under rocks, and on plants.

Carla: I'm going to look for a butterfly and a ladybug!

Sam: Look! There's a butterfly in the flower garden. Let's go see it!

Neisha: We're really enjoying our insect zoo adventure. I'll bug Mrs. Spellman to let us come back soon.

▲ spider

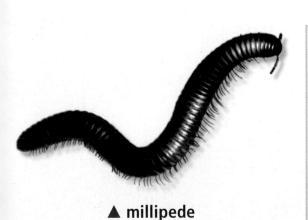

▲ millipede

Sharing Ideas

1. **READING CHECK** What is a good way to identify insects?

2. **WRITE ABOUT IT** Insects such as stick bugs and praying mantises use camouflage. Why do you think this is important?

3. **TALK ABOUT IT** Discuss ways insects help farmers and gardeners.

Lesson 3

Which Animals Lived Long Ago?

Why It Matters...

Triceratops and other dinosaurs died out millions of years ago. Scientists have learned about dinosaurs by studying their bones and footprints. They now know what dinosaurs looked like, where they lived, and even what they ate. This information helps scientists understand how dinosaurs were similar to the animals that are alive today.

PREPARE TO INVESTIGATE

Inquiry Skill

Classify When you classify, you sort objects into groups according to their properties.

Materials

- fossil A
- fossil B
- hand lens

Science and Math Toolbox

For step 2, review **Using a Hand Lens** on page H2.

Fossil Clues

Procedure

1. **Collaborate** Work with a partner. In your *Science Notebook*, make a chart like the one shown.

2. **Observe** Use a hand lens to examine fossil A and fossil B. A **fossil** is the very old remains of a plant or animal.

3. **Infer** Try to identify whether a plant or an animal made fossil A. Try to identify the parts of the living thing that fossil A came from. Record your ideas in your chart.

4. Repeat step 3 for fossil B.

Conclusion

1. **Classify** What parts of the living thing do you recognize from its fossil? What living things did they come from?

2. **Infer** What kind of environment do you think the organism that made fossil A lived in? What makes you think this?

3. **Infer** What kind of environment do you think the organism that made fossil B lived in? What makes you think this?

STEP 1

Fossil	Plant or Animal	Parts that Made Fossil
A		
B		

STEP 2

STEP 4

Investigate More!

Research Find out about fossil hunting in your state or region. What kinds of fossils have been found? What do these fossils tell about the living things of long ago?

Extinct Animals

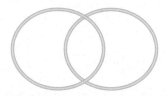
MAIN IDEA If the needs of a living thing are not met by its environment, it may not survive.

Animals of Long Ago

Dinosaurs were animals that lived millions of years ago. There were many species (SPEE-sheez) of dinosaur. A species is a group of living things that can produce living things of the same kind.

Scientists know about dinosaurs because they left behind fossils (FAHS uhlz). A **fossil** is the very old remains of a plant or animal. Scientists have found many bones, teeth, and footprint fossils of dinosaurs.

The diplodocus (dih PLAHD-uh kuhs) may have become extinct because the plants it ate died out.

Fossils help scientists understand what environments were like long ago. Fossils also help scientists learn about plants and animals that are extinct (ihk STIHNGKT). An **extinct species** is one that has disappeared. Species may become extinct if their habitat (HAB ih tat) changes. A **habitat** is the place where a plant or animal lives. If a habitat changes, the living things there may not be able to find food, water, or shelter.

Using fossil bones, scientists have made models of some extinct animals. Woolly mammoths are an extinct species. We know what they looked like from their fossils and from old drawings on the walls of caves.

Dodo (DOH doh) birds are also extinct. People destroyed the forests where dodos lived, so the birds could not find food. People also hunted dodos.

▲ The dodo had a very large body with short wings. It could not fly.

▶ **COMPARE AND CONTRAST** What is the difference between an extinct species and one that is not extinct?

Woolly mammoths were mammals that had a thick coat, curved tusks, and a large head.

Extinct and Modern Animals

Many modern animals are similar to extinct animals. The woolly mammoth looked like the modern elephant. Fossils show that the rhinoceros (ry NAHS ur-uhs) and the extinct indricothere (IHN-druh koh THIHR) are related. Rhinos, like the indricothere, are mammals, eat leaves, and have feet with three toes.

The emu (EE myoo) is a large bird that cannot fly. It shares several traits with the extinct diatryma (dih A trih mah). However, fossils show that the two birds are not related.

Diatryma

A diatryma was a large bird that is now extinct. It could not fly.

Indricothere

Indricothere was the largest land mammal ever known. It was 5.5 m (18 ft) tall.

▲ An emu is a large modern bird from Australia. It cannot fly.

◄ Although the modern rhinoceros looks fierce, it eats only leaves and grass.

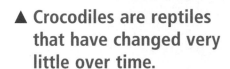

▲ Crocodiles are reptiles that have changed very little over time.

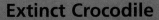
Extinct Crocodile

This extinct crocodile species was similar to modern crocodiles. The environment of the modern animal may be similar to that of the extinct species.

The saber-toothed cat was a fierce-looking mammal. It had two 18-cm (7-in.) teeth. Its jaws were used to rip apart the animals it hunted. It was not a fast runner because its legs were short.

This animal is not related to modern wild cats. But it has been compared to the Bengal tiger. Bengal tigers are larger and have shorter teeth and longer legs than saber-toothed cats.

▶ **COMPARE AND CONTRAST** How is a diatryma like an emu?

Saber-toothed Cat

Saber-toothed cats likely became extinct when the animals they ate died out.

◀ Bengal tigers and saber-toothed cats share some traits, but they are not related.

A59

Endangered Animals

Plant and animal species are still becoming extinct. An **endangered species** (ehn DAYN jurd SPEE sheez) is one that has so few members that the entire species is in danger of becoming extinct.

Laws have been passed to protect endangered species. There have been some success stories. For example, bald eagles are returning to areas where they were once almost extinct.

▶ **COMPARE AND CONTRAST** Does a greater number of animals belong to a species that is endangered than to one that is not?

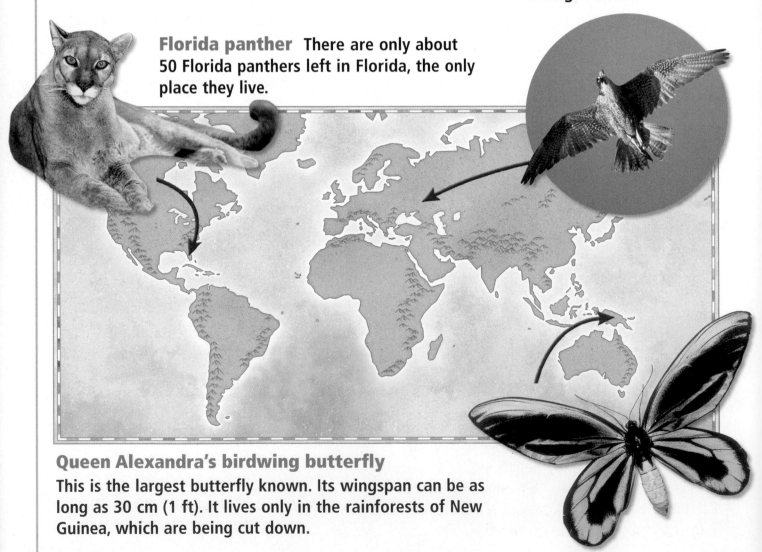

Eurasian peregrine falcon
These birds were unable to reproduce because they ate poisons used for killing insects.

Florida panther There are only about 50 Florida panthers left in Florida, the only place they live.

Queen Alexandra's birdwing butterfly
This is the largest butterfly known. Its wingspan can be as long as 30 cm (1 ft). It lives only in the rainforests of New Guinea, which are being cut down.

Visual Summary

Living things may become extinct if they cannot find food, water, or shelter.

Some modern animals resemble extinct animals. These animals may or may not be related.

Unless endangered species are protected, they could become extinct.

LINKS for Home and School

TECHNOLOGY Recreate a
Dinosaur Scientists use computers to create pictures of dinosaurs. Choose two types of dinosaurs. Use the Internet to find computer-generated pictures of these dinosaurs. Use the pictures to create your own sketches of what these dinosaurs probably looked like.

SOCIAL STUDIES Write a
Letter Some endangered species have been saved from extinction by people's efforts. Choose an animal on the endangered species list. Write a letter to a newspaper to tell people why that species should be saved.

Review

❶ **MAIN IDEA** Why might a species become extinct if its habitat is destroyed?

❷ **VOCABULARY** What is a fossil?

❸ **READING SKILL: Compare and Contrast** What is the difference between an endangered species and an extinct species?

❹ **CRITICAL THINKING: Evaluate** Suggest a way you could help an endangered animal from becoming extinct.

❺ **INQUIRY SKILL: Classify** Classify the following animals as either extinct or endangered: dodo bird, Florida panther, Eurasian falcon, saber-toothed cat, Queen Alexandra's birdwing butterfly, diatryma.

 TEST PREP
All of the following can become a fossil except ___.

A. water.

B. bones.

C. teeth.

D. footprints.

 Technology
Visit **www.eduplace.com/scp/** to find out more about extinct animals.

No Brain, No Bones, No Problem!

A "jellyfish" is not a fish! It isn't jelly, either. In fact, jellies, to use their scientific name, are invertebrates: animals that get along fine without a spine. Everything about the giant Antarctic jelly shown here is extreme. Its bell (the rounded shape at the top) can be over three feet wide. Its tentacles can be 30 feet long. Jellies use their long tentacles to sting and catch their food.

Scientists think jellies have been around since before the dinosaurs. Not bad for an animal with no bones, no blood, no heart ... not even a brain!

Most jellies, like these moon jellies, are much smaller than the Antarctic jelly.

⟶

Most jellies simply
float wherever
the ocean currents
take them. Others, like
the Antarctic jelly, can
move through the water
by expanding and
contracting their bells.

Vocabulary

Complete each sentence with a term from the list.

1. A sponge, a worm, a squid, and a spider is each an example of a/an _____.

2. The place where a plant or animals lives is its _____.

3. The very old remains of a living thing is a/an _____.

4. An animal that has hair or fur and produces milk for its young is a/an

5. A species that is no longer found on Earth is a/an _____.

6. An animal that has gills when it is young and lungs as an adult is a/an _____.

7. An animal that has a backbone is a/an _____.

8. A vertebrate having lungs, wings, and feathers is a/an _____.

9. An animal that has jointed legs and an exoskeleton is a/an _____.

10. The series of bones that runs down the back of some animals is a/an _____.

amphibian A40
arthropod A48
backbone A36
bird A38
endangered species A60
extinct species A57
fish A39
fossil A56
habitat A57
invertebrate A46
mammal A37
reptile A41
vertebrate A36

Test Prep

Write the letter of the best answer choice.

11. Which animals have gills?

   A. reptiles
   B. fish
   C. mammals
   D. birds

12. Which of the following is a trait found in reptiles?

   A. scales
   B. wings
   C. hair
   D. feathers

13. Arthropods do NOT have _____.

   A. legs.
   B. eyes.
   C. backbones.
   D. an exoskeleton.

14. A species that has very few members is _____.

   A. extinct.
   B. endangered.
   C. doomed.
   D. a fossil.

Inquiry Skills

15. Use Models What materials could you use to make a model of an arthropod?

16. Classify Invertebrates can be classified by their traits. For example, they can be grouped by whether or not they have a head, an exoskeleton, or tentacles. Choose one of these traits. List which of the following animals have that trait: coral, worm, lobster, sea star, squid, spider.

Map the Concept

Complete the concept map using the following terms.

amphibians   gills
fish   reptiles
fur   wings

Critical Thinking

17. Apply How do you think scientists know that saber-toothed cats ate meat?

18. Synthesize What might happen to the animals that live in an area where humans are moving in?

19. Evaluate Suppose someone tells you that carrier pigeons, an extinct species, will return to an area if its habitat is restored. Is this statement accurate?

20. Analyze Which animals breathe in a similar way: whales and cats or whales and sharks? Explain.

Performance Assessment

Design an Animal
Design a new mammal that lives on land. Draw and describe what your animal looks like. List what it eats. Tell about its habitat.

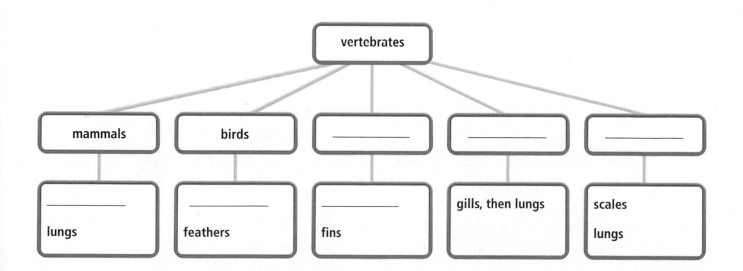

Chapter 3

Living Things Grow and Reproduce

LESSON

1

A flower, a fruit, and an insect—how do they help plants reproduce?

Read about it in Lesson 1.

LESSON

2

A turtle hatches from an egg and a caterpillar changes into a butterfly— how do the life cycles of animals compare?

Read about it in Lesson 2.

LESSON

3

Red flower or yellow flower, big dog or small dog—why do plants and animals of the same species sometimes look different?

Read about it in Lesson 3.

© Thomas Weiwandt / www.wildhorizons.com

What Are Plant Life Cycles?

Why It Matters...

When you look outside, you probably see many types of plants. You may see huge trees or small flowers. Perhaps you see vegetables in a garden or fruits on a vine. By understanding how plants grow, people can produce the food supplies that they need.

PREPARE TO INVESTIGATE

Inquiry Skill

Observe When you observe, you gather information using your senses and tools such as hand lenses.

Materials

- clear plastic cup
- gravel
- potting soil
- pea seed
- plastic spoon
- water
- pencil
- metric ruler
- hand lens
- goggles

Science and Math Toolbox

For step 2, review **Using a Tape Measure or Ruler** on page H6.

Growing Greens
Procedure

Seed Growth	Drawing	Observation
Day 1		
Day 2		
Day 3		
Day 4		
Day 5		

1. **Observe** In your *Science Notebook*, make a chart like the one shown. Work with a partner. Use a hand lens to look closely at a pea seed. Draw the seed and record your observations. **Safety:** Wear goggles.

2. **Measure** Place a 2-cm layer of gravel in the bottom of a cup. Use a ruler to help you measure. Then fill the cup with soil.

3. **Experiment** Use a pencil to make a small hole in the soil. Place the pea seed in the hole and cover it with soil. Add a few spoonfuls of water. Place the cup near a sunny window.

4. **Observe** After a few days, measure the plant and observe it with a hand lens. Add water if the soil is dry. Make a drawing. Record your observations and measurements in your chart.

5. **Observe** Repeat step 4 each day for the next four days.

Conclusion

1. **Compare** Exchange charts with a partner. How are your observations similar?

2. **Predict** You have seen two stages in a plant's life cycle. What stage will you see next if your plant keeps growing?

Investigate More!

Design an Experiment
Observe the inside of a tomato. Based on your observation, infer how a tomato plant grows. Design an experiment to test your idea.

VOCABULARY

conifer	p. A72
fruit	p. A70
life cycle	p. A70
seed	p. A70

READING SKILL

Main Idea and Details
Use a chart to show three details about the life cycle of a flowering plant.

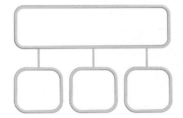

Plant Life Cycles

MAIN IDEA Plants have life cycles, during which they grow, reproduce, and die.

Flowering Plants

Both plants and animals have life cycles (SY kuhlz). A **life cycle** is the series of changes that a living thing goes through during its lifetime. Different living things have different life cycles. Flowering plants, such as this apple tree, have similar life cycles.

A flower, or blossom, is the part of the plant that makes fruit (froot) and seeds. A **seed** is the first stage of most plants. For a plant to produce seeds, pollen (PAHL uhn) must first move from one part of a flower to another. Pollen is a powdery material found inside flowers. The wind, insects, and other animals can move pollen.

A **fruit** is the part of the plant that contains the seeds. The apple blossoms on this tree will produce many apples. The seeds inside the apples can grow into new apple trees.

When a seed is planted in the soil it will sprout and develop into a seedling. As the seedling grows, it becomes a young tree, or sapling. When the sapling becomes an adult, the life cycle begins again. Most plants continue this cycle for many years until they die.

▶ **MAIN IDEA** What part of a flowering plant contains seeds?

Life Cycle of an Apple Tree

blossom

sapling

fruit

seedling

seed in fruit

Conifers

Not all plants have flowers. Some plants have cones instead of flowers. A **conifer** (KAHN uh fur) is a plant that makes seeds inside cones. Pine trees are conifers. Conifers use their cones to reproduce. The diagram below shows the stages in the life cycle of a conifer.

 **MAIN IDEA** **What is a conifer?**

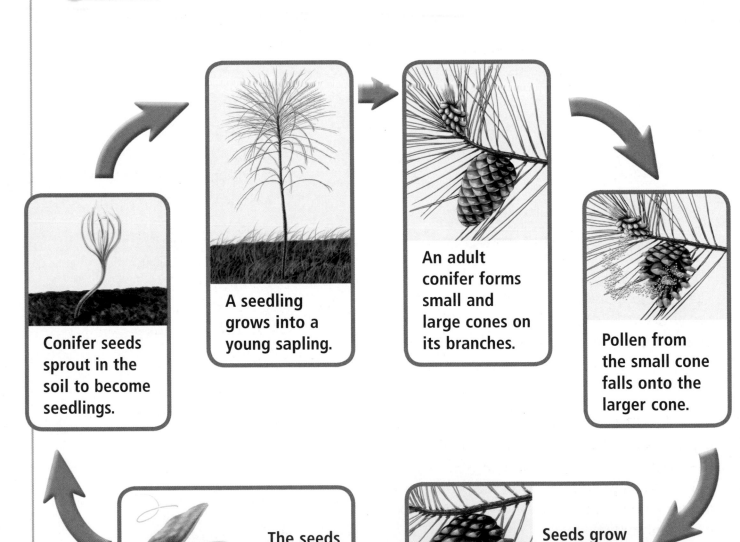

Conifer seeds sprout in the soil to become seedlings.

A seedling grows into a young sapling.

An adult conifer forms small and large cones on its branches.

Pollen from the small cone falls onto the larger cone.

The seeds fall to the ground.

Seeds grow inside the larger cone.

Visual Summary

Flowering plants grow and reproduce by making fruits and seeds from flowers.

Conifers grow and reproduce by making seeds from cones.

LINKS for Home and School

MATH Continue the Pattern The scale-like parts on pinecones are called bracts. Bracts are arranged in spirals. The number of bracts in each spiral follows a pattern. Look at this pattern: 1, 2, 3, 5, 8. What are the next two numbers in the pattern?

ART Draw a Diagram Choose a flowering plant or a conifer. Find photos or real-life examples of the plant to use as models. Draw a detailed diagram of the plant at each stage in its life cycle. Show differences in size, shape, color, and texture.

Review

① MAIN IDEA What are two things that happen during a plant's life cycle?

② VOCABULARY Write a sentence using the term *life cycle*.

③ READING SKILL: Main Idea and Details List three details about the life cycle of a conifer.

④ CRITICAL THINKING: Analyze How is the seed of a flowering plant different than the seed of a conifer?

⑤ INQUIRY SKILL: Observe You see a plant that has white blossoms and small berries with seeds inside. Is the plant a flowering plant or a conifer? Explain.

 TEST PREP
A young tree is called a ___.
A. conifer.
B. seed.
C. fruit.
D. sapling.

 Technology
Visit **www.eduplace.com/scp/** to find out more about the life cycles of plants.

A73

What Are Some Animal Life Cycles?

Why It Matters...

Like some kinds of animals, an elephant grows inside its mother's body until it is born. Other kinds of animals hatch from eggs. Some animals grow in size until they become adults. Some animals may change form. You can learn a lot about animals by studying their life cycles.

PREPARE TO INVESTIGATE

Inquiry Skill

Communicate When you communicate, you present information using words, sketches, charts, and diagrams.

Materials

- disposable gloves
- plastic container and lid
- butterfly habitat
- paper towel
- leaves
- twigs
- caterpillar food
- hand lens
- tape
- caterpillars

Caterpillar Change

Procedure

① In your *Science Notebook*, make a chart like the one shown.

② **Experiment** Place a folded paper towel, leaves, and twigs in a plastic container. Carefully put caterpillars and their food in the container and close the lid. **Safety:** Wear gloves and handle the caterpillars gently.

③ **Observe** Look closely at the caterpillars with a hand lens. Make a drawing and record your observations in your chart.

④ Repeat step 3 every other day for 7 to 10 days. When the caterpillars are hanging from the paper disk at the top of the container and are enclosed in a casing, remove the paper disk with the casings attached. Use tape to hang it on the wall of the butterfly habitat, as shown.

⑤ Repeat step 3 every other day for another 7 to 10 days.

Conclusion

1. **Compare** Compare two stages of the butterfly life cycle.

2. **Communicate** Explain how a caterpillar becomes a butterfly.

STEP 1

Drawing	Observation

STEP 3

STEP 4

Investigate More!

Research Choose an animal that lives in your area. Use library books or search the Internet to find out how the animal is born and how it changes as it grows.

Animal Life Cycles

VOCABULARY

chrysalis	p. A76
larva	p. A76
offspring	p. A78
pupa	p. A76
tadpole	p. A77

READING SKILL

Sequence
Use a chart to show the life cycle of an animal.

1	
2	
3	
4	

MAIN IDEA Different animals have different life cycles, but they are all born, grow, reproduce, and die.

Life Cycle of Insects

Animals follow similar stages in their life cycles. They are born, grow, reproduce, and die. But butterflies and most other insects change more than many other animals do.

The first stage in the life cycle of most insects is the egg. The second stage is a wormlike stage called the **larva** (LAHR vuh). The third stage is the pupa (PYOO puh). During the **pupa** stage, the butterfly changes into an adult. Butterflies form a case called a **chrysalis** (KRIHS uh lihs). The fourth stage is the adult. The life cycle starts again when the adult female butterfly lays eggs.

Life Cycle of a Butterfly

Egg The adult female butterfly lays eggs on a leaf.

Larva A larva, called a caterpillar, hatches from the egg.

Pupa The caterpillar becomes a pupa and makes a case called a chrysalis.

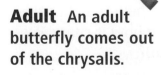

Adult An adult butterfly comes out of the chrysalis.

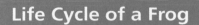

Eggs An adult female frog lays many eggs in the water.

Tadpole Tadpoles hatch from the eggs.

Frog The adult frog has no tail and breathes with lungs.

Young frog The tadpole becomes a small frog with legs and a tail.

Life Cycles of Amphibians and Reptiles

Like insects, amphibians, such as frogs, change form during their life cycles. After a frog hatches from its egg, it is called a tadpole (TAD pohl). A **tadpole** lives in water and has a long tail, gills, and no legs. It looks very different from an adult frog.

Reptiles have a different life cycle from amphibians. The adult female reptile lays eggs, usually on land. After the eggs hatch, young reptiles increase in size and grow into adults. Unlike amphibians, reptiles do not change form as they grow. A young reptile looks similar to its parents.

▶ **SEQUENCE** Female insects, amphibians, and reptiles lay eggs during which stage of their life cycles?

Life Cycles of Birds and Mammals

Birds lay eggs, just as insects, amphibians, and reptiles do. Young birds have traits similar to their parents.

The offspring (AWF sprihng) of mammals grow and develop inside the bodies of adult females. **Offspring** are the living things that result when an animal reproduces. The offspring of mammals are born live. They do not hatch from eggs. At birth they look much like adult mammals. Dogs, cats, and humans grow and develop in this way.

▶ **SEQUENCE** **Can a mammal be an adult as soon as it is born? Explain.**

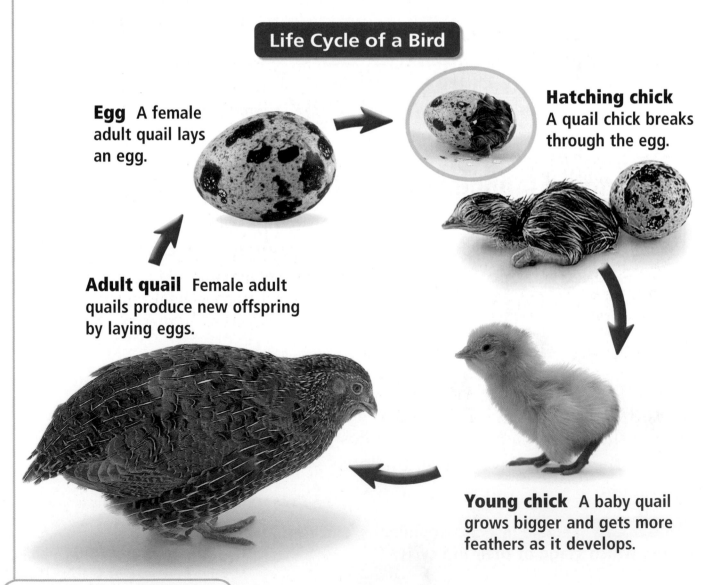

Life Cycle of a Bird

Egg A female adult quail lays an egg.

Hatching chick A quail chick breaks through the egg.

Adult quail Female adult quails produce new offspring by laying eggs.

Young chick A baby quail grows bigger and gets more feathers as it develops.

Visual Summary

Some animals are born live and other animals hatch from eggs.

↓

Animals grow in size or change into different forms as they develop.

↓

Adult animals reproduce and make new offspring.

LINKS for Home and School

MATH **Calculate the Number** Suppose a farmer has 6 hens. Each hen has an equal number of eggs in her nest. When all the eggs hatch, there are 12 chicks. How many eggs did each hen have in her nest?

WRITING **Narrative** Imagine that you are a young frog. Write a narrative story about your life. Include details about how your body is changing as you grow from a tadpole into a frog.

Review

❶ **MAIN IDEA** What do the life cycles of all animals have in common?

❷ **VOCABULARY** Write a sentence using the terms *offspring* and *tadpole*.

❸ **READING SKILL: Sequence** Describe the stages in the life cycle of a bird.

❹ **CRITICAL THINKING: Analyze** Suppose that Animal A is an adult animal that hatched from an egg, once had gills, and once had a tail. What type of animal is Animal A?

❺ **INQUIRY SKILL: Communicate** Draw a diagram of the life cycle of a reptile.

 TEST PREP
An example of an animal that lays eggs but does not change forms as it grows is ___.

A. an insect.

B. an amphibian.

C. a reptile.

D. a mammal.

 Technology
Visit **www.eduplace.com/scp/** to find out more about animal life cycles.

Jane Goodall

She Dreamt of Africa. When she was a child, Jane Goodall dreamed of working with wild animals. At age 23, she left her home in England and sailed to Africa. Dr. Louis Leakey, a famous archaeologist, hired her to study chimpanzees in the Gombe forest.

At first, the chimps were afraid of Jane. She watched them from afar for months. Finally, she gained their trust. Jane spent hours observing the chimpanzees. Over time, Jane realized that chimps make and use tools, communicate with each other, and form family relationships.

In 1977, Jane founded the Jane Goodall Institute. This organization works to protect wildlife. Today, Jane travels the world, teaching people about chimpanzees and the importance of protecting the environment.

Gombe National Park is in Tanzania, a country in East Africa.

Gombe National Park is full of thick forests and steep valleys. It is a perfect environment for chimpanzees.

Baby chimps depend on their mothers for survival.

Sharing Ideas

1. **READING CHECK** How did Jane gain the chimps' trust?

2. **WRITE ABOUT IT** What are some things Jane learned about chimps?

3. **TALK ABOUT IT** Discuss the importance of protecting the African forest.

A81

How Can Living Things Vary?

Why It Matters...

These two animals look very different from one another, but they are both dogs. Living things of the same kind do not always look the same. Some may be tall and some may be short. Some may have spots and some are a solid color. Scientists study living things of the same kind to learn how they are alike and different.

PREPARE TO INVESTIGATE

Inquiry Skill

Use Numbers You use numbers when you measure, estimate, and record data.

Materials

- 4 pea pods
- index cards
- marking pen
- metric ruler

Science and Math Toolbox

For step 6, review **Making a Bar Graph** on page H3.

Peas in a Pod
Procedure

STEP 1

Pea Pod	Length of Pod	Number of Peas	Color of Peas
A			
B			
C			
D			

1. In your *Science Notebook*, make a chart like the one shown.

2. **Experiment** Label four index cards *A*, *B*, *C*, and *D*. Place a pea pod on each of the labeled cards.

3. **Measure** Use a ruler to measure the length of each pea pod. Record the data in your chart.

STEP 4

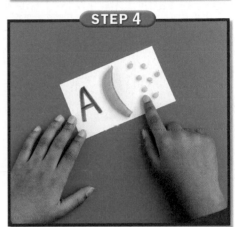

4. **Record Data** Open each pea pod. Count the number of peas in each pod. Record the data in your chart.

5. **Observe** Look at the color of the peas in each pod. Record your observations in your chart.

STEP 6

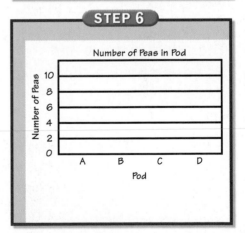

6. **Use Numbers** In your *Science Notebook*, copy the bar graph grid shown. Use the data in your chart to complete the graph.

Conclusion

1. **Analyze Data** Find the greatest and the least number of peas in your data. Combine this data with that of your classmates. Make a line plot to show the class data.

2. **Predict** Suppose you measured and observed four additional pea pods. Would you expect the data to be similar to the class data? Explain your answer.

Investigate More!

Research Use books or the Internet to learn about one kind of apple. Write a report about that apple type. Find out if all apples of that type have the same number of seeds.

▶ **READING SKILL**

Compare and Contrast
Use a chart to compare
and contrast living things
of the same kind.

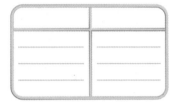

Similarities and Differences

MAIN IDEA Most living things look similar to their parents. This is true because parents pass traits to their offspring.

Family Resemblance

"He has his father's eyes!" "Oh, she has her mother's smile!" You may have heard people talk about children this way. In some families, children look similar to their parents. Young plants and animals also often look like their parents. They grow to be about the same height as their parents. The color of a plant's flowers is usually similar to that of its parent plant. The color of an animal's fur is often similar to the fur of one or both of its parents.

The adult tortoise and its young have a similar design on their shells. ▼

▲ **The adult and baby rabbit look very similar.**

Although offspring and their parents may look similar, they do not look exactly alike. A young horse may grow to be taller or a different color than its parents. A child may have a different eye color than either parent. A grown tree may have fewer flowers or fruit than the tree from which it came.

Differences in appearance between parents and offspring are not extreme. Have you ever seen a turtle the size of a house? A turtle may grow to be larger than either of its parents. But a turtle cannot grow to be as large as a house. Similarly, a large animal, such as a giraffe, does not produce offspring that stay very small.

▲ The adult penguin and its offspring do not look exactly alike.

▶ COMPARE AND CONTRAST Compare ways in which plants and animals may resemble their parents.

This adult orca whale and its baby have a similar pattern on their skin.

These petunias come in many different colors.

Individuals Vary

In a crowd, you can see lots of different people—some are tall, some are short, some have blue eyes, some have brown eyes—but they are all humans. Although all people are humans, each person has different features.

There are also many differences within groups of plants and animals. One petunia flower may have red petals. Another petunia may have pink petals. A dog may have very short fur. Another dog may have so much fur that you can barely see its face! Petal color and fur length are just two examples of differences among individuals (ihn duh VIHJ oo uhlz). An **individual** is a single member of a species. Can you think of some other differences among individuals?

These are all domestic cats. Notice how different they look from one another. ▼

When living things reproduce, they pass on traits to their offspring. This explains why offspring usually look similar to their parents. Look at the three sheep shown here. The parents of the first sheep probably also had black heads. The parents of the second sheep likely had curled horns. The wooly third sheep probably had wooly parents, as well.

A living thing's environment may also affect its traits. For example, a plant that does not receive enough sunlight and water may not grow as tall as its parent plant.

Living things may also get traits from interacting with their environment. These traits are not passed on to their offspring. For example, suppose a young girl scrapes her arm. The scrape leaves a scar. She did not get this trait from her parents, and she will not pass it on to her children.

▶ **COMPARE AND CONTRAST** **Name two traits that can be different among individuals.**

▲ These animals look different, but they are all sheep.

Visual Summary

Living things usually look similar to, but not exactly like, their parents.

Individuals of the same kind usually vary in appearance.

LINKS for Home and School

MATH **Make an Organized List** Suppose a cat has a litter of kittens. The mother cat has long, white fur and the father cat has short, black fur. What might the kittens look like? Make a list of the possible combinations of fur color and fur length.

TECHNOLOGY **Compare and Contrast** Fertilizer is a material that is put in soil to give it extra nutrients. Farmers use fertilizer as a tool for growing healthy crops. Suppose you had two plants that you gave the same amount of water and light. Imagine that you give fertilizer to only one of them. How do you think these individual plants would differ?

Review

❶ **MAIN IDEA** Why do most offspring look similar to their parents?

❷ **VOCABULARY** Define the term *individual*.

❸ **READING SKILL: Compare and Contrast** How are the sheep on page A87 similar? How are they different?

❹ **CRITICAL THINKING: Evaluate** You have two flowers that are the same color. Your friend says that the flowers are definitely the same species. Is this statement accurate? Explain.

❺ **INQUIRY SKILL: Use Numbers** The number of petals for six flowers of the same kind are: *8, 7, 9, 7, 8, 6*. What can you infer about the number of petals usually found on this kind of flower?

✔ **TEST PREP**
Which trait can be passed on from an adult human to a child?

A. scar

B. hair color

C. sunburn

D. sprained ankle

 Technology
Visit **www.eduplace.com/scp/** to learn more about how individuals vary.

Veterinary Assistant

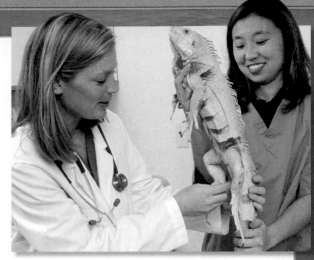

Do you enjoy caring for animals? As a veterinary assistant, you might help a veterinarian bandage the broken leg of a dog or calm a cat during an examination. You would also feed, water, and exercise animals. You would clean cages and exam rooms and take notes during exams. Veterinary assistants work at animal shelters, humane societies, and animal hospitals.

What It Takes!

- A high-school diploma.
- Courses in biology; some knowledge of medicine or dentistry

Marine Biologist

You might think marine biologists spend all their time swimming in the ocean while they study plants and animals. In fact, much of a marine biologist's work is done in a submarine or a laboratory. They use computers to track the movements of sea creatures like whales, dolphins, and sea turtles. Understanding the habits of these creatures can help scientists protect them.

What It Takes!

- A degree in biology, oceanography, or zoology
- The ability to work with computers

EXTREME Science

Mama Croc!

This mother crocodile isn't eating her baby! She's carrying it in her mouth to keep it safe from harm. Most reptiles just bury their eggs and leave them. The crocodile fiercely guards her buried eggs from other predators.

When she hears peeping from the buried eggs, she digs them out. Sometimes she even uses her huge teeth to help her babies out of their shells. After carrying them to the water, she watches over them until they are big enough to protect themselves.

This baby will grow fast—and big. Some full-grown crocodiles are longer than a family car and weigh more than a ton!

A91

Review and Test Prep

Vocabulary

Complete each sentence with a term from the list.

1. When a frog first hatches from an egg, it is called a/an _____.

2. The part of the plant that contains seeds is the _____.

3. The third stage of an insect's life cycle is the _____.

4. The series of changes a living thing goes through during its lifetime is called a/an _____.

5. A single member of a species is called a/an _____.

6. Living things that result when animals reproduce are called _____.

7. The first stage in the life cycle of most plants is the _____.

8. The case that butterflies form in their pupa stage is a/an _____.

9. A plant that grows cones is a/an _____.

10. The worm-like stage of an insect's life cycle is called the _____.

chrysalis A76
conifer A72
fruit A70
individual A86
larva A76
life cycle A70
offspring A78
pupa A76
seed A70
tadpole A77

Test Prep

Write the letter of the best answer choice.

11. Living things and their parents _____.

    A. often look similar.
    B. never look similar.
    C. are always the same size.
    D. do not interact with their environment.

12. The offspring of birds grow and develop in _____.

    A. water.   **C.** the adult female's body.
    B. eggs.   **D.** a plant.

13. Adult frogs _____.

    A. give birth to live young.
    B. live only in water.
    C. have tails.
    D. breathe with lungs.

14. The part of a plant that makes fruit and seeds is the _____.

    A. flower.   **C.** sapling.
    B. stem.   **D.** leaf.

15. Observe Suppose that you observe an orange tree with blossoms on it. Describe what must happen so that the tree can produce fruit and seeds.

16. Communicate A cottonwood leaf beetle has a life cycle that is similar to that of a butterfly. Write a paragraph to describe the life cycle of a cottonwood leaf beetle.

Map the Concept

Place the following terms in the concept map to describe the life cycle of an insect.

pupa   egg
adult   larva

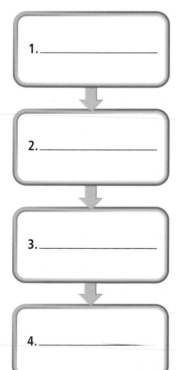

1. _____

2. _____

3. _____

4. _____

17. Apply Suppose you have a long-haired male dog and a long-haired female dog. You have each dog's hair cut short. If these dogs reproduce, are their puppies likely to have long hair or short hair? Explain.

18. Evaluate Suppose your friend says that an apple seed is similar to a frog's egg. Do you agree or disagree with this statement? Explain your answer.

19. Synthesize When walking in the park, you see pine cones on the ground. What can you conclude about some of the trees in that park?

20. Analyze How are plant life cycles and animal life cycles similar? How are they different?

Performance Assessment

Draw a Life Cycle
Choose one of the following animals: frog, hawk, mouse. Make a diagram of the life cycle of that animal. Include a drawing, label, and brief explanation of each stage of the cycle.

Write the letter of the best answer choice.

1. Which do both plants and animals have?

   A. seeds
   B. life cycles
   C. taproots
   D. larvae

2. Which pair of invertebrates are both arthropods?

   A.

   B.

   C.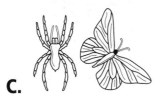

   D.

3. A carrot has a long, thick root. The veins in its leaves have many branches. Which terms describe a carrot?

   A. taproot, netted veins
   B. taproot, woody stem
   C. fibrous root, netted veins
   D. fibrous root, smooth leaves

4. All vertebrates have _____.

   A. fur.
   B. scales.
   C. a shell.
   D. a backbone.

5. A species for which there are fewer individuals each year is said to be _____.

   A. endangered.
   B. extinct.
   C. a fossil.
   D. reproducing.

6. Which plant stores most of its food in its stem?

A.

B.

C.

D.

7. Which shows the life cycle of a frog in the correct order?

A.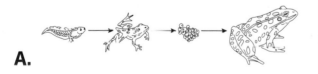

B.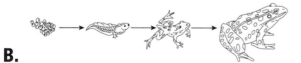

C.

D.

8. Which is NOT needed by a seed for it to grow into a new plant?

    A. soil

    B. water

    C. sunlight

    D. wind

Answer the following in complete sentences.

9. The picture below shows a mother giraffe and her young. Describe how the two giraffes are BOTH alike and different.

10. Florida panthers are an endangered species. Explain why they are endangered.

Discover!

Because dolphins and people have traits in common, they belong to many of the same animal groups. They are both vertebrates, which means they both have a backbone. They are also mammals. They produce milk for their young. Also, they use lungs to breathe. Dolphins and people are considered intelligent animals. They have large brains for their body size.

Both people and dolphins have lungs for breathing. To breathe, a dolphin swims to the surface of the water. It takes in air through an opening, called a blowhole, on the top of its head. A human breathes air through the nose and mouth.

Like most mammals, dolphins are born live. That means they don't hatch from eggs. When they are born, they look like adult dolphins, only smaller. Human babies are also born live and look like very small adults.

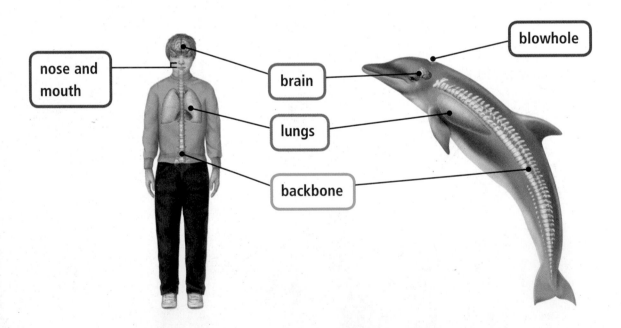

nose and mouth

blowhole

brain

lungs

backbone

Compare a dolphin and a human. Go to **www.eduplace.com/scp/** to learn more about the features that these animals have in common.

LIFE · UNIT B · SCIENCE

Living Things in Their Environment

Living Things in Their Environment

Independent Reading

A Hungry Red Hawk

Amazing Adaptations

Forced Out

Polar bears live on the frozen coasts of the Arctic. They hunt from the edges of ice platforms. These bears can run as fast as 40 kilometers (about 25 miles) in an hour without slipping. Why doesn't a polar bear slip on the ice when it runs? You will have the answer to this question by the end of the unit.

Chapter 4

Survival of Living Things

LESSON

1

Water, air, a place to live—why do you need these to survive?

Read about it in Lesson 1.

LESSON

2

Bald eagles and bears both eat fish—what happens to these animals if there are not enough fish?

Read about it in Lesson 2.

LESSON

3

From the leaves of a plant to the feet of a duck— how do their parts help living things survive?

Read about it in Lesson 3.

LESSON

4

A fire spreads through a forest—can a forest fire ever be good for living things?

Read about it in Lesson 4.

What Are the Needs of Living Things?

Why It Matters...

You probably know that a turtle is alive and that a rock is not alive. But how do you know this? What does it mean to be alive? You and all other living things share some of the same traits. All living things also share the same basic needs.

PREPARE TO INVESTIGATE

Inquiry Skill

Collaborate When you collaborate, you work with others to share ideas, data, and observations.

Materials

- aquarium
- water
- gravel
- goldfish
- fish food
- piece of elodea plant

Science and Math Toolbox

For step 2, review **Making a Chart to Organize Data** on page H10.

Staying Alive
Procedure

1. **Collaborate** Work with a partner. One partner should observe a goldfish. The other partner should observe an elodea (ah LOH dee ah), which is a type of water plant.

2. **Observe** In your *Science Notebook,* make a chart like the one shown. Watch your living thing for a few minutes. In your chart, record the name of the living thing and everything you observe. Include its surroundings and any movements it makes.

3. **Infer** Based on your observations, write two or three things that you think your living thing needs to stay alive.

4. **Collaborate** Compare charts with your partner. Circle the needs that are alike for the fish and the plant.

Conclusion

1. **Compare** What does the goldfish need that the elodea plant does not need?

2. **Hypothesize** If you put the elodea plant in sunlight, it releases tiny bubbles of gas. Where do you think this gas comes from? What does the goldfish do that might be similar?

STEP 2

Observing Living Things	
Observations	Needs

STEP 2

STEP 4

Investigate More!
Research What animal would you like to have as a pet? Use the library to find books about what that animal needs to stay alive and healthy.

B5

▶ **VOCABULARY**

ecosystem   p. B10
energy   p. B7
environment   p. B10
organism   p. B8

▶ **READING SKILL**

Draw Conclusions Fill in the diagram with details about an object. Conclude whether the object is alive or not.

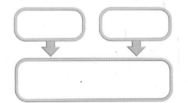

Needs of Living Things

MAIN IDEA Everything is either living or nonliving. Living things depend on both the living things and nonliving things around them to meet needs.

Living and Nonliving Things

As you look at the picture on this page, you see many things. There are flowers, bushes, sunlight, soil, a dog, and humans. Some of these things are living, and others are nonliving. A living thing is alive and is able to carry out life processes (PRAHS ehs ihz).

There are living and nonliving things in this picture. Identify as many of each kind as you can.

What are life processes? Think of the things your body does. For example, you grow and develop. You also react to the things around you. Another life process of living things is the ability to reproduce (ree pruh DOOS), or to produce young. All of these life processes use energy (EHN-ur jee). **Energy** is the ability to cause change.

Not all things are alive. A nonliving thing is not alive, so it cannot carry out life processes. What traits could you look for to decide whether something is living or nonliving? The five traits of living things are described in the table below.

▶ DRAW CONCLUSIONS **What might happen to a living thing that doesn't get any energy?**

Traits of Living Things

Made of Cells		All living things are made of tiny parts called cells. Some living things are made up of only one cell. Humans are made of many millions of cells!
Obtain and Use Energy		Plants, such as apple trees, get energy from the Sun. Apples contain food energy. Animals obtain energy from food and use that energy to power their activities.
Respond to Surroundings		When a plant bends toward the light, it is responding to its surroundings. All living things react to changes in their surroundings.
Grow and Develop		All living things grow and develop. When you get taller, you are growing. When your body changes during your lifetime, you are developing.
Reproduce		All living things have the ability to reproduce. This means that they can produce offspring, or young that are like themselves.

Energy Leaves capture the energy in sunlight. The plant uses this energy to make food.

Nutrients Roots and stems carry nutrients and water from the soil to all parts of the plant.

Needs of Living Things

You watch a bee flying just above a flower. A bee and a plant don't seem to have much in common, but both are organisms (AWR guh nihz uhmz). An **organism** is a living thing. All organisms carry out the same life processes. They also have similar basic needs. What do plants, animals, and all other organisms need to survive?

Energy Moving, growing, and breathing all require energy. All living things need a source of energy. They use food as a source of energy, but they get this food in different ways. Plants use energy from sunlight to make food. Animals cannot make food. They get energy by eating plants or other animals.

Nutrients Nutrients (NOO tree uhnts) are materials in food and soil that living things need for energy and for growth.

Air Air is a mixture of gases that living things need. One of the gases in air is oxygen (AHK sih juhn). Most living things need oxygen to survive. When plants make food they give off oxygen into the air. Animals depend on this oxygen to survive.

Shelter All animals need a place to live. An animal's home gives it shelter and provides it with protection from enemies. Some animals use plants for shelter.

Water Living things are made mostly of water. In fact, more than three fourths of your blood is water. Most living things can live for only a short time without water.

▶ **DRAW CONCLUSIONS** Could most plants live in soil that contained no nutrients? Why or why not?

Shelter Caves give bats shelter. The insects that bats eat and the water bats drink are found in or near caves.

Air When you exercise, you need a lot of oxygen. Oxygen is used to break down nutrients.

Water The body needs water to break down food, to move things from place to place, and to make cells.

Interactions

Living things are found in every kind of environment (ehn VY ruhn muhnt). An **environment** is all the living and nonliving things that surround an organism.

A Florida mangrove swamp is one kind of ecosystem (EE koh sihs tuhm). An **ecosystem** is all the living and nonliving things that exist and interact in one place. To survive, the organisms in an ecosystem depend on each other and on the nonliving things that share their ecosystem.

▶ **DRAW CONCLUSIONS** What might happen if all of one type of organism in an ecosystem died?

Herons build nests in the leafy branches.

Mangrove trees use sunlight to make food.

Mangrove roots prevent soil from washing away.

Pelicans depend on fish for food.

Red snapper and other fish live in the water.

Oysters and crabs use mangrove roots for shelter.

Lesson Wrap-Up

Visual Summary

Living things are made up of cells, obtain and use energy, react, grow and develop, and produce offspring.

Living things need energy, nutrients, air, water, and shelter.

In an ecosystem, organisms interact with other organisms and with nonliving parts of their environment.

LINKS for Home and School

ART Design a Mural Design a mural that shows an ecosystem near your school. Include living as well as nonliving things. Try to show how the living and nonliving things interact.

LITERATURE Write a Log Entry Imagine you are a space explorer and your ship has landed on a faraway planet. What strange life forms do you see? How can you tell if they are alive? Write a log entry that describes the life processes and environment of one life form.

Review

❶ **MAIN IDEA** What are the five traits of living things?

❷ **VOCABULARY** Write a sentence using the term *environment*.

❸ **READING SKILL: Draw Conclusions** You receive a gift that grows in sunlight and does not need to be fed. Would you conclude that this gift is a plant or an animal? Explain.

❹ **CRITICAL THINKING: Apply** Give an example of how a nonliving thing might affect the living things in a desert ecosystem.

❺ **INQUIRY SKILL: Collaborate** Name a basic need of living things. Explain to a classmate how that basic need can be met for a mouse.

✓ **TEST PREP**
Plants do, but animals do NOT ___.

A. produce offspring.

B. need water.

C. use sunlight to make food.

D. grow and develop.

 Technology
Visit **www.eduplace.com/scp/** to find out more about the needs of living things.

How Do Living Things Compete?

Why It Matters...

"It's mine!" "No, it's mine!" If birds and squirrels could speak to each other, this is what they might say. When food is limited in an environment, animals must compete. An animal that loses a competition might lose a meal or a place to live.

PREPARE TO INVESTIGATE

Inquiry Skill

Use Variables A variable is the condition that is being tested in an experiment. All conditions in an experiment must be kept the same, except for the variable.

Materials

- 4 paper plates
- 4 sheets of paper
- pretzels (1 per student)

Science and Math Toolbox

For step 5, review **Making a Bar Graph** on page H3.

Investigate

Competition
Procedure

1. **Use Variables** Your teacher will set up four model ecosystems. Each ecosystem is represented by a plate covered with a sheet of paper. Some plates contain many pretzels, some contain few pretzels, and some contain no pretzels.

2. **Use Models** Stand in the center of the room. When your teacher says "Go," choose an ecosystem and walk to it. **Safety:** Do not run or push others.

3. Peek under the paper. If there is a pretzel, take the pretzel and stand by the ecosystem. If there are no pretzels, move on to another ecosystem.

4. Repeat step 3 until you find a pretzel.

5. **Communicate** When every student has found a pretzel, make a bar graph like the one shown. The graph should show how many ecosystems each student visited before finding food.

STEP 2

STEP 3

STEP 5
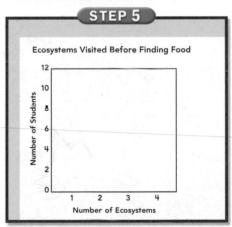

Ecosystems Visited Before Finding Food

Number of Students (y-axis: 0, 2, 4, 6, 8, 10, 12)

Number of Ecosystems (x-axis: 1, 2, 3, 4)

Conclusion

1. **Analyze Data** How many ecosystems did most people visit before they found food? Why?

2. **Predict** How might an organism be affected if the food in its ecosystem were eaten by other organisms?

Investigate More!

Solve a Problem Take away several pretzels, then repeat the activity. Think of ways that each student could still get some food. Share your ideas with your classmates.

► **VOCABULARY**

community	p. B15
population	p. B14
resource	p. B15

► **READING SKILL**

Main Idea and Details
As you read, write down details that describe the ways in which organisms compete.

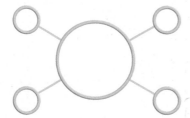

Living Things Compete

MAIN IDEA Organisms compete for resources when they live in the same ecosystem and have similar needs.

Competing for Food and Water

Look around. You, your classmates, your teachers, your family, and all the people who live in your neighborhood make up a population (pahp yuh LAY shuhn) of humans. A **population** is all the organisms of the same kind that live together in an ecosystem. All the ants living in a forest make up the ant population of that forest ecosystem. Every oak tree in a forest is a member of the oak tree population of that ecosystem.

snake

coyote

skunk

prairie chicken eggs

In a prairie ecosystem, coyotes, snakes, and skunks compete with each other for prairie chicken eggs.

All the populations in an ecosystem make up a community (kuh MYOO nih tee). A **community** is a group of plants and animals that live in the same area and interact with each other. The ants, oak trees, robins, and other living things in a forest ecosystem are part of the same community.

A pond ecosystem is home to animal populations such as fish, frogs, and insects. Plants such as cattails and populations of algae also live there. Living things in nature must be able to get enough resources (REE-sawrs ehz) to survive. A **resource** is a thing found in nature that is useful to organisms. Food, water, shelter, and air are resources. If there is not enough of a resource for all the organisms that need it, they must compete for the resource.

In a pond community, cattails and algae compete for nutrients in the water. Members of the same population may also compete for a resource. If there are not enough resources to meet the needs of all the organisms, some will die. For example, if there are too many frogs, some will not catch enough insects and will not survive.

▶ **MAIN IDEA** What are four resources for which living things compete?

above surface

below surface

▲ **Pond Community**
Competition in a community keeps populations from getting too large.

Competing for Space

In addition to food and water, organisms need living space. Many birds need tree branches and holes in tree trunks to build nests. Trees need space underground for their roots to spread out. They need space above ground for their leafy branches to capture energy from sunlight.

Wolves live in family groups called packs. Sometimes there isn't enough space for all the wolf packs in an area to live and raise offspring. Some of the packs may leave the area to find more space.

Sea lions live on rocks at the edge of the ocean. If a sea lion population in a rocky area becomes too crowded, the animals will fight for space. Some sea lions are injured or killed as a result of those fights.

▲ Wolf packs may move to new areas to find more space.

Sea lions compete with one another for space. ▼

Moose are big animals. They need large areas where they can roam in search of food, water, and shelter. Sometimes humans build houses in areas where moose live. The moose no longer have enough space to meet their needs. As moose populations become crowded, moose wander into areas where humans live. This can be dangerous for both the moose and the humans.

People need space, too. When people are crowded together, as in some large cities, they may compete for space. Competition for space might take place on a busy street or on a crowded bus.

▲ In a crowded city, people compete for space.

▶ **MAIN IDEA** What can happen if a population becomes too crowded?

Moose often roam into areas where humans live. ▼

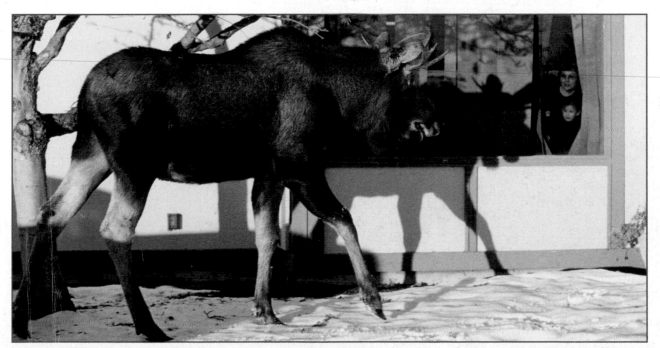

Resources and Population Size

The resources in an area affect the size of populations that depend on those resources. One hundred years ago, wild horses roamed the desert in southern Nevada. They ate grasses and small shrubs that grew there. Some horses were killed by other animals, such as mountain lions. This kept the horse population from becoming too large.

As humans moved into the area, they hunted and killed many of the mountain lions. With fewer enemies, the wild horse population grew. More horses ate more grass and shrubs. As plant resources disappeared, horses began to starve and die. As the number of horses decreased, the plant population grew again.

Today, the number of wild horses does not change much. When the number of horses becomes too great for the amount of plant resources, the United States government captures some horses. The government finds new homes for them.

▶ **MAIN IDEA** **What caused the wild horse population to decrease?**

The size of a population of wild horses is limited by the amount of food resources that are available. ▼

Visual Summary

All the populations that live in an area and interact make up a community.

Organisms in a region compete for resources such as food, water, air, and space.

The size of a population depends on the available resources in an area.

LINKS for Home and School

MATH **Find the Product** You are observing a frog in a pond ecosystem. You see that the frog eats 18 crickets each week. If there were 8 frogs in the pond that each ate the same amount as the first frog, how many crickets would they eat in all in one week? What problem did you solve to find the answer?

SOCIAL STUDIES **Write an Interview** Humans and animals often compete for living space and resources. Research competition between elephants and farmers in Africa. Write an interview with a farmer. Then write an interview with an elephant to show the other side of the story.

Review

❶ MAIN IDEA When do organisms compete for resources?

❷ VOCABULARY How is a population different from a community?

❸ READING SKILL: Main Idea and Details Explain how frogs compete for resources in a pond.

❹ CRITICAL THINKING: Apply How might a community of rabbits, grass, and coyotes change if most of the grass died?

❺ INQUIRY SKILL: Use Variables An experiment is designed to find out how the amount of food in an aquarium affects the size of the fish. What is the variable?

✔ TEST PREP
If a robin and a blue jay try to build their nests on the same branch, the birds are competing for ___.

A. food

B. space

C. water

D. air

Technology
Visit www.eduplace.com/scp/
to read more about competition.

How Do Adaptations Help Living Things?

Why It Matters...

Suppose you were an insect that lived on green leaves. What would be a good way to hide from birds that wanted to make you their dinner? Green katydids look just like the leaves they live on. All living things have special body parts or ways that they act that help them stay alive.

PREPARE TO INVESTIGATE

Inquiry Skill

Infer When you infer, you use facts you know and observations you have made to draw a conclusion.

Materials

- foods: wheat nugget cereal, shredded wheat cereal softened in water, sunflower seeds, grapes
- water bottle with water
- tools: tweezers, chopsticks, dropper, salad tongs, pliers, hand-held strainer or slotted spoon
- goggles

Science and Math Toolbox

For step 1, review **Making a Chart to Organize Data** on page H10.

Best Bird Beak
Procedure

1. **Record Data** In your *Science Notebook*, make a chart like the one shown. **Safety:** Wear goggles during this activity. Do not eat any of the foods.

2. **Experiment** Use each tool to pick up softened shredded wheat. Each tool represents a type of bird beak. Which tool works best? Write the name of that tool next to "softened shredded wheat" on your chart.

3. Repeat step 2 for each of the other materials. Record results in your chart.

4. The bottle of water represents a trumpet-shaped flower containing a sweet liquid called nectar. Repeat step 2 to find out which tool works best to remove water from the bottle.

5. **Communicate** Share your results with your classmates. Then, decide which tool you think is best for handling each material.

Conclusion

1. **Use Models** Which tool would be best for getting nectar from a flower?

2. **Infer** From your results, make an inference about how the shape of a bird's beak is related to what it eats.

STEP 1

Material	Best Tool
softened shredded wheat	
wheat nuggets	
sunflower seeds	
grapes	
water	

STEP 2

STEP 4

Investigate More!

Research Look in books, in magazines, and on the Internet for pictures of bird beaks that work like the tools in the activity. Try to find one beak for each tool. How does each bird's beak help it eat?

B21

VOCABULARY

adaptation   p. B22
behavior   p. B22

READING SKILL

Problem-Solution Use the chart to identify an extreme environment. Give an example of an organism that has body structures that allow it to survive in that environment.

Problem	Solution

Adaptations Help Living Things

MAIN IDEA Body parts and behaviors are adaptations that help an organism survive.

Getting Food

Did you ever wish that you were invisible so you could take a snack without being seen? Many animals have adaptations (ad dap TAY-shuhnz) that let them become almost invisible. Then they can sneak up on food or hide from enemies. An **adaptation** is a behavior (bi HAYV-yur) or a body part that helps a living thing survive in its environment. A **behavior** is the way an animal typically acts in a certain situation.

A cat's ability to sneak up on a mouse is a behavior that is an adaptation. ▼

▲ Some spiders have body parts that they use to spin webs that trap insects.

Many types of animal behaviors are adaptations. A bee dancing to tell other bees where food can be found is an adaptation that helps that population of bees survive.

Adaptations for getting food help an organism survive. Certain adaptations let an organism get food that others can't. A hummingbird has a long, thin beak that can reach nectar deep inside a flower. The arms of sea stars have suction cups that they use to pull open the shells of clams.

Plants have adapted parts, too. Some rainforest plants have long stems that let them reach to the tops of trees. Although their roots are in the ground, their leaves are up high where sunlight can shine on them.

▲ Venus flytraps live where soil has few nutrients. They get nutrients by trapping insects.

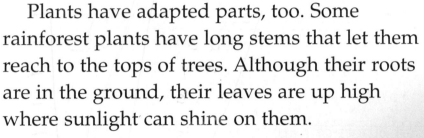 **PROBLEM AND SOLUTION** **What two kinds of adaptations help a living thing survive?**

The long-necked giraffe can eat tree leaves that are out of reach of other animals. ▶

Surviving Harsh Conditions

Living conditions in an alpine, high-mountain, ecosystem are harsh. Temperatures are low and it often snows. The land is steep and rocky. Organisms there have adaptations that help them survive.

The growing season is short. The fact that plants sprout, grow, and produce seeds quickly is an adaptation. Many plants are small. Small plants lose little water when it's windy.

Animals also have adaptations that help them survive the cold. Thick fur and layers of fat keep some animals, such as marmots and sheep, warm. Some animals sleep during very cold periods.

Some plants and animals have adaptations that are slightly better than those of others. These organisms are more likely to survive than others of their kind.

▶ **PROBLEM AND SOLUTION** Describe an adaptation that helps an animal survive in cold temperatures.

Needle-shaped leaves of some trees help prevent water loss.

Ptarmigans have white feathers in winter which help them blend in with the snow. In summer, their feathers are brown which helps them hide on rocky ground.

ptarmigans

Self-Defense

Most organisms have adaptations for self-defense. These are behaviors or structures that help keep an organism from being eaten by enemies. For example, when an enemy approaches, many animals will run away or hide. Some plants have spines or thorns that prevent them from being eaten. Some plants and insects contain bad-tasting chemicals. The bad taste makes them a poor choice for a meal.

Some organisms have markings, such as spots or stripes that make it hard to see them in their environment. Still other plants and animals look like other organisms that are poisonous. These harmless organisms fool their enemies into thinking they are poisonous, so they are left alone.

▶ **PROBLEM AND SOLUTION** **How does a self-defense adaptation help an organism survive?**

▲ A barrel cactus is covered with long, sharp spines, which keeps animals away.

An octopus can change its color or release a cloud of ink to help it hide. ▼

Lesson Wrap-Up

Visual Summary

Adaptations help organisms:
- get food
- survive harsh conditions
- defend themselves from enemies

Body structures help organisms:
- survive
- grow
- reproduce

Behaviors help organisms:
- survive
- grow
- reproduce

LINKS for Home and School

MATH **Convert Measurements** Ernie is a 9,800-pound, 37-year-old Asian male elephant. Ernie is 9 feet tall and drinks 30 gallons of water each day. There are 4 quarts in a gallon. How many quarts of water does Ernie drink each day? Did you need to use all the numbers provided in this problem?

TECHNOLOGY **Write a Paragraph** In nature, adaptations can take millions of years to develop. But scientists might someday discover a way to adapt an organism in a very short time. Choose an organism. How could that organism be better adapted to what it does every day? Write a paragraph to describe the adaptation and how it would help that organism.

Review

1 MAIN IDEA Why are adaptations important?

2 VOCABULARY Use the term *behavior* in a sentence about animal adaptations.

3 READING SKILL: Problem-Solution How might a plant adapt to living in a desert?

4 CRITICAL THINKING: Apply Describe an adaptation an organism might have if it lived on ice and ate animals that lived under the ice.

5 INQUIRY SKILL: Infer What can you infer about an animal's environment if the animal has body structures that can store large amounts of water?

✓ TEST PREP

Which is NOT an example of self-defense?

A. An octopus squirts a cloud of ink.

B. A bee injects poison with a stinger.

C. A harmless butterfly looks like a poisonous butterfly.

D. A sea star uses its suction cups to open a clam shell.

 Technology
Visit **www.eduplace.com/scp/** to learn more about adaptations.

The Wump World is a story about fictional creatures that must adapt to a changing environment. The Wumps are forced to live underground when their planet becomes polluted. Read an excerpt from *The Wump World* below. In *Deer, Moose, Elk, and Caribou*, read about how real-life animals adapt to changes in their environment.

The Wump World
by Bill Peet

THE WUMP WORLD

written and illustrated by BILL PEET

... the poor Wumps remained underground wandering aimlessly through the caverns feeding on the fuzzy green moss growing on the ledges and the mushrooms clustered in the crannies, and sipping the sweet water from pools fed by underground springs. But they were very unhappy. For all they knew, they might have had to spend the rest of their days down there.

Deer, Moose, Elk, & Caribou
by Deborah Hodge

To survive, the deer family needs wild, wooded areas. When people clear land for houses and roads, wild areas get smaller. The number of cougars and wolves also shrinks. With fewer enemies, too many deer end up in one area. Food becomes scarce, and some deer die. Others eat farmers' crops to stay alive.

Sharing Ideas

1. **READING CHECK** How did the Wumps adapt when their environment became polluted?

2. **WRITE ABOUT IT** Do you think that deer are able to adapt? Give reasons for your answer. If you think deer are able to adapt, compare the way that the Wumps adapted to the way that deer adapt.

3. **TALK ABOUT IT** Tell a story about a group of fictional characters that must adapt to a changing environment.

What Happens When Habitats Change?

Why It Matters...

You may have seen headlines about an oil tanker accidentally spilling oil into water. The oil coats the fur and feathers of water animals. An animal can't keep warm with oil on its body. Oil-coated birds can't float or fly, and may drown. Organisms are affected in different ways when their environments change.

PREPARE TO INVESTIGATE

Inquiry Skill

Use Models You can use a model of an object, process, or idea to better understand or describe how it works.

Materials

- large feather
- baby oil
- balance
- water
- dropper
- disposable gloves
- aluminum pan

Science and Math Toolbox

For step 3, review **Using a Balance** on page H9.

Feather Failure
Procedure

STEP 4

1 **Communicate** Work with a partner. In your *Science Notebook*, make a two-column chart with the headings *Dry* and *Oily*.

2 **Observe** Examine a dry feather. Smooth it with your fingers. Wave it in the air. Record your observations.

3 **Measure** Use a balance to find the mass of the feather. Record the mass.

STEP 5

4 **Experiment** Smooth the feather. With a dropper, sprinkle several drops of water on the feather. Record your observations.

5 Put on disposable gloves. Pour baby oil into an aluminum pan. Dip the feather into the oil. Spread the oil over the entire feather.

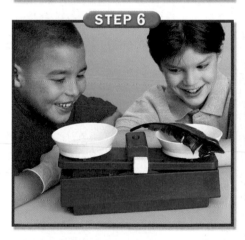
STEP 6

6 Using the oily feather, repeat steps 2, 3, and 4.

Conclusion

1. **Use Models** What features of the dry feather might help a bird survive?

2. **Hypothesize** How did the oil affect the feather? How might an oil spill affect the bird population of an ecosystem?

Investigate More!

Design an Experiment Make a plan to find out how to remove the oil from bird feathers. Choose your materials and get permission from your teacher to carry out your plan. Share your results.

VOCABULARY

habitat   p. B32

pollution   p. B34

READING SKILL

Cause and Effect Use the diagram to show three changes in a forest habitat that are caused by a forest fire.

Habitats Change

MAIN IDEA Changes to an environment can have good and bad effects on the organisms that live there.

Fire and Water

How does a fire change a forest? Small plants that some animals eat are destroyed. Thick bushes that provide shelter may vanish.

But a change that is harmful to some organisms can be good for others. A fire can create new habitats (HAB ih tats). A **habitat** is a place where an organism lives.

After a flood, people and animals may lose their homes. Plants die as muddy water covers them and blocks sunlight. But when the water dries up, nutrient-rich soil is left behind. New plants can grow where they might not have grown before the flood.

Forest fires destroy habitats, but they also create conditions that allow new plants and animals to live. ▶

Plants and Animals

Living things change an environment in many ways. When beavers build a dam across a stream, the water builds up behind the dam. A pond may form. Plants or animals that lived in the once dry area may die or have to find new homes. However, new plants and animals may make the pond their habitat.

Kudzu (KUD zoo) is a fast-growing vine. It was brought to the United States from Japan. It rapidly changes the environment in which it grows. Kudzu vines grow so fast that they can cover houses and trees in a short time. The trees die because they cannot get enough sunlight.

▶ **CAUSE AND EFFECT** **How is a forest fire harmful to the organisms that live in a forest?**

Beavers cut down trees to build dams. The areas where the trees once grew get more sunlight. ▼

Pollution

Some human activities harm the environment, and some help it. People are always building. They build houses, roads, farms, and cities. In the process, they may destroy the habitats of plants and animals.

Human activities can produce pollution (puh-LOO shuhn). **Pollution** is any harmful material in the environment. For example, chemicals that are dumped into rivers can cause fish to die. Smoke can pollute air, harming all organisms that breathe it. Garbage dumps pollute the land when harmful materials in them leak into water or soil.

It's not all bad news, though. Humans can also help the environment. People have passed laws to protect natural resources. Laws that limit hunting and fishing can help protect wildlife populations. Wildlife habitats are also protected by laws. In some places, land has been set aside for parks and wildlife reserves. And farmers plant crops in ways that keep soil healthy.

▶ **CAUSE AND EFFECT** What human activities result in a better environment?

Pollution can destroy wildlife habitats. ▶

Visual Summary

Fires and floods destroy natural habitats, but they also create new ones.

Plants and animals can cause both good and bad changes in their environment.

Humans create pollution, but they also work to protect the environment.

LINKS for Home and School

MATH **Interpret Data** Around the year 1800 in England, there were about 2 dark-colored moths for every 98 light-colored moths. By 1900 there were about 95 dark-colored moths for every 5 light-colored moths. Think about how many dark- and light-colored moths there might have been in 1825, in 1850, and in 1875. Make a graph to display your guesses.

WRITING **Explanatory** Find an example of pollution in your area. Look up ways it might affect the plants, animals, and people where you live. Explain the steps that you would take to clean up or prevent the pollution. Use your ideas to write a letter to your local newspaper.

Review

①ℹ MAIN IDEA How might a change in the environment affect an organism that lives in that environment?

② VOCABULARY Define the word *habitat*.

③ READING SKILL: Cause and Effect How can a beaver dam cause a pond to form?

④ CRITICAL THINKING: Evaluate A forest fire can benefit living things. Give evidence to support this statement.

⑤ INQUIRY SKILL: Use Models Describe a model that shows how thick vines covering a tree can cause harm to the tree.

✔ TEST PREP

An example of air pollution is ___.

A. smoke caused by burning a pile of old tires.

B. dumping chemicals into a river.

C. making a garbage dump.

D. destroying a habitat by building a road.

 Technology
Visit **www.eduplace.com/scp/** to find out more about changing environments.

EXTREME Science

Super Tongue

What in the world is it? It looks like a cross between a bird, a skunk, and a reptile. Meet the giant anteater of Central and South America!

At seven feet long and 80 pounds, the giant anteater is the largest anteater in the world. It may look odd, but when you get to know this creature, its unusual body parts make perfect sense.

The anteater's tongue is two feet long and is covered with tiny spines and sticky saliva to help trap ants.

A giant anteater can eat about 30,000 ants in a day!

Tail Anteaters use their long, fan-like tail to cover their head and body when resting.

Feet Huge claws help the anteater dig up the ants and termites it loves to eat. It also uses its claws to fight off enemies.

Snout Its snout is long, but its mouth is very small.

B37

Chapter 4 Review and Test Prep

Vocabulary

Complete each sentence with a term from the list.

1. All the living and nonliving things that exist and interact in one place are a/an _____.

2. A living thing is also called a/an _____.

3. The ability to cause change is _____.

4. A behavior that helps a living thing survive is a/an _____.

5. All living things of the same kind in an ecosystem are a/an ____.

6. Something found in nature that is useful to living things and can help them meet their needs is a/an _____.

7. The way an animal acts in a situation is called a/an _____.

8. Harmful chemicals in a water supply are a kind of _____.

9. The place where a plant or animal lives is its _____.

10. Plants and animals that live in the same area and interact with each other are members of a/an _____.

adaptation B22
behavior B22
community B15
ecosystem B10
energy B7
environment B9
habitat B32
organism B8
pollution B34
population B14
resource B15

Test Prep

Write the letter of the best answer choice.

11. Which of the following is NOT a need of all living things?

    A. water
    B. energy
    C. nutrients
    D. carbon dioxide

12. Sea lions on the same crowded rock are competing for which resource?

    A. space   **C.** water
    B. energy   **D.** algae

13. An example of behavior is _____.

    A. the long neck of a giraffe.
    B. a spider spinning a web.
    C. the thick fur of a polar bear.
    D. the spines of cactus.

14. The environment of a blue whale is a/an _____.

    A. ocean   **C.** forest
    B. desert   **D.** mangrove swamp

15. Infer Suppose a population of mice and a population of owls live in a grassy meadow. Owls eat mice. About half of the mice have white fur and half have brown fur. By the end of summer, only brown mice are left. What can you infer about the overall color of the grass in the meadow? Explain how this could affect which color mice survive and which do not.

16. Use Variables A package of bean seeds says to plant the seeds 5 cm apart. You plant two groups of seeds. For one group, you plant the seeds 5 cm apart. For the other group, you plant the seeds 2 cm apart. How do you think the variable of space will affect each group? Explain.

Map the Concept

Write the terms to fill in the concept map. Organize the terms by their size relationship in the environment. The smallest unit should go in the smallest oval, the next-largest unit should go in the next-largest oval, and so on.

population   **organism**
ecosystem   **community**

1. _____
2. _____
3. _____
4. _____

Critical Thinking

17. Apply Two populations of birds live in the same habitat. Both kinds of birds eat insects. Explain how it is possible that the two populations do not compete for food.

18. Synthesize The cones of some types of pine trees release their seeds only after they have been heated to high temperatures. Explain how this adaptation improves the pine's chances of producing new trees after a forest fire.

19. Evaluate Is setting aside land for parks a good way to help the environment? Explain.

20. Analyze Imagine that you are given a fake plant and a real plant that look very similar. How can you tell which plant is real? Discuss at least three traits of living things in your answer.

Performance Assessment

Publicity Poster
Make a poster that tells other students why it is important to conserve water and land resources. How will you tell your classmates how to save resources? Display your poster at school.

Food Chains

Lesson Preview

LESSON 1

From birds in the air to plants on the ground—how do living things get energy?

Read about it in Lesson 1.

LESSON 2

A frog, an insect, a leaf, the Sun—how are these things connected?

Read about it in Lesson 2.

LESSON 3

Sea stars, snails, jellies—how do these creatures depend on each other?

Read about it in Lesson 3.

How Do Living Things Get Energy?

Why It Matters...

A hummingbird flies above a flower, sipping nectar. Its wings beat so rapidly that they make a humming sound. The hummingbird needs a lot of energy to move its wings so quickly. Hummingbirds, like all living things, need energy to survive.

PREPARE TO INVESTIGATE

Inquiry Skill

Compare When you compare two things, you observe how they are different and how they are alike.

Materials

- 2 plastic cups containing soil and grass seedlings
- marking pen
- metric ruler
- aluminum foil
- plastic wrap
- plastic spoon
- water

Science and Math Toolbox

For step 2, review **Using a Tape Measure or Ruler** on page H6.

Soak Up the Sun
Procedure

1. **Collaborate** Work with a partner. Use a marking pen to label one cup of grass seedlings *Light*. Label another cup *Dark*. In your *Science Notebook*, make a chart like the one shown.

2. **Measure** Measure the height of the grass in each cup. Record the measurements on your chart.

3. Count as you add spoonfuls of water to one cup until the soil is wet. Add the same amount of water to the other cup.

4. **Use Variables** Use aluminum foil to wrap the *Dark* cup. Use plastic wrap to wrap the *Light* cup. Place both cups where they will receive indirect sunlight.

5. **Record Data** After 5 days, unwrap both cups. Observe the appearance of the grass. Then measure and record the height of the grass in each cup.

Conclusion

1. **Compare** In which cup did the height of the grass increase?

2. **Infer** Plants need energy to grow. How do you think the grass plants got the energy to grow?

STEP 1

	Height of grass (Light)	Height of grass (Dark)
Day 1		
Day 5		

STEP 2

STEP 4

Investigate More!
Design an Experiment
Does the amount of water grass gets affect how it grows? Write a hypothesis to explain what you think. Then, plan and carry out an experiment to find out. Share your results.

VOCABULARY

cell   p. B45
solar energy   p. B44

READING SKILL

Main Idea and Details
As you read, record one
main idea and two details
for each section.

Getting Energy

MAIN IDEA All organisms need energy to grow
and survive. The Sun is the source of energy for
almost all living things.

Energy from the Sun

Imagine a bright winter day. The air is cold,
but your face feels warm as you tilt it toward
the Sun. Sunlight feels warm on your face
because light is energy. Energy is the ability to
cause change.

Energy that comes from the Sun is called
solar energy. Solar energy provides Earth
with light and heat. Light and heat are energy.
The Sun provides energy that plants need to
make food. Most living things could not exist
without solar energy.

Plants use sunlight
to make food.

Plants Make Food

How does a plant get something to eat? It doesn't. Plants make food using water, air, and sunlight. The food they make is called sugar. And although plants don't "eat," they do use the food they make. Plants use the energy in the food they make to survive, to grow, and to make new plants. Dandelions use the food they make to produce new flowers. Apple trees make apples. Moss spreads and makes new plants.

Plants store some of the food they make in their cells (sehlz). A **cell** is the basic unit that makes up all living things. Plants can use this stored food when the Sun is not shining.

▶ **MAIN IDEA** What do plants need to make food?

Almost all energy on Earth comes from the Sun. ▼

Plants use the food they make to survive.

Animals Get Energy from Plants

Unlike plants, animals can't make food. Animals must take in food in order to get the energy that they need to survive. When an animal eats, the energy is transferred from the food source to that animal. Many animals eat plant parts. Each time an animal eats a plant, energy is transferred from the plant to that animal.

Not all of the energy that a plant gets from the Sun is transferred to an animal that eats the plant. Some energy is used by the plant for its survival. Some is stored in the plant's cells.

▶ MAIN IDEA **How do animals get energy from plants?**

A tomato plant stores energy from the Sun. Animals get some of this energy by eating the plant.

slug

human

groundhog

crow

Visual Summary

Energy from the Sun is called solar energy.

Plants use energy from the Sun to make food.

Animals that eat plants get energy from plants.

LINKS for Home and School

WRITING **Expository** People have been growing crops for thousands of years. Modern scientists use technology to improve crops. Research the history of farming. Write a paragraph about a new technology that farmers are using today.

HEALTH **Make a Chart** Nutrients are in food. Nutrients include sugar, protein, fat, vitamins, and minerals. List the main ingredients of your favorite food. Make a chart that shows each ingredient, its animal or plant source, and the nutrients it provides.

Review

❶ **MAIN IDEA** Why do living things need energy?

❷ **VOCABULARY** Write a sentence using the term *solar energy*.

❸ **READING SKILL Main Idea and Details** List three details that support the idea that some animals get energy from plants.

❹ **CRITICAL THINKING: Synthesize** A population of grass-eating leafhoppers live in a field. What would happen if all the grass in the field died?

❺ **INQUIRY SKILL: Compare** How does the way plants get energy compare with the way animals get energy?

 TEST PREP
Plants survive by ___.

A. getting food from water in the soil

B. making food from water, air, and sunlight

C. getting food from the air

D. using energy from animals

Technology
Visit **www.eduplace.com/scp/** to find out more about how living things get energy.

What Is a Food Chain?

Why It Matters...

Zip! A frog's long, sticky tongue flicks out of its mouth and captures an insect—the frog's next meal. What might the insect have eaten for its last meal? And will another living thing eat the frog? All animals must eat food, and most animals are food for others.

PREPARE TO INVESTIGATE

Inquiry Skill

Classify When you classify, you sort things into groups according to their properties.

Materials

- plant and animal picture cards
- string
- scissors
- construction-paper Sun
- transparent tape

Food-Chain Mobile
Procedure

1 **Collaborate** Work in a group. Use tape to attach a paper Sun to a string. Cut out a set of picture cards.

2 **Classify** Find the two living things that use sunlight to make food. Use string and tape to hang one of these cards from the Sun. Look at the remaining picture cards. Find the animals that eat plants. Hang one of these cards from the hanging plant card.

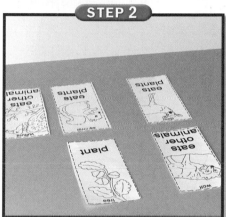

3 **Classify** Now, find the animals that eat other animals. Hang one of these cards from the hanging plant-eater card. You have made a model of a food chain. A **food chain** shows how organisms get energy.

4 **Use Models** Cut the string that connects the plant card to the plant-eater card.

5 Repeat steps 2–4 with the other cards.

Conclusion

1. **Infer** How could you organize your mobile using other card groupings?

2. **Use Models** Think about step 4. How would animals be affected if the plants they ate died out?

Investigate More!

Research Choose a plant-eating animal from your mobile. Do research to learn which plants this animal eats. Find out which animals eat this animal. Make a mobile to present to the class.

Food Chains

READING SKILL

Sequence Use the chart to trace the flow of energy in a food chain. Start with the Sun.

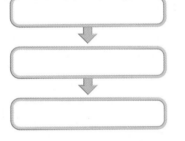

MAIN IDEA When one animal eats another animal or eats a plant, it becomes part of the flow of energy in a food chain.

Links in the Chain

Suppose you labeled each link of a paper chain with the name of an organism. If each organism was linked to an organism that it used for food, you would have a model of a food chain. A **food chain** is the path that energy takes through a community as one living thing eats another.

All animals depend on plants for their energy. When an insect eats a plant and then a frog eats that insect, energy is passed from organism to organism. The plant produced its own food using the energy in sunlight. Some of the Sun's energy captured by the plant passed to the insect and then to the frog.

Savanna Food Chain

Producer Savanna grass uses sunlight to make food.

Parts of a Food Chain

No matter what organisms are part of a food chain, the Sun is always the first link in the chain. Plants are the second link. A plant is called a **producer** (pruh DOO-sur) because it produces its own food.

An animal is a **consumer** (kuhn SOO mur). A consumer is an organism that eats other living things in order to get energy. Consumers are classified by their food source. An animal that eats only other animals is a **carnivore** (KAHR nuh vawr). Lions, hawks, and spiders are carnivores.

An animal such as a zebra, horse, or deer that eats only plants is an **herbivore** (HUR buh vawr). An animal that eats both plants and animals is an **omnivore** (AHM-nuh vawr). Most humans are omnivores, although some people are vegetarians. That means they don't eat meat. Producers, carnivores, herbivores, and omnivores are all parts of a food chain.

▶ **SEQUENCE** Why can't a consumer be the first link in a food chain?

Herbivore The zebra is a consumer that eats only plants.

Carnivore The lion is a consumer that eats only other animals.

Linked Food Chains

An African savanna is home to many producers and consumers. These organisms form links in different food chains. Grasses, bushes, and trees are the producers in the savanna.

Lions are carnivores. They hunt and eat zebras and gazelles.

Fire ants are omnivores that eat almost anything they can find. They eat grass seeds, small insects, and even small birds.

Visual Summary

Plants are producers. Plants are the first living link in every food chain.

Herbivores eat only plants. Carnivores eat only other animals.

Animals that eat plants and also eat other animals are omnivores.

LINKS for Home and School

MATH Multiply With 100 One 8-pound eagle must eat 8 rabbits to get enough energy to survive. Each rabbit must eat 100 pounds of grass. How many pounds of grass must be in the food chain so that one eagle can get enough energy?

LITERATURE Write a Song or Poem Some poems or songs repeat lines, and then add a new line at the end of each verse. One popular song of this kind is "I Knew an Old Lady Who Swallowed a Fly." Write a song or a rhyme about a food chain using this repeating style.

Review

❶ MAIN IDEA What is a food chain?

❷ VOCABULARY Write a short paragraph using the terms *producer* and *consumer*.

❸ READING SKILL: Sequence Describe the correct sequence of a food chain that has a carnivore, a producer, and an herbivore.

❹ CRITICAL THINKING: Analyze What are the relationships among a carnivore, an herbivore, and an omnivore?

❺ INQUIRY SKILL: Classify Suppose an animal eats only mosquitoes. Is the animal a producer or a consumer? If you classify it as a consumer, what kind of consumer is it?

✔ TEST PREP
Which of the following is an example of an herbivore?

A. rabbit

B. lion

C. maple tree

D. hawk

 Technology
Visit **www.eduplace.com/scp/** to discover more about food chains.

B55

Exploring Underwater

In 1977, a submersible called *Alvin* allowed scientists to dive deeper than ever before. Scientists used the *Alvin* to explore the bottom of the ocean. There, they discovered many new life forms, including the giant tubeworm.

Tubeworms are worms that can be as long as 2.4 m (8 ft). They have no mouth or eyes. Until the discovery of the tubeworm, scientists believed that all food chains began with energy from the Sun. When scientists studied this amazing animal, they learned something that surprised them. Tubeworms contain bacteria that change chemicals in the water into food for the tubeworms.

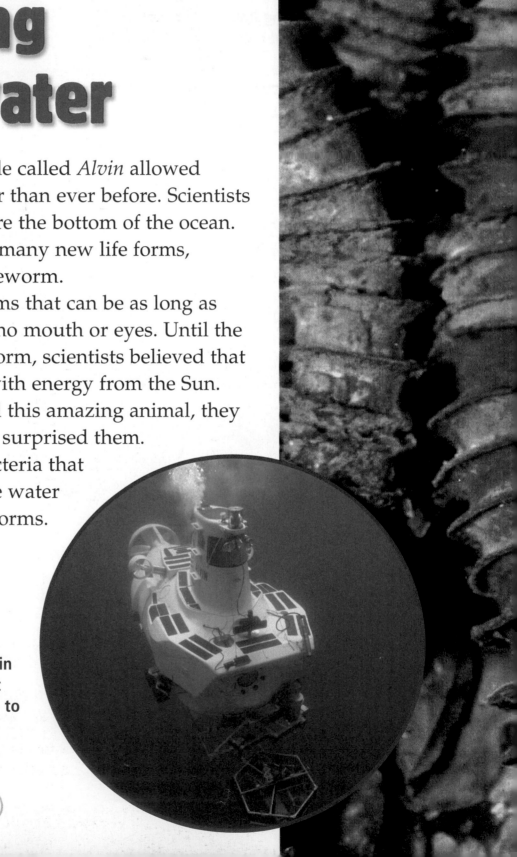

The *Alvin* was built in 1964. It was rebuilt and improved in 1977. These changes made it possible for the *Alvin* to dive to the ocean floor.

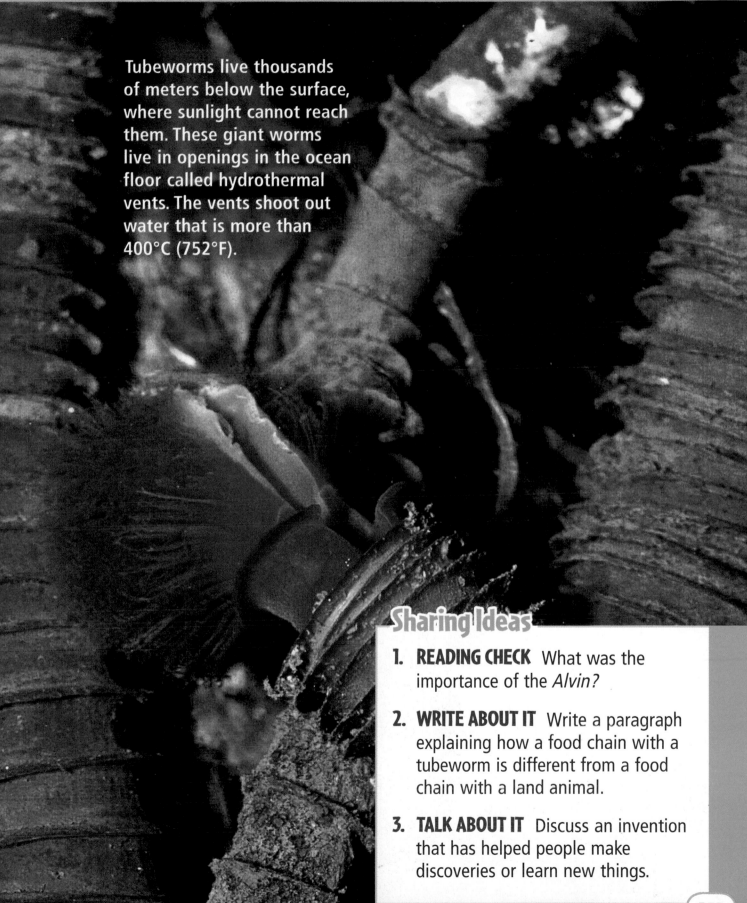

Tubeworms live thousands of meters below the surface, where sunlight cannot reach them. These giant worms live in openings in the ocean floor called hydrothermal vents. The vents shoot out water that is more than 400°C (752°F).

Sharing Ideas

1. **READING CHECK** What was the importance of the *Alvin?*

2. **WRITE ABOUT IT** Write a paragraph explaining how a food chain with a tubeworm is different from a food chain with a land animal.

3. **TALK ABOUT IT** Discuss an invention that has helped people make discoveries or learn new things.

What Are Some Different Food Chains?

Why It Matters...

Food chains exist wherever living things are found. In an ocean food chain, tiny floating plants and seaweed use solar energy to make food. The fish eat the plants and seaweed. Later, some of the fish may become a meal for a shark.

PREPARE TO INVESTIGATE

Inquiry Skill

Research When you do research, you learn more about a subject by looking in books, searching the Internet, or asking science experts.

Materials

• plant and animal picture cards

Science and Math Toolbox

For step 1, review **Making a Chart to Organize Data** on page H10.

Match Things Up

Procedure

1. **Collaborate** Work in a group. In your *Science Notebook*, make a chart like the one shown.

2. **Classify** Cut out a set of plant and animal picture cards provided by your teacher. Find cards that show plants and animals that live in a desert. Group these cards together. Write the names of these organisms in your chart.

3. **Research** Repeat step 2 for an ocean environment and for a rainforest environment. If necessary, use reference books or the Internet to check where an organism lives.

4. **Use Models** When all of the organisms have been classified in your chart, make a food chain for each environment. Line the cards up in order. Each food chain should start with a producer. Write or draw each food chain in your *Science Notebook*.

Conclusion

1. **Infer** What is the role of the Sun in each food chain?

2. **Communicate** Explain why you arranged each food chain the way you did.

STEP 1

Environments		
Desert	Ocean	Rainforest

STEP 2

STEP 4

Investigate More!

Solve a Problem
Suppose you want to set up an aquarium with several kinds of fish. What would you need to know about the fish's food chains?

► **VOCABULARY**

aquatic habitat   p. B60
terrestrial   p. B62
    habitat

► **READING SKILL**

Compare and Contrast
Use a chart to compare
and contrast food chains
in aquatic habitats and
terrestrial habitats.

Food Chains in Environments

MAIN IDEA Food chains exist wherever living
things are found. The organisms in each food chain
vary based on their environment.

Food Chains in Water

Animals live in many different places, or
habitats. Tide pools are the habitat of some
ocean animals. A tide pool is an area at the
edge of the ocean where water collects in
spaces between rocks.

A tide pool is one kind of aquatic (uh-
KWAT ihk) habitat. An **aquatic habitat** is a
place where organisms live in or on water.
In tide pools, seaweed and algae are the
producers. Like producers on land, they use
the energy from sunlight to make food.

Portuguese man-of-war

periwinkle

minnow

shrimp

blue crab

bladderwort
seaweed

An aquatic habitat is also home to herbivores, carnivores, and omnivores. Look at the picture of the tide pool. What food chains can you find?

▶ **COMPARE AND CONTRAST** **Compare a producer that lives in an aquatic habitat with one that lives on land.**

oystercatcher bird

cordgrass

oyster

sea star

blue crab

Tide Pool Food Chain

 →  →

Cordgrass
This grass captures energy from the Sun to make food.

Periwinkle snail
This snail eats and scrapes plants from rocks with its mouth.

Blue crab
This crab uses its strong claws to capture and eat snails.

Food Chains on Land

People live in terrestrial (tuh REHS tree uhl) habitats. A **terrestrial habitat** is a place where organisms live on land. A desert is one kind of terrestrial habitat.

Desert regions usually get little rainfall, so they are very dry. Organisms that live in the desert are adapted to the dry conditions there. Desert producers include grasses, wildflowers, and cactuses. Cactuses store large amounts of water in their cells.

Desert herbivores include insects and small animals like rabbits. Desert herbivores that eat cactus are able to get both energy and water from the plants they eat.

prickly pear cactus

black-collared lizard

road runner

white-tailed antelope squirrel

Desert Food Chain

Evening primrose
This plant blooms at night, when desert temperatures are cool.

Antelope squirrel
This squirrel eats primrose, seeds, and small animals.

Rattlesnake
This snake eats rabbits, mice, squirrels, and birds.

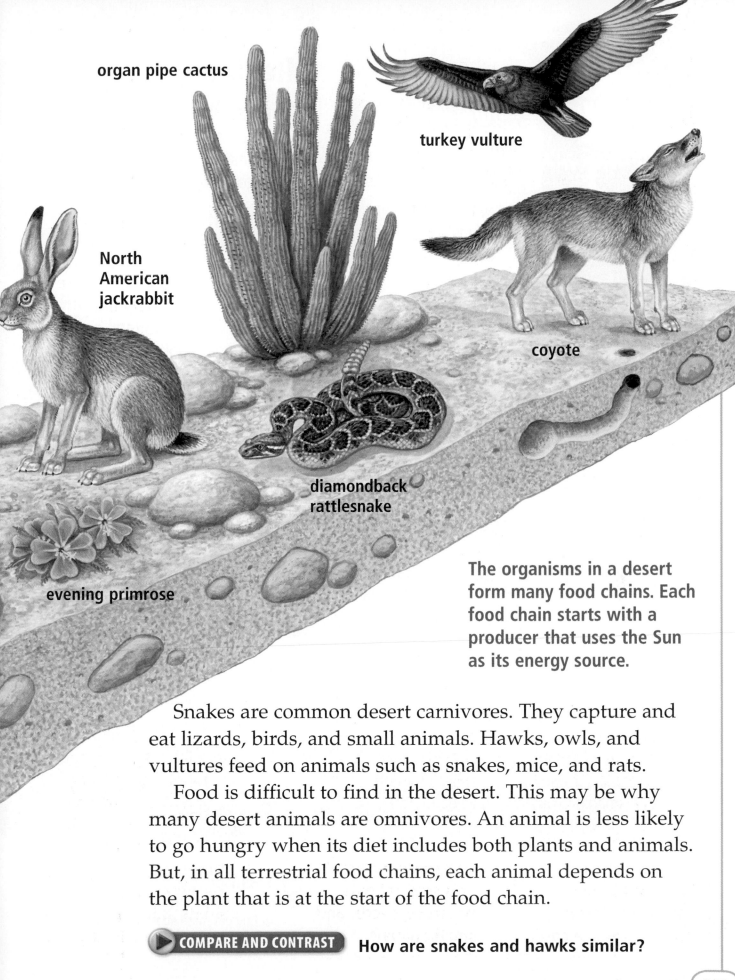

organ pipe cactus

turkey vulture

North American jackrabbit

coyote

diamondback rattlesnake

evening primrose

The organisms in a desert form many food chains. Each food chain starts with a producer that uses the Sun as its energy source.

Snakes are common desert carnivores. They capture and eat lizards, birds, and small animals. Hawks, owls, and vultures feed on animals such as snakes, mice, and rats.

Food is difficult to find in the desert. This may be why many desert animals are omnivores. An animal is less likely to go hungry when its diet includes both plants and animals. But, in all terrestrial food chains, each animal depends on the plant that is at the start of the food chain.

▶ **COMPARE AND CONTRAST** How are snakes and hawks similar?

Visual Summary

Food chains in aquatic habitats are made up of plants and animals that live in or on water.

Food chains in terrestrial habitats are made up of plants and animals that live on land.

LINKS for Home and School

MATH Draw Lines of Symmetry Suppose that an enormous sea star has been discovered in the Pacific Ocean. Draw the sea star with five arms. Draw a line of symmetry. Suppose the sea star loses one arm, and in its place two new arms grow back. Draw the sea star with its new arms. Does it have the same line of symmetry as the first sea star you drew?

SOCIAL STUDIES Write a Journal Entry The Inuit are a people who live near the ocean in the snowy Arctic. The Yanomano live in the hot rainforests of South America. Imagine you have traveled to visit both groups. Write a journal entry comparing the food sources of each group.

Review

❶ **MAIN IDEA** What do food chains in aquatic and terrestrial habitats have in common?

❷ **VOCABULARY** What does *terrestrial habitat* mean?

❸ **READING SKILL: Compare and Contrast** How are food chains in aquatic and terrestrial habitats different?

❹ **CRITICAL THINKING: Apply** What would happen to the number of herbivores in a food chain if most of the producers disappeared?

❺ **INQUIRY SKILL: Research** How could you find out what food is best to feed a pet iguana?

 TEST PREP
In an aquatic habitat, the producer in a food chain ___.

A. gets its food from water.

B. is likely to be an herbivore.

C. uses solar energy to make food for other producers.

D. uses solar energy to make its own food.

 Technology
Visit **www.eduplace.com/scp/** to find out more about terrestrial habitats.

Soil Conservationist

Soil conservationists are experts on soil. They develop ways to help farmers keep their land fertile, moist, and rich in nutrients. They also advise government agencies and businesses on how to use land without harming it.

What It Takes!

• A degree in environmental studies, forestry, or agriculture

• Investigative and research skills

Ecotourist Guide

As an ecotourist guide, you could find yourself leading safaris in Africa, exploring South American rainforests, or hiking glaciers in Alaska. Ecotourist guides take adventure-seekers on vacations to natural areas. They teach people about protecting wildlife and the environment.

What It Takes!

• A high-school diploma

• An interest in nature, ecology, and adventure

Big Mouth!

Its jaws are as long as a rowboat. The amount of food It eats each day can weigh more than a car. So this humpback whale must eat lots of really *big* fish—right?

Wrong! The humpback mainly eats krill—tiny creatures smaller than your pinky. Why? Krill are one of the most plentiful foods in the ocean. They are part of a food chain that begins with tiny ocean plants called phytoplankton. Krill eat these microscopic plants, and whales and many fish eat the krill. There are so many krill in the ocean, the humpback can eat them by the ton!

The krill is a crustacean, similar to a shrimp. It has a hard shell and no backbone.

No teeth, no problem! Instead of teeth, the humpback has baleen. These comb-like plates hang from the whale's upper jaw. The whale scoops up water in its huge mouth and squeezes it through the baleen, which traps the krill.

Review and Test Prep

Vocabulary

Complete each sentence with a term from the list.

1. The path that energy takes through a community as one living thing eats another is a/an _____.

2. An animal that eats only plants is a/an _____.

3. Lions, zebras, and grass are all found in a/an _____.

4. An organism that makes its own food is a/an _____.

5. An animal that only eats animals is a/an _____.

6. Plants are able to make food by capturing ___ from the Sun.

7. An organism that eats other living things in order to get energy is a/an _____.

8. Fish and other water organisms live in a/an _____.

9. The basic unit that makes up all living things is a/an _____.

10. An animal that eats both plants and animals is a/an _____.

aquatic habitat B60
carnivore B51
cell B45
consumer B51
food chain B50
herbivore B51
omnivore B51
producer B51
solar energy B44
terrestrial habitat B62

Test Prep

Write the letter of the best answer choice.

11. Which is a terrestrial habitat?

   A. desert.
   B. river.
   C. ocean.
   D. lake.

12. In the following food chain, the producer is the _____.

   plant caterpillar bird cat

   A. bird.   C. plant.
   B. caterpillar.   D. cat.

13. In a food chain, consumers _____.

   A are usually the first link in the chain.
   B. eat other living things.
   C. use solar energy to make food.
   D. get energy from air.

14. The organism that would most likely be last in a food chain is a _____.

   A. seaweed.   C. maple tree.
   B. human.   D. caterpillar.

15. **Classify** Classify each organism in this food chain as a producer or consumer.

    grass   cow   human

16. **Compare** Suppose a tree is planted in a small grassy field. As years pass, the tree grows. Over time, the grass beneath the tree dies. For what reason might the grass die? Compare the conditions for grass growing under the tree with the conditions for grass growing in the rest of the field.

Map the Concept

The chart shows two categories. Classify each organism on the list. Check that you have placed each organism in the correct category.

dandelion   **crab**
seaweed   **grass**
squirrel   **zebra**

Producer	Consumer

Critical Thinking

17. **Apply** A sparrow, a hawk, a rosebush, and a beetle are links in the same food chain. Put the parts of the food chain in order to trace the path of energy. What is the original source of the energy in the food chain?

18. **Synthesize** A plant on your dresser appears to be dying. Your friend suggests that you move the plant to a windowsill. What does your friend think the plant needs?

19. **Evaluate** Suppose you had to prepare a classroom display of pet animals. Your classmates have brought a turtle, a frog, a snake, and a hamster for the display. How would you decide which animals, if any, could be displayed together in the same container?

20. **Analyze** If living conditions became difficult, why might an omnivore be better able to survive than either an herbivore or a carnivore?

Performance Assessment

Plan a Dinner

Choose one of the three kinds of consumers: herbivore, omnivore, or carnivore. Plan a dinner menu for your consumer. Be creative. You might include a soup, a salad, a main course, and a dessert. Describe the ingredients in each of the menu items. Explain why your consumer would eat each menu item.

Write the letter of the best answer choice.

1. Which is NOT an example of a structure that is an adaptation?

   A. needle shaped leaves

   B. suction cups on the arm of a sea star

   C. the long, thin beak of a hummingbird

   D. a cat sneaking up on a mouse

2. Which is the source of energy for plants?

   A.

   B.

   C.

   D.

3. For which resource do squirrels and birds drinking from a birdbath compete?

   A. air

   B. food

   C. space

   D. water

4. Which organism in this food chain is an herbivore?

   A. coyote

   B. day lily

   C. rat

   D. snail

5. BOTH plants and animals   .

   A. reproduce.

   B. give off oxygen.

   C. look for a home.

   D. use sunlight directly for energy.

6. Which is MOST likely to be an adaptation for self-defense?

   A. the thick fur coat of a bear

   B. a thick plant stem that stores water

   C. the webbed feet of a bird that lives in water

   D. a rabbit that has brown fur in summer and white fur in winter

7. Which is NOT an adaptation of a living thing to its environment?

    A. the very sharp claws of a cat

    B. the thick winter coat of a rabbit

    C. the spines that cover a desert cactus

    D. the very long stem of a rainforest plant

8. Which organism could be a consumer in an aquatic habitat?

A.

B.

C.

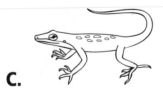
D.

Answer the following in complete sentences.

9. Beavers build a dam across a stream. Which is likely to benefit MORE from the dam—the fish in the stream or the trees along the stream? Explain your answer.

10. The following organisms live in a desert habitat.

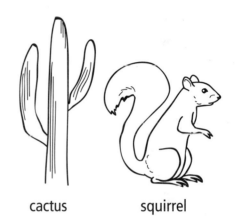

cactus   squirrel

rabbit   rattlesnake

Which two organisms are most likely to compete for food? Explain why you made your choice.

Wrap-Up

Discover!

Polar bears are adapted to the cold, icy environment of the Arctic. Thick fur and a layer of fat keep them warm in freezing temperatures. Even their paws are adapted for their environment. These adaptations make it easy for polar bears to walk on ice without slipping.

Polar bears have four paws that can be over 25 cm (about 10 in.) wide. Each paw has five toes, and each toe has a long sharp claw. These claws help polar bears grip the ice.

Each polar bear paw has seven footpads. The footpads are made of a thick, black layer of skin and are covered with small bumps. The bumps on the bear's footpads are like the treads on a sport shoe. They grip the ice and keep the bear from slipping when it runs.

Long fur between the footpads and toes keeps polar bears from slipping, too. Webbing that is under the fur between the toes helps polar bears swim.

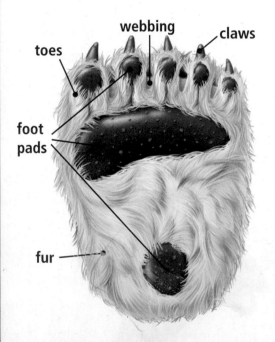

Learn more about animal adaptations. Go to **www.eduplace.com/scp/** to see how polar bears and other animals adapt to their environments.

EARTH

UNIT C

SCIENCE

Earth's Surface

EARTH SCIENCE

UNIT C

Earth's Surface

═══ Independent Reading ═══

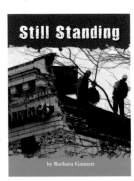

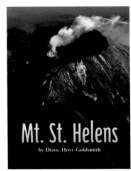

Fishing Family **Still Standing** **Mt. St. Helens**

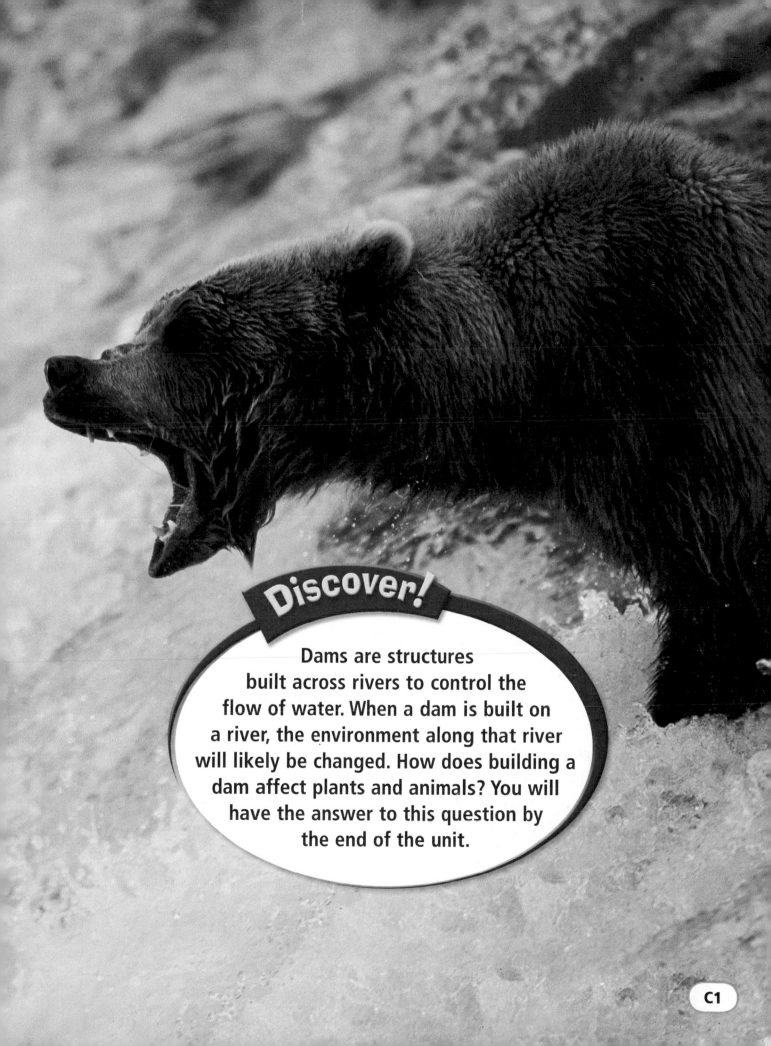

Discover!

Dams are structures built across rivers to control the flow of water. When a dam is built on a river, the environment along that river will likely be changed. How does building a dam affect plants and animals? You will have the answer to this question by the end of the unit.

Chapter 6

Earth's Crust

LESSON 1

Tall mountains and huge oceans—what other features of Earth's surface can you find on a map?

Read about it in Lesson 1.

LESSON 2

An iron golf club, gold bars, and the salt on a pretzel—what do these things have in common?

Read about it in Lesson 2.

LESSON 3

From sandy deserts to lush forests—how does soil form in these very different places?

Read about it in Lesson 3.

What Is Earth's Surface Like?

Why It Matters...

This island in the southern Pacific Ocean looks like a giant mushroom. Of course, it's made of rock. As surrounding ocean water wears away the edges of the rock, the island becomes mushroom-shaped. Like this island in the ocean, the surface of Earth is made of rock.

PREPARE TO INVESTIGATE

Inquiry Skill

Compare When you compare two things, you observe how they are alike and how they are different.

Materials

- 4 clear plastic cups
- metric measuring cup
- water
- sand
- marking pen

Science and Math Toolbox

For steps 2, 3, and 4, review **Measuring Volume** on page H7.

Earth's Surface
Procedure

STEP 2

1. **Use Models** Work with a partner. Use a marking pen to label each of three clear plastic cups *Water*. Label another clear plastic cup *Land*.

2. **Measure** Measure 150 mL of sand. Pour the sand into the cup labeled *Land*. The sand in this cup represents the amount of land on Earth's surface.

3. **Measure** Measure 150 mL of water. Pour the water into one cup labeled *Water*.

STEP 4

4. Repeat step 3 twice, adding water to the remaining two cups labeled *Water*. The water in these three cups represents the amount of water on Earth's surface.

5. **Use Models** Look at the cups of sand and water. Compare the amount of sand with the amount of water. Record your comparison in your *Science Notebook*.

STEP 5

Conclusion

1. **Compare** How does the amount of land on Earth compare with the amount of water?

2. **Use Numbers** Use numbers to complete this sentence: The Earth's surface is ____ parts water and ____ part land.

Investigate More!

Research Use resource books or the Internet to find out how much of the water on Earth's surface is fresh water and how much is salt water. Write two fractions to show these amounts in hundredths.

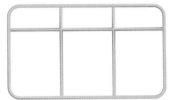

READING SKILL

Compare and Contrast
Use the chart to compare
three kinds of landforms.

Surface of Earth

MAIN IDEA Earth's surface is made up of water
and land. Landforms, such as mountains and
valleys, can be found on Earth's surface.

Water on Earth's Surface

Some people think that from space,
Earth looks like a big blue marble. Earth is
sometimes called the blue planet because
about three-fourths of its surface is covered by
water. The remaining one-fourth of the surface
is land.

Most of Earth's water is salt water. Salt
water is found in the oceans and seas. Lakes,
rivers, and streams have a different kind of
water, called fresh water. Water you use for
drinking, washing, and cooking is fresh water.

**Niagara Falls is a waterfall on the
Niagara River.** ▼

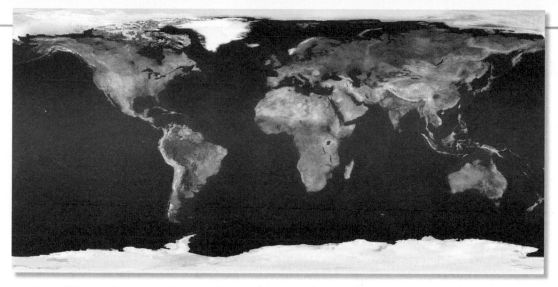

▲ Satellite photos show that almost three-fourths of
Earth's surface is water.

Only a very small amount of all the water on Earth is
fresh water. And only a tiny amount of this fresh water
is usable by living things. The rest of the fresh water
is unavailable. It cannot be used because it is frozen in
huge masses of ice called glaciers (GLAY shurz).

You have already learned that
fresh water is found in rivers, lakes,
and streams. It's also found in
soil, air, and large spaces in deep
underground rock.

COMPARE AND CONTRAST Is there more
salt water or fresh water on Earth's
surface?

Earth's Water

3 percent
fresh water

97 percent
salt water

Earth's Landforms

You have probably seen several different features of the land. Perhaps you have gone hiking to the top of a mountain (MOWN tuhn). A mountain is a landform (LAND fawrm). A **landform** is a part of Earth's surface that has a certain shape and is formed naturally. Earth has several kinds of landforms.

The most visible landform is a mountain. A mountain is a raised part of the land, usually with steep sides, that rises above the area around it. Some mountains are high, rocky, and topped with snow. Others are lower and covered with trees.

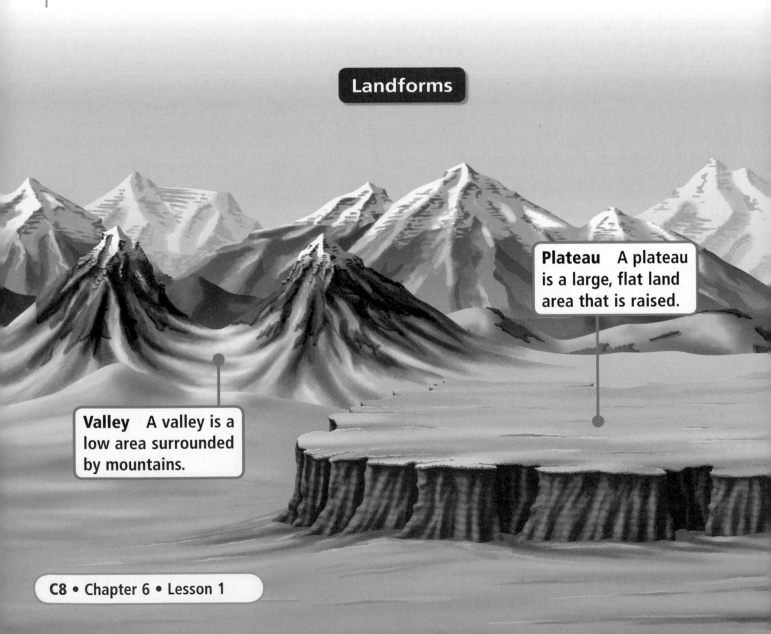

Landforms

Plateau A plateau is a large, flat land area that is raised.

Valley A valley is a low area surrounded by mountains.

The low area of land between mountains, hills, or other high areas is called a valley (VAL ee). Some valleys are wide and flat. Others are narrow with steep sides. A canyon (KAN yuhn) is a narrow and deep valley that often has a stream or river flowing through it.

A plain is a large land area that is mostly flat. The middle part of the United States is a large plain. Plains often have rich soil and make good farmland. Another type of landform is a plateau (pla TOH). Plateaus are flat areas of land that are higher than the land around them. The sides of a plateau are often steep.

 **COMPARE AND CONTRAST** How are plateaus and plains different?

Mountain The highest mountain peak on Earth is Mount Everest.

Canyon A canyon is a deep valley that forms when rivers cut through layers of rock.

Plain A plain is a large, flat area of Earth's surface.

Mapping Landforms

If you want to know what kinds of landforms are found in an area, you can look at a map. Many maps show rivers, mountains, and valleys. A landform map tells you about the shape of the land's surface. Mountains are drawn to look like mountains and valleys are drawn to look like valleys.

Some maps use symbols to represent different kinds of landforms. On these maps, a key tells what each symbol stands for.

▶ **COMPARE AND CONTRAST** What are two different ways that maps show landforms?

West Virginia has a variety of landforms.

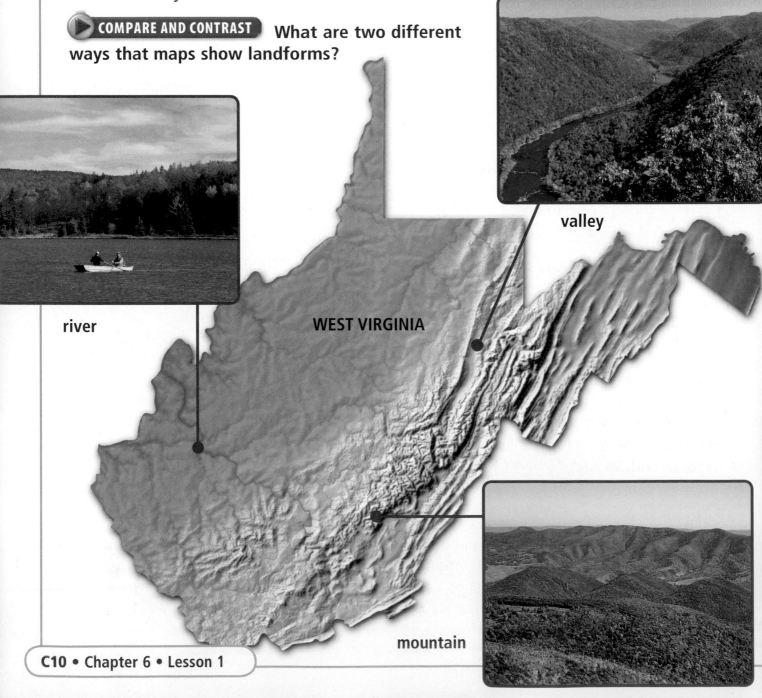

valley

river

WEST VIRGINIA

mountain

Visual Summary

About three-fourths of Earth's surface is covered by water. And 97% of that water is salt water.

Earth's surface has mountains, valleys, canyons, plains, and plateaus.

Some maps show the shape of the land's surface.

LINKS for Home and School

MATH **Make Circle Graphs** About $\frac{3}{4}$ of Earth's surface is covered by water, the other $\frac{1}{4}$ of Earth's surface is land. About $\frac{97}{100}$ of Earth's water is salt water, and $\frac{3}{100}$ is fresh water. Make a poster with two circle graphs that show this data.

ART **Make a Map** Make up a name for an imaginary country. Draw a map of this country. Use different colors to show oceans, rivers, mountains, plains, and other landforms. Label each landform with a name you make up. Be sure to include a key for your map.

Review

❶ **MAIN IDEA** How does the amount of land compare with the amount of water on Earth's surface?

❷ **VOCABULARY** What does the term *landform* mean?

❸ **READING SKILL: Compare and Constrast** What is the difference between a valley and a canyon?

❹ **CRITICAL THINKING: Apply** When your friend looks out the windows, he sees mountains rising above him on both sides. Identify the kind of landform where he is likely to be located.

❺ **INQUIRY SKILL: Compare** Compare the features of a mountain with a valley.

TEST PREP

A very narrow and deep valley is called a ____.

A. plateau.

B. plain.

C. mountain.

D. canyon.

 Technology
Visit **www.eduplace.com/scp/** to find out more about Earth's surface.

How Does Earth's Crust Change?

Why It Matters...

Scientists that study volcanoes are called volcanologists. They wear suits designed to protect them from the hot melted rock that flows out of volcanoes. When melted rock reaches Earth's surface, it cools and hardens quickly. When a volcano erupts, Earth's surface changes.

PREPARE TO INVESTIGATE

Inquiry Skill

Use Models You can use a model of an object to better understand or describe how it works.

Materials

- small plastic cup
- modeling clay
- grass, leaves, twigs
- red and yellow food coloring
- liquid dishwashing detergent
- dropper
- baking soda
- vinegar
- metric measuring cup
- plastic spoon
- goggles

Volcano Blast!

Procedure

STEP 1

1. **Collaborate** Work in small groups to build a volcano. Place a plastic cup on a flat surface. Use modeling clay to build a volcano around the cup. Leave an opening in the volcano, directly over the opening in the cup.

2. Place grass, leaves, and twigs around the sides of the volcano. Stand some of the twigs up to look like trees. **Safety:** Wear goggles during this activity.

STEP 3

3. Carefully put 2 spoonfuls of baking soda in the cup. Add 1 drop each of red and yellow food coloring. Use a dropper to add 6 drops of dishwashing detergent. Stir the mixture.

STEP 4

4. **Observe** Pour 125 mL of vinegar into a metric measuring cup. To cause your model volcano to "erupt," slowly add the vinegar to the mixture. Record your observations in your *Science Notebook*.

Conclusion

1. **Use Models** What happened to the grass, leaves, and twigs on the sides of the volcano during the eruption?

2. **Hypothesize** How do you think a real lava flow would affect the land near a real volcano?

Investigate More!

Design an Experiment
Use more modeling clay to change the shape of the volcano. Then cause the volcano to erupt again. How does the shape affect the lava flow?

READING SKILL

Classify Use the chart to list and describe the main layers of Earth.

Earth's crust is the layer of Earth on which we live. This cave is part of Earth's crust. ▶

Changes in Crust

MAIN IDEA Earth is made of three layers. Earth's surface may change slowly or quickly.

Earth's Layers

Earth is made of three layers. Imagine using a peach as a model of Earth. The skin of the peach represents the thin outermost layer of Earth, called the **crust** (kruhst). The fruit beneath the skin represents Earth's mantle (MAN tl). The **mantle** is the middle layer of Earth. The pit of the peach represents the **core** (kohr), Earth's deep innermost layer.

Earth's crust is most familiar to you. It is where humans and other organisms live. Underground caves and the bottom of the ocean are also part of the crust.

The mantle is the thickest layer. It is made of rock. Some rock of the mantle is a thick fluid that will move when it is squeezed.

The core extends to the center of Earth. It is made mostly of the metals iron and nickel. Part of the core, called the inner core, is solid. The outer core is melted metal.

You may wonder why some of the materials inside Earth are melted. The temperature of Earth increases toward the center. Deep inside Earth, it is hot enough to melt rock and metal.

▶ **CLASSIFY** On which layer of Earth are living things found?

The crust is much thicker under land than under the oceans. ▼

crust

Inside Earth

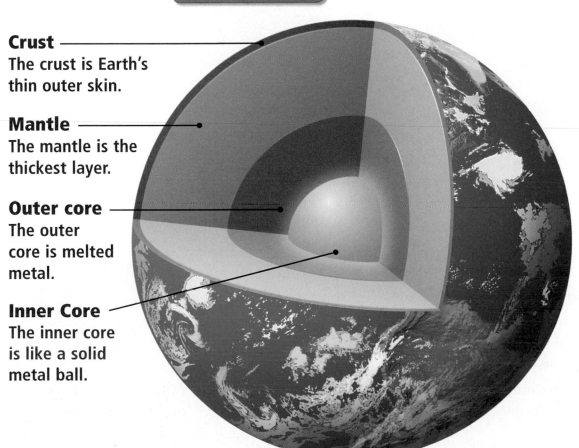

Crust
The crust is Earth's thin outer skin.

Mantle
The mantle is the thickest layer.

Outer core
The outer core is melted metal.

Inner Core
The inner core is like a solid metal ball.

Minerals

Have you ever played a game to guess an unknown object? The first question you might ask is whether the object is an animal, vegetable, or mineral (MIHN ur uhl). A **mineral** is a material that is found in nature and that has never been alive. There are many kinds of minerals. Metals, such as gold and iron, are minerals. The graphite (GRAF yt) in your pencil is a mineral. Salt that you put on food is also a mineral.

Minerals have certain properties that can be used to identify them. Color, hardness, and texture are some properties of minerals. Gold is yellow and shiny. Graphite is black, soft, and feels greasy. The mineral talc is so soft you can scratch it with a fingernail.

 **CLASSIFY** **What properties can be used to classify minerals?**

Rock Gabbro is a rock that contains the minerals shown. ▶

Mineral Olivine is a hard, dark-green mineral.

Mineral Pyroxenes are important rock-forming minerals.

Mineral Feldspars are common minerals in Earth's crust.

How Minerals Are Used

Titanium is a lightweight metal used in eyeglass frames and airplanes.

titanium

Zincite is used to make sunscreen.

Quartz is used in the glass that covers this watch and in the parts that help it run.

bauxite

quartz

Talc, the softest mineral, is used to make talcum powder.

zincite

Aluminum comes from the mineral bauxite.

talc

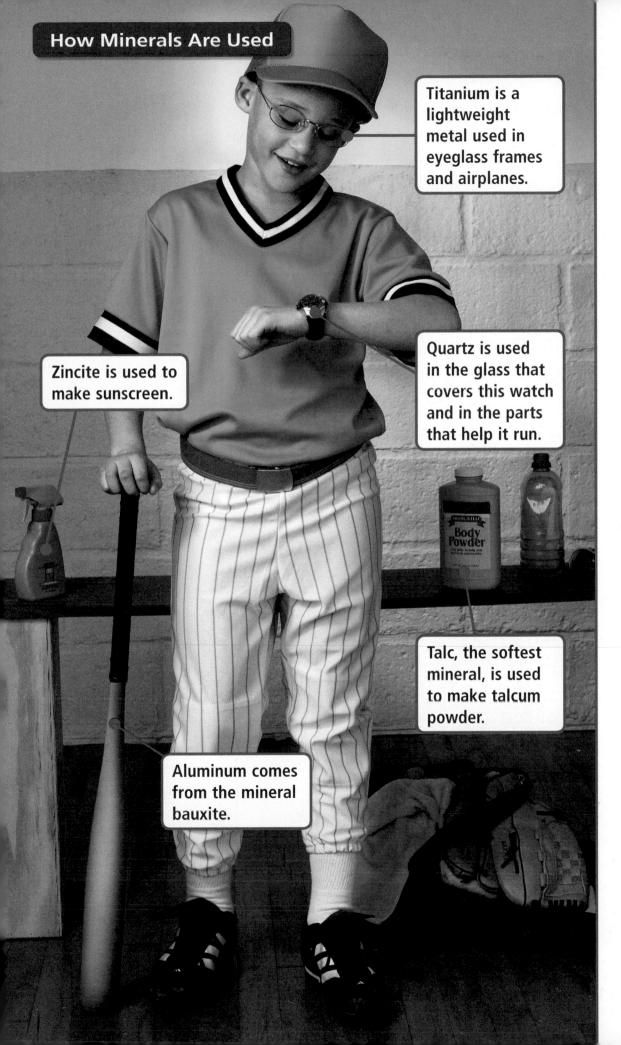

How Rocks Form

Rocks make up Earth's crust. Rock is a solid material made of minerals. A rock may contain one mineral or several minerals. The rock granite contains quartz, feldspar, mica, and hornblende.

Rocks are grouped according to how they are formed. There are three kinds of rock. **Igneous rock** (IHG nee uhs rahk) forms when melted rock from inside Earth cools and hardens. **Sedimentary rock** (sehd uh MEHN tuh ree rahk) forms when sediment, or sand and small bits of stone are cemented, or glued, together. **Metamorphic rock** (meht uh MAWR fihk rahk) forms when other rocks are changed by heat and pressure. Each type of rock has specific traits.

Traits of Rocks

	Igneous	Sedimentary	Metamorphic
Rock	obsidian	red sandstone	slate
Texture	glassy, smooth, no grains	gritty, medium grains	smooth, small grains, wavy bands
Color	black	red-brown	dark gray
Layering	no	yes	yes

Types of Rocks

Igneous Rock	Sedimentary Rock	Metamorphic Rock
obsidian	red sandstone	slate
granite	conglomerate	quartzite
pumice	gypsum	marble

Igneous   If melted rock cools inside Earth's crust, it hardens slowly. Then large mineral grains form. If rock cools on Earth's surface, it hardens quickly. Then, if mineral grains form, they are small.

Sedimentary   Sedimentary rock forms from layers of sediment that are deposited, usually on the bottom of rivers, lakes, and oceans. The layers become pressed together, and they harden to form rock. You can often see layers of different colors in sedimentary rocks.

Metamorphic   Metamorphic rock forms when rock inside Earth is heated and squeezed. Although the heat and pressure are not enough to melt the rock, they change it into a different kind of rock.

▶ **CLASSIFY**   What determines whether a rock is classified as igneous, sedimentary, or metamorphic?

Slow Changes

Did you ever build a sand castle on the beach, only to have waves wash it away? Water changes Earth's crust by breaking down rocks and carrying them away. Unlike sand washing away at the beach, the process of breaking down rock is slow.

Wind carrying sand can also break down rock. Wind, which is moving air, blows against rock. Over time, the sand it carries wears the rock away.

Ice changes the shape of Earth's surface, too. A glacier is a large mass of slow-moving ice. Glaciers carrying small rocks grind down large rocks. As glaciers move over some rocks, they pick up the rocks. When the glacier stops moving or melts, it drops the rocks.

▲ The action of water on rock causes changes to the rock over time.

The sedimentary rock layers of the Grand Canyon formed over millions of years. ▼

Rapid Changes

Although it is rare to feel them move, parts of Earth's crust are always moving. A crack in the crust, called a fault (fawlt), may form where the crust moves.

When parts of the crust move against each other, stress can build up. Over time, the stress can become so great that the crust suddenly snaps back. An **earthquake** (URTH kwayk) is caused by a sudden movement of large sections of rock beneath Earth's surface. Earthquakes cause rapid changes to Earth's surface. Mountains can form as the crust bends, folds, and is pushed up.

If two sections of crust pull apart, melted rock may rise to the surface. At the surface, this melted rock is called lava. A volcano (vahl KAY noh) is an opening in the crust through which hot ash, gases, and melted rock move from deep inside Earth to the surface.

▶ **CLASSIFY** What are two causes of rapid changes to Earth's surface?

▲ When a volcano erupts, new landforms may form and old ones may be destroyed.

▲ Lava forms new crust when it cools and hardens.

Fossils and Earth's Past

A **fossil** (FAHS uhl) is the remains of a once-living plant or animal. Fossils can tell stories about living things of long ago and how they have changed over time. Fossils can also tell what Earth's surface was like long ago.

Scientists study fossils to find clues about the environment in which the fossil plant or animal once lived. For example, fossils of trees and a fly found near the South Pole have helped scientists understand that this area was once much warmer than it is today.

By examining fossils of plants or animals that no longer exist, scientists can tell what they looked like. By learning the age of the rock layers around a fossil, they can tell when the plant or animal that formed the fossil lived.

> ▶ **CLASSIFY** How can scientists use a fossil to tell when an animal once lived?

Most fossils form from living things that had hard parts, such as bones, shells, and wood. ▼

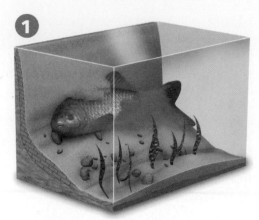

1 A living thing dies and is buried under layers of sand and soil.

2 Over a long period of time, the sand and soil harden and turn into rock.

3 As the crust moves, rock containing the fossil is slowly brought closer to the surface.

Lesson Wrap-Up

Visual Summary

Minerals can be classified according to their color, hardness, and texture.

The three types of rocks are igneous, sedimentary, and metamorphic.

Slow and rapid changes take place on Earth's surface.

LINKS for Home and School

WRITING Persuasive Suppose you find a deep, rocky canyon with a stream at the bottom. Do you suppose the canyon was created by gradual changes, or by a sudden change? Write a persuasive essay to explain your choice. Be sure to include detailed evidence.

SOCIAL STUDIES Historical Interview At 5:12 A.M., on April 18, 1906, one of the worst earthquakes in American history shook San Francisco. Write a news broadcast as if you were a reporter at the scene.

Review

❶ **MAIN IDEA** What are Earth's three layers?

❷ **VOCABULARY** How do igneous rocks form? Give an example of an igneous rock.

❸ **READING SKILL: Classify** What are three kinds of rocks?

❹ **CRITICAL THINKING: Analyze** Which kind of rock is most likely to contain fossils? Why?

❺ **INQUIRY SKILL: Use Models** What materials could you use to model the layers of Earth? Explain your choices.

✔ **TEST PREP** Which of the following is NOT a mineral?

A. granite

B. graphite

C. gold

D. feldspar

 Technology
Visit **www.eduplace.com/scp/** to find out more about changes in Earth's crust.

C23

Volcano Visit
Watching Lava Form Land

What does lava look like? The Mendez family is about to find out. They are hiking near Kilauea (kee law AY uh), an active volcano in Hawaii Volcanoes National Park. Lava is erupting from a vent on the southeast side of the volcano. A park ranger is leading them to the perfect viewing spot.

Characters

Alana Smith: park ranger

Andre: age 8

Kim: age 10

Margaret Mendez: mother of Andre and Kim

Bill Kato: volcanologist

Ranger Smith: OK, we're almost at the lava flow. Is everybody ready to walk out to the observation area?

Kim: I can't wait to see real lava! How close will we be?

Andre: Are you sure we'll be safe?

Ranger Smith: Just follow me. I've been leading tours here for 15 years. You'll be a safe distance from the flow. But you'll still feel the lava's heat and smell volcanic gases.

Andre: Wow, it's hotter already. Is it always like this?

Ranger Smith: It's extra hot today because there's a big flow from a vent on the southeast side of the volcano.

Kim: But I thought lava burst out of the big hole at the top.

Ranger Smith: That big hole, or crater, is called a caldera (kal DAIR uh). Lava did flow from the caldera in 1983, when Kilauea started erupting. But lava also flows from the volcano's vents, tubes, and small craters. Hawaiian volcanoes are famous for smooth, gentle flows. They're called pahoehoe (puh HOH eh hoh eh) flows. *Pahoehoe* is a Hawaiian word for "runny."

Margaret Mendez: That lava looks like a river of fire!

Kim: How hot is it?

Ranger Smith: When lava erupts, it's temperature is about 1,100 degrees Celsius.

Andre: Hey, something smells terrible! What *is* that? [*Andre pinches his nose.*]

Ranger Smith: That's sulfur dioxide, a volcanic gas. It helps make lava erupt.

Kim: How?

Ranger Smith: Combined with the pressure and heat inside Earth, it pushes the lava up and out of the surface.

Margaret Mendez: [*pointing*] Who's that man in the astronaut suit?

[*Enter Mr. Kato*]

Ranger Smith: That's Bill Kato. He's a volcanologist. Bill works at the volcano observatory. He wears that heat-resistant suit and face mask when he works close to lava. Hi, Bill. What are you working on today?

Bill Kato: Aloha, Ranger. I've been collecting lava samples and measuring craters. I'm looking for clues that will help predict eruptions. The more that scientists know about volcanoes, the safer people will be.

Margaret Mendez: Oh, wow! The sight of that lava flowing to the sea is breathtaking!

Andre: There's a lot of steam down by the water. How come?

Bill Kato: When the hot lava touches the cool water, it creates big, puffy clouds of steam.

Ranger Smith: What else have you been studying lately, Bill?

Bill Kato: Well, I'm writing a report on how the volcano has affected our coastline. In the past 20 years, Kilauea has added almost 550 acres of land to the Big Island of Hawaii. That's nearly 550 football fields!

Margaret Mendez: How does that happen?

Bill Kato: When flowing lava cools, it hardens and forms new crust on Earth's surface. When the lava flows down to the ocean, it extends the coastline and makes the island bigger.

Ranger Smith: Well, it's getting late, and we have a long walk back. We'd better get going, folks. Thanks for all the info, Bill!

Bill Kato: Anytime. Aloha!

Ranger Smith, Margaret Mendez, Andre, and Kim: Aloha!

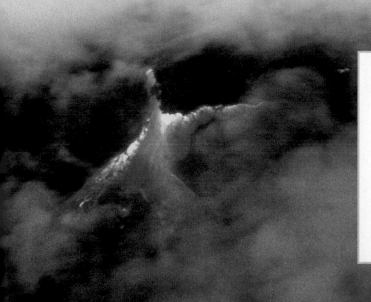

Sharing Ideas

1. **READING CHECK** From what parts of a volcano might lava erupt?

2. **WRITE ABOUT IT** Describe what happens when lava flows into the ocean.

3. **TALK ABOUT IT** Discuss why volcanologists study volcano activity.

Where Does Soil Come From?

Why It Matters...

When you eat a carrot, your body takes in nutrients such as vitamins and minerals. Where did the carrot get these nutrients? It got them from the soil in which it grew. Without soil, most carrots, tomatoes, and other plants people use for food could not grow.

PREPARE TO INVESTIGATE

Inquiry Skill

Infer When you infer, you use facts you know and observations you have made to draw a conclusion.

Materials

- pieces of sandstone
- 2 sheets of waxed paper
- plastic spoon
- water
- hand lens
- sand
- goggles

Science and Math Toolbox

For steps 1 and 4, review **Using a Hand Lens** on page H2.

Stones and Sand
Procedure

1. **Observe** Work with a partner. Place a piece of sandstone on a sheet of waxed paper. Examine the rock with your hand lens. In your *Science Notebook*, make a drawing of what you see. **Safety:** Wear goggles during this activity. Be careful when handling sandstone.

2. **Record Data** Pour one spoonful of water onto the piece of sandstone. Record your observations below your drawing.

3. **Experiment** Place another sheet of waxed paper on the table. Rub two dry pieces of sandstone together over the waxed paper.

4. **Observe** Examine what you see on the waxed paper with your hand lens. Make a drawing of it in your *Science Notebook*.

5. Add two spoonfuls of sand to what you see on the waxed paper. Add a spoonful of water to the sand. Record your observations.

STEP 2

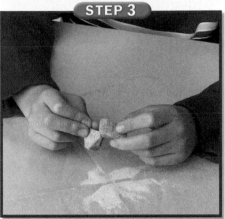

STEP 3

STEP 5

Conclusion

1. **Infer** Which absorbed more water, sandstone or sand? Based on your observations, would a plant grow better in sandstone or sand?

2. **Hypothesize** What natural processes might cause sandstone to become sand?

Investigate More!
Design an Experiment
Is soil alike wherever it is collected? Make a plan to find an answer. List the materials you will need. Then get permission to carry out your investigation.

Soil

VOCABULARY

erosion	p. C31
humus	p. C32
soil	p. C30
weathering	p. C30

READING SKILL

Sequence Use the chart to sequence layers of soil and rock from the surface down.

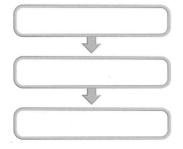

MAIN IDEA Water, wind, ice, plant roots, and gravity can break up rocks and carry the loose material away.

Soil and Weathering

If you have ever grown a plant, you know that plants need soil. **Soil** is the loose material that covers much of Earth's surface. Soil is made up of bits of rock, minerals, and material that was part of once-living things.

Soil forms when rocks are worn away. The breaking up or wearing away of rock is a process called **weathering** (WEHTH ur ihng). Large rocks become smaller rocks. Small rocks become gravel and sand. After thousands of years of wearing away, rocks become soil. Five causes of weathering are water, wind, ice, plant roots, and gravity.

Water often falls into small cracks in rock. When water freezes, it expands and enlarges the crack. ▶

As rock is weathered, small pieces are carried to other places. This process of carrying weathered rock from one place to another is called **erosion** (ih ROH zhuhn).

Sometimes erosion moves materials quickly. Water and wind can pick up sand and soil and move them quickly to other places. Erosion can also happen slowly. In a river or stream, water flows over soil on the bottom. Small amounts of soil are constantly carried away.

Gravity also causes erosion. Gravity is the force that causes things to be pulled toward the center of Earth. Because of gravity, soil on a hill slowly moves to the bottom of the hill. Glaciers, too, move materials downhill.

▲ Plant roots often grow into cracks in rock and force the rock to split.

> **SEQUENCE** How does weathering cause large rocks to become soil?

This arch is rock that has been broken down by weathering and carried away by erosion.

Topsoil The top layer of soil is called topsoil. Rich topsoil contains a lot of humus. The particles, or pieces, that make up topsoil are dark and small. Plants grow best in topsoil.

- -

Subsoil The bottom layer of soil, called subsoil, contains little humus. The soil particles are larger and lighter in color than in topsoil. Subsoil also contains small pieces of rock.

- -

Bedrock The solid rock that lies below the lowest layer of soil is bedrock. Some of the materials in the soil above may have come from the bedrock.

Soil Layers

When wind, moving water, and moving ice slow down or stop, they drop the materials they are carrying. Sand, soil, and pieces of rock build up and form layers.

In addition to weathered rock, soil also contains humus (HYOO muhs), air, and water. **Humus** is the decayed remains of plants and animals. The kinds of materials in soils and their amounts vary from place to place. Different kinds of soils contain different amounts of weathered rock, minerals, humus, air, and water.

Some kinds of soil can hold more water than others. Sandy desert soil can hold only a small amount of water. Soils that contain a lot of clay can hold a lot of water.

▶ **SEQUENCE** Starting at the surface, list three layers of soil and rock.

Visual Summary

Rocks are worn away by wind, moving water, ice, plant roots, and gravity.

Wind, flowing water, glaciers, and gravity move weathered materials from place to place.

Topsoil and subsoil are soil layers that lie above bedrock.

LINKS for Home and School

MATH **Count the Faces** Suppose a stone shaped like a cube is broken into two pieces. The two pieces are rectangular prisms. How many faces did the cube have? How many faces does each prism have? How many faces do the two prisms have in all?

SOCIAL STUDIES **Write a Letter** English settlers who reached Massachusetts in the 1600s found rocky soil. The pioneers went west in the 1800s in search of fertile ground to farm. Imagine you are a pioneer in the 1800s. Write a letter to relatives in the east, telling them about the soil conditions.

Review

1 MAIN IDEA How does wind cause weathering of rock?

2 VOCABULARY Write a sentence using the term *humus*.

3 READING SKILL: Sequence Describe the steps that a rock particle goes through during weathering and erosion.

4 CRITICAL THINKING: Synthesize Suppose you visit a place where the weather is wet and very cold. You notice large boulders that are surrounded by smaller rock pieces. Where might these rock pieces have come from?

5 INQUIRY SKILL: Infer Why is topsoil likely to contain more humus than subsoil contains?

 TEST PREP
Sticky soils that can hold a lot of water are mostly made of ___.

A. sand

B. air

C. clay

D. rocks

 Technology
Visit **www.eduplace.com/scp/** to read and write more about soil.

the Galloping Glacier

Imagine a river made of ice!

That's what a glacier is — a huge river of ice creeping downhill. Most glaciers move just a few inches or feet in a year. But some glaciers gallop! Hubbard Glacier in Alaska, shown here, is one example. Glaciers like this can move 10 to 100 times faster than average. Scientists are studying Hubbard glacier to understand why it moves so fast compared to other glaciers.

Hubbard is the largest glacier in North America. This picture only shows the six-mile wide front of it. The rest of this extreme river of ice stretches back 76 miles to the mountains where it begins.

Typical glaciers move a few inches to a few feet a year. The Hubbard glacier can move 100 feet in a single day!

Vocabulary

Complete each sentence with a term from the list.

1. When sand and small bits of stone harden, _____ is formed.

2. Earth's innermost layer is the _____.

3. The decayed remains of plants and animals found in topsoil is _____.

4. The loose material made up of bits of rock, minerals, and material from once-living things is _____.

5. Heat and pressure can change different kinds of rock into _____.

6. The sudden movement of rock beneath Earth's surface can cause a/an _____.

7. A canyon or a plain is an example of a/an _____.

8. A natural material that has never been alive is a/an _____.

9. The process in which weathered rock is carried from one place to another is called _____.

10. The remains of something that was once alive is a/an _____.

core C14
crust C14
earthquake C21
erosion C31
fossil C22
humus C32
igneous rock C18
landform C8
mantle C14
metamorphic rock C18
mineral C16
sedimentary rock C18
soil C30
weathering C30

Test Prep

Write the letter of the best answer choice.

11. The layer of Earth on which living things are found is the _____.

   A. crust.
   B. mantle.
   C. outer core.
   D. inner core.

12. Earth's middle layer is called the _____.

   A. crust
   B. mantle
   C. soil
   D. humus

13. Which of the following is a cause of slow changes to Earth's surface?

   A. volcanoes
   B. earthquakes
   C. weathering
   D. floods

14. When melted rock cools and hardens, which of the following is formed?

   A. sedimentary rock
   B. igneous rock
   C. slate rock
   D. metamorphic rock

15. **Infer** A fossil of a clam that could only live in the ocean is found on land. Infer what this land area was like in the past.

16. **Compare** You find a black rock that looks like glass. It has no layers and does not seem to have any mineral grains. You also find a red-brown rock that has layers of different colors. Compare how each of these rocks was probably formed.

Map the Concept

Use the following terms to fill in the blanks in the diagram:

weathering
erosion
volcano
earthquake
glacier

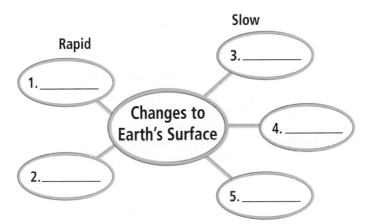

Rapid

Slow

1. _____

2. _____

3. _____

Changes to Earth's Surface

4. _____

5. _____

Critical Thinking

17. **Apply** Do you think most plants are able to grow well in sand? Explain why or why not.

18. **Synthesize** A barrier island is a long, narrow island near a coast. On the side of the island facing the ocean, there are often large waves and strong winds. How would land changes on the side facing the ocean differ from those on the side facing the land?

19. **Evaluate** Suppose a friend tells you that Earth's entire core is made of solid metal. How would you evaluate this statement?

20. **Analyze** A factory receives large shipments of graphite. What product might be made at the factory?

Performance Assessment

Rock Collection
Make a rock collection. Collect several rocks in your neighborhood. Use a rock identification guide from the library to classify your rocks as sedimentary, metamorphic, or igneous. If possible, try to find out the name of each rock.

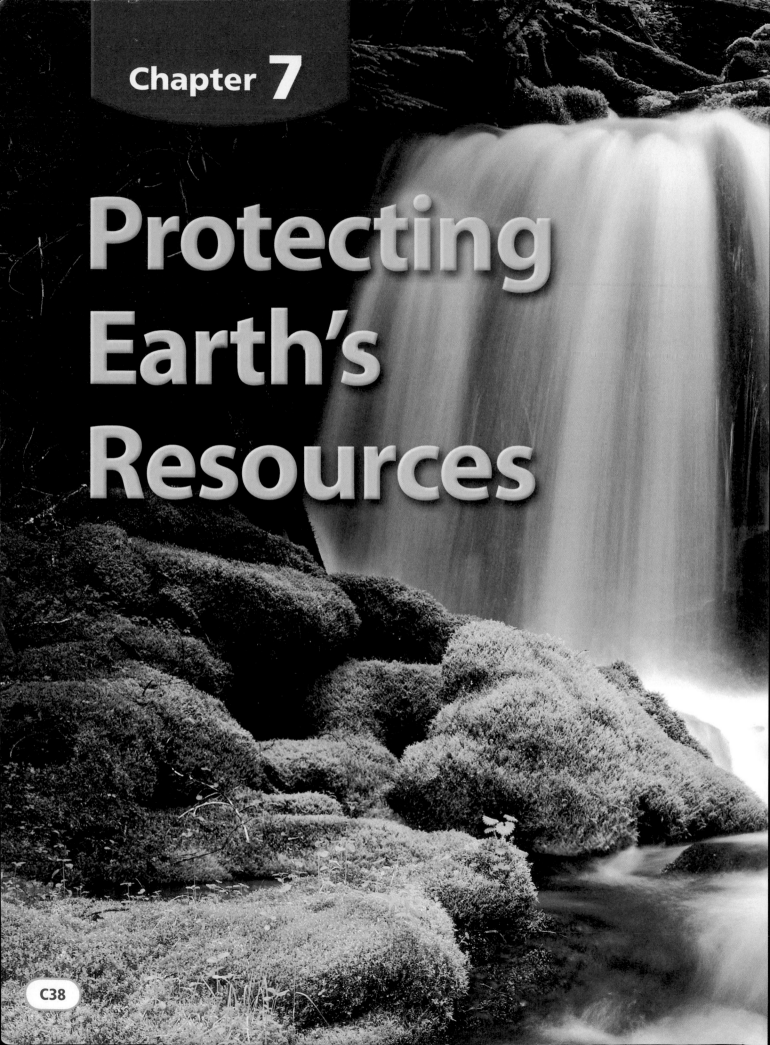

Chapter 7

Protecting Earth's Resources

Lesson Preview

LESSON 1

A pebble on the ground, gas in a car, water in a lake—which of these materials is replaced naturally?

Read about it in Lesson 1.

LESSON 2

From the lights in your classroom to the bus that brings students to school—where does the energy to use these things come from?

Read about it in Lesson 2.

LESSON 3

Reduce, reuse, recycle—how can these three steps help save resources?

Read about it in Lesson 3.

What Are Natural Resources?

Why It Matters...

What do an automobile, a pair of eyeglasses, and a doghouse have in common? They are all made of materials such as metal, glass, and wood that come from nature. These natural materials are used to make things that people use every day.

PREPARE TO INVESTIGATE

Inquiry Skill

Classify When you classify, you sort objects into groups according to their properties.

Materials

• set of objects

Science and Math Toolbox

For step 2, review **Making a Chart to Organize Data** on page H10.

What It's Made Of
Procedure

1. **Collaborate** Work with a partner. Get a set of objects from your teacher. Place them on a desk.

2. **Record Data** In your *Science Notebook*, make a chart like the one shown.

3. **Classify** Examine each object. Group together objects that are made of metal. Then group together objects that are made of wood. Finally, group together objects that are made of materials other than metal or wood.

4. **Record Data** Record your groupings in your chart.

Conclusion

1. **Communicate** Explain why you grouped the objects as you did.

2. **Use Numbers** How many objects are made of metal? How many are made of wood? How many are made of another material?

3. **Infer** Based on your data, what is the most common material that the objects in your set are made of? Make an inference about the effects that a shortage of this material would have on Earth.

STEP 2

Metal	Wood	Other Material

STEP 3

STEP 4

Investigate More!

Research List all the materials that spoons are made of. Use the library or Internet to find out where each material comes from. Share your findings with your classmates.

VOCABULARY

natural   p. C42
  resource
nonrenewable   p. C44
  resource
ore   p. C42
renewable   p. C44
  resource

READING SKILL

Main Idea and Details
Write the main idea and
two details from the
lesson on the chart.

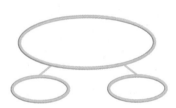

Natural Resources

MAIN IDEA Humans depend on natural resources
for all their daily activities.

Earth's Natural Resources

A home-improvement store sells everything
you might need to build or fix a home. It has
wood for floors and walls, metal for pipes
and wiring, and glass for doors and windows.
Where did all these materials come from?

Almost everything around you comes
from natural resources. A **natural resource**
is a material from Earth that is useful to
people. The wood sold as lumber in a home-
improvement store comes from trees. The
metal used to make pipes and wires comes
from ores (awrz). An **ore** is a rock that
contains metal or other useful minerals.
The glass for the windows is made from
melted sand.

Natural resources provide you with the air,
water, food, clothing, and shelter you need
to live. Materials for books, toys, and sports
equipment come from natural resources.
Natural resources help provide electricity for
television and gas for cars.

▶ **MAIN IDEA** Where do natural resources come
from?

Using Natural Resources

Natural Resource	Uses	Example
Plants	food, lumber, furniture, paper, cardboard, rubber, cork, beauty products, cotton, medicines	
Animals	food, clothing, wool, leather, fertilizer	
Rocks, Soil, and Minerals	concrete, bricks, growing crops, gardening, salt, talcum powder, gems, glass (melted sand), ceramics (heated clay)	
Oil	plastics, human-made fabrics, food containers, safety equipment, fuel, machine and engine grease, beauty products	
Water	drinking, bathing, washing, cooking, growing crops, gardening	
Metals	tools, building materials, plumbing, transportation, wiring, cans, coins, jewelry	

Renewable and Nonrenewable Resources

Imagine that you pick flowers from a daisy plant. As time passes, the plant grows new flowers. Now imagine that you collect some pebbles from the ground. Unlike the flowers, the stones cannot grow back.

Some resources, like the flowers, are renewable resources. A **renewable resource** is a natural resource that can be replaced by nature. Others are nonrenewable resources. A **nonrenewable resource** is in limited supply. It cannot be replaced or takes thousands or even millions of years to be replaced.

This sailboat is powered by the wind, a renewable resource. ▶

Trees are renewable resources. Lumber is made from trees. It is used to construct buildings and make furniture. ▶

▲ Coal is removed from Earth in mines, like the one shown.

Plants are examples of renewable resources. They can grow back. Water and air are also renewable. Fresh water is renewed each time it rains. Air can be used over and over again.

Metal ores and coal arc examples of nonrenewable resources. Coal is used to produce electricity and to make iron and steel. Once metal ores and coal are removed from Earth and used, they cannot be replaced.

▶ MAIN IDEA   What are renewable resources?

Comparing Resources

The items that people use come from either renewable or nonrenewable resources. Renewable resources include water, plants, animals, and air. The first three materials can be replaced in a few weeks, months, or years. If air becomes dirty, it does not take a very long time for it to become clean again.

Nonrenewable resources include materials from Earth such as oil, metals, and minerals. Wise use of these resources is important. That's because it takes many thousands of years for them to form.

▶ **MAIN IDEA** Name one renewable and one nonrenewable resource.

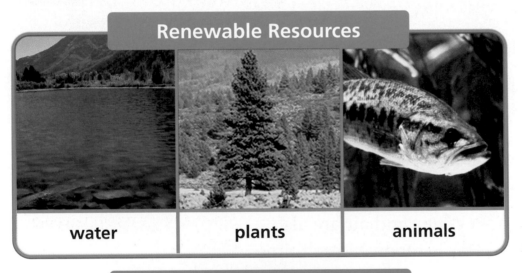

Renewable Resources

| water | plants | animals |

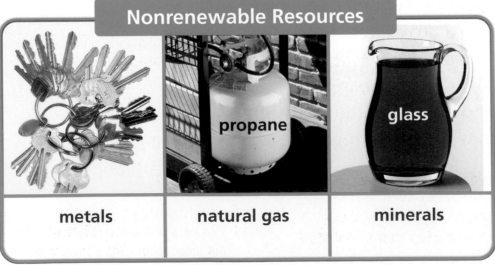

Nonrenewable Resources

| metals | natural gas | minerals |

propane

glass

Visual Summary

Everything that people use comes from natural resources.

Some natural resources are renewable. They can be replaced.

Some resources are nonrenewable. They cannot be replaced.

LINKS for Home and School

MATH Write Mixed Numbers Each American uses about $\frac{5}{3}$ tons of paper every five years. If you used only recycled paper for one year, you would save about $\frac{17}{3}$ trees. Find the improper fractions in this problem. Write them as mixed numbers.

TECHNOLOGY Make a Poster Some resources, especially minerals and metals, might be found elsewhere in our solar system. Research the Moon or another planet. Make a poster that shows some resources that scientists think might be found there.

Review

❶ **MAIN IDEA** Why are natural resources important?

❷ **VOCABULARY** What is the difference between a renewable resource and a nonrenewable resource?

❸ **READING SKILL: Main Idea and Details** Write two details that support the main idea that a natural resource is renewable or nonrenewable.

❹ **CRITICAL THINKING: Apply** A boat could be made of metal or wood. Which would you use to save nonrenewable resources? Explain.

❺ **INQUIRY SKILL: Classify** Choose ten items in your classroom. Decide whether each item comes from a renewable or nonrenewable resource.

✔ **TEST PREP** Natural resources _____.

A. are always renewable

B. are materials found on Earth

C. can never be used up

D. are made by people

 Technology Visit **www.eduplace.com/scp/** to find out more about natural resources.

What Are Energy Resources?

Why It Matters...

A steady breeze spins the blades of wind turbines. Wind turbines are machines that turn the motion of the wind into electricity. Electricity is used in homes, schools, and workplaces every day. Only a small amount of this electricity is produced by wind power. But turbines like these are slowly becoming more common.

PREPARE TO INVESTIGATE

Inquiry Skill

Collaborate Each member of a team should be free to reach his or her own conclusions.

Materials

- pizza box with flap cut in the top
- aluminum foil
- black construction paper
- heavy-duty plastic wrap
- masking tape
- ruler
- clay
- thermometer
- clock

Science and Math Toolbox

For step 4, review **Using a Thermometer** on page H8.

Solar Oven
Procedure

STEP 2

1. **Collaborate** Work in a group. Use aluminum foil to cover the inside of the flap cut in a pizza box. Make sure the shinier side of the foil is showing. Tape the foil in place.

2. Open the box and cover the inside bottom with foil. Tape the foil in place. Tape sheets of black paper over the foil bottom so the foil is covered.

STEP 3

3. Tape plastic wrap across the inside of the pizza box lid so it forms a tight seal over the flap opening.

4. **Measure** Place a thermometer in the box. Record the temperature in your *Science Notebook*.

STEP 5

5. **Observe** Put the oven outdoors. Adjust the flap so that it reflects sunlight onto the thermometer. Use a ruler with clay on both ends to prop the flap open. After 2 hours, record the temperature again. **Safety:** Do not touch the aluminum foil. The oven may be hot.

Conclusion

1. **Predict** What might happen to a slice of cheese placed in your solar oven?

2. **Infer** During what season of the year will your solar oven work best?

Investigate More!

Design an Experiment
How does your solar oven work at different times of the day? Test it in the morning and afternoon. Use a bar graph to display the temperatures you measured.

VOCABULARY

alternate energy
  resource   p. C52

fossil fuel   p. C50

geothermal
  energy   p. C52

hydroelectric
  energy   p. C52

READING SKILL

Text Structure Read the headings in this lesson. Write three energy resources you will learn about.

Energy Resources

MAIN IDEA People use fossil fuels and alternate energy resources to meet their energy needs.

Fossil Fuels

Oil is used to make products such as plastics and asphalt for roads. It is an important energy resource. An energy resource is anything that can be used to produce energy that people use. For example, oil is used to produce gasoline, which powers cars.

Oil, coal, and natural gas are fossil fuels. A **fossil fuel** is a fuel that forms over time from the remains of plants and animals. These fuels are burned to make heat, run engines, and produce electricity.

A pipeline from this oil platform reaches oil that lies below the ocean floor. A pump is used to bring the oil to the surface. ▶

▲ Most cars burn gasoline, which is made from oil.

People use fossil fuels for many energy needs. Trucks and buses run on diesel fuel made from oil. Many people use natural gas for cooking and to heat homes. Much of the electricity in homes and businesses comes from burning coal.

Fossil fuels are nonrenewable resources. Once they are used up, it takes millions of years for them to be replaced. It's possible that people could use up all of the fossil fuels on Earth. Scientists have studied how quickly fossil fuels are being used. They have concluded that Earth's fossil fuels could be used up in the next hundred years. As fossil fuels begin to run out, they will become more and more costly.

▲ Natural gas is used for cooking on stoves.

▶ TEXT STRUCTURE If there was a heading on this page, what might it be?

Sources of Electricity

Iceland

- fossil fuels
- geothermal
- hydroelectric

United States

- geothermal
- hydroelectric
- other
- fossil fuels

▲ Which country uses more fossil fuels to make electricity?

▲ The Blue Lagoon, a swimming area in Iceland is heated by geothermal energy.

Alternate Energy Resources

An energy resource other than fossil fuel is called an **alternate energy resource**. Most of these are renewable resources. **Geothermal energy** is heat from inside Earth. In some places, such as sections of Iceland, this heat is found very close to Earth's surface. People can use this energy to cook and to heat their homes. Power plants like the one shown use geothermal energy to make electricity.

Hydroelectric energy is electricity produced by using the force of moving water. Moving water is the most widely used alternate energy resource. Many power plants are built near dams and waterfalls.

When dams are built on rivers, lakes are created. Often the lakes are used as water supplies for cities. Dam building can also cause flooding of land areas.

The Sun is an important alternate energy resource. Solar panels are devices that change sunlight into electricity. You may have seen solar panels on the roofs of homes or on phone boxes along the highway. Perhaps you have seen small solar panels on a calculator.

Cars use huge amounts of fossil fuels. Many people are working to invent cars that run on alternate energy resources. Cars that run partly on electricity are already on the road. Experimental solar cars are powered by sunlight. Hydrogen (HY druh juhn) is a gas that can be used as a fuel. Its only waste product is water. Hydrogen-powered cars are being tested by several car-makers.

▲ A solar panel provides power for this phone.

TEXT STRUCTURE What would be a good heading for the last paragraph on this page?

Alternate energy sources used to power cars, such as methanol, burn cleaner than gasoline does. ▼

Windmill Wind power has been used for hundreds of years.

Wind Turbine Modern wind turbines are placed where the winds are steady and strong.

Wind Power

Wind power is one of the most promising alternate energy resources. Wind is a clean energy source found almost everywhere. Wind turbines are becoming less costly to produce and run. However, some people believe that wind turbines are noisy, ugly, and may be harmful to birds and other wildlife.

There are both benefits and problems in using each type of energy resource. But the major drawback of fossil fuels is that they are nonrenewable. Because most alternate energy resources are renewable, they are the energy sources of the future.

▶ **TEXT STRUCTURE** What do the photos on this page suggest about wind power?

Visual Summary

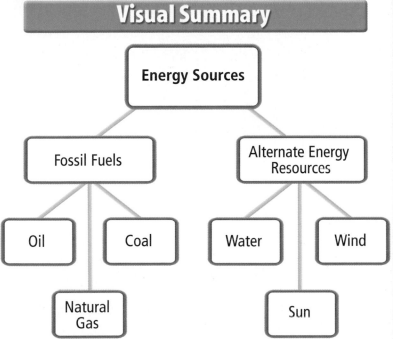

Energy Sources

Fossil Fuels — Alternate Energy Resources

Oil — Coal — Water — Wind

Natural Gas — Sun

 LINKS for Home and School

MATH **Use Hundredths** In the United States, 0.39 of the energy used comes from oil. The other sources of energy are shown below. Make a grid of 100 squares. Use a different color to shade the squares in the grid to stand for each energy source.

SOURCE OF ENERGY	AMOUNT USED
Natural gas	0.24
Coal	0.23
Nuclear power	0.08
Hydroelectric power	0.03
All other sources	0.03

SOCIAL STUDIES **Make a List**

Think about all the activities you do each day that use fossil fuels. Choose one activity. List all the ways you can think of that fossil fuels were used in that activity.

Review

❶ MAIN IDEA What do people use to meet their energy needs?

❷ VOCABULARY Define the term *fossil fuels*.

❸ READING SKILL: Text Structure Review the section titled *Wind Power*. Under which of the other headings could you place this text? Explain your answer.

❹ CRITICAL THINKING: Apply Think about where you live. Are there any alternate energy resources that your community might be able to use?

❺ INQUIRY SKILL: Collaborate Work with a partner. Think of how you could get to and from school in a way that saves fossil fuels.

TEST PREP
Which of the following is a renewable energy resource?

A. coal

B. geothermal energy

C. oil

D. natural gas

 Technology
Visit **www.eduplace.com/scp/** to find out more about energy resources.

CAPTURING THE SUN

People have been using the Sun's energy for thousands of years. Today, as Earth's nonrenewable resources run out, solar power is more important than ever. You can see how people throughout history have captured the Sun.

Ancient Greeks build cities in checkerboard patterns so every home faces south. This way, even in winter, the houses are warmed by the Sun.

In 1948 Dr. Maria Telkes designs the heating system for the first solar house.

The Pueblo Indians build "Sky City" in the 1300s. The floors are stacked to allow the Sun's rays to warm each level.

Modern solar ovens are used to cook food throughout the world.

Sharing Ideas

1. **READING CHECK** Why did the ancient Greeks design their cities in checkerboard patterns?

2. **WRITE ABOUT IT** Why is the Sun an important natural resource?

3. **TALK ABOUT IT** Which solar power invention shown do you think is most important? Discuss your ideas with classmates.

How Can Resources Be Conserved?

Why It Matters...

For most people, old milk containers are garbage. And they could be, if they are not reused. These boys used old milk containers to build a boat. Making new things from old materials saves resources.

Inquiry Skill

Compare When you compare two things, you observe how they are alike and different.

Materials

- 4 plastic bowls
- water
- marking pen
- clock
- plastic-foam packing peanuts
- pieces of crumpled newspaper
- plastic bubble wrap
- cellulose packing peanuts

Science and Math Toolbox

For steps 3 and 4, review **Measuring Elapsed Time** on page H12.

Long-Lived Litter
Procedure

1. **Collaborate** In your *Science Notebook*, make a chart like the one shown. Work with a partner. Use a marking pen to label each of four bowls with a different packing material listed in the chart.

2. **Experiment** Fill each bowl halfway with water. Put a few small pieces of each packing material into its labeled bowl.

3. **Record Data** After 1 hour, look at the packing material in each bowl. Feel whether the material has softened or has begun to break down. Record your observations in your chart.

4. **Observe** Repeat step 3 every few hours for the rest of the day.

Conclusion

1. **Compare** By the end of the day, which packing materials have begun to break down? Which materials have not?

2. **Infer** Suppose each packing material were thrown away as trash and buried under soil in a landfill. Which packing materials would not break down?

STEP 1

Packing Materials	Observation			
	1	2	3	4
cellulose peanuts				
newspaper				
foam peanuts				
bubble wrap				

STEP 2

STEP 3

Investigate More!

Design an Experiment
How could you break down the newspaper and biodegradable peanuts faster? Design an experiment to test your ideas. Get permission from your teacher to carry out your plan.

VOCABULARY

conservation	p. C62
pollution	p. C60
recycle	p. C62

READING SKILL

Problem-Solution As you read, write down three ways to reduce pollution.

Problem	Solution

Conserving Earth's Resources

MAIN IDEA People can reduce pollution and save resources by practicing conservation.

Land Pollution

A small plane sprays insect poison over a field of crops. After the crops are picked, some of the chemicals remain in the soil where they may continue to harm living things.

Other human activities also cause pollution (puh LOO shuhn). **Pollution** is the addition of harmful materials to the environment. After mining metals, harmful materials are often left behind. Some materials that are thrown away can also be a source of pollution. These include paints, cleaning products, and batteries. When these materials are thrown away, they may cause land pollution.

A crop-duster can cause pollution by spraying chemicals on the land.

Polluted water Water pollution affects people, other animals, and plants.

Cleaned-up water Water pollution can be cleaned up and water quality improved.

Water and Air Pollution

Chemicals that pollute land can also become a source of water pollution. This happens when rainwater washes chemicals into streams and rivers. These chemicals can poison fish, insects, and water plants. They can also harm living things that drink the water or eat fish from the water.

Air pollution comes from a variety of sources. The burning of fossil fuels is a major source of air pollution. Air pollution can harm people, wildlife, and plants.

Many people are trying to reduce the amount of trash that is put in landfills. People are also working to clean up areas that have already been polluted.

▶ **PROBLEM AND SOLUTION** What are two ways that people are trying to solve the problem of pollution?

Conserving Resources

There is some good news about how people affect the environment. Many people are now practicing conservation (kahn sur VAY shuhn). **Conservation** is the safe-keeping and wise use of natural resources.

One way to practice conservation is to clean up litter, polluted land, and water. Some people buy products packaged in paper instead of plastic. Paper breaks down in a landfill. Plastic does not. Setting aside land as a safe area for wildlife is a way to practice conservation. Saving resources by using alternate energy resources is another.

You can practice conservation, too. To help save resources and reduce pollution, use the three R's: *Reduce, Reuse,* and *Recycle* (ree SY kuhl). To **recycle** is to collect old materials, process them, and use them to make new items. The more you conserve, the more resources you will save for the future.

▶ PROBLEM AND SOLUTION **How does recycling help reduce pollution?**

Recycling helps the environment by reducing the amount of garbage.

Reduce, Reuse, Recycle

Reuse When you reuse objects, you produce less trash and help save resources. Old tires can be made into toys. At home, you can wash used plastic bags and containers and reuse them.

Reduce
Recycle
Reuse

Recycle Plastic bottles and jugs can be turned into fibers. The fibers can be woven into fleece cloth, which is used to make blankets and clothing.

Reduce When you reduce, you use fewer resources. Reduce your energy use by turning off lights when they are not needed. Reduce trash by buying products with less packaging and with packaging that will break down over time.

Visual Summary

Human activities often cause land, water, and air pollution.

People practice conservation in order to keep natural resources safe.

Reducing, reusing, and recycling are three easy steps that help save resources.

LINKS for Home and School

WRITING Story Imagine that it is 150 years in the future. Are people wasting Earth's resources, or are they following the Reduce, Reuse, Recycle rules? Write a science fiction story to tell what you think the future of Earth's environment will be like.

HEALTH Make a Poster Farmers often use pesticides to protect crops. However, pesticides can be harmful if eaten. Research ways to make fruits and vegetables safe to eat. Make a poster including pictures of these foods and instructions on how to make sure they are safe.

Review

❶ MAIN IDEA How can people reduce pollution?

❷ VOCABULARY Write a sentence using the term *conservation*.

❸ READING SKILL: Problem-Solution Describe something that you can do to help solve the problem of pollution.

❹ CRITICAL THINKING: Evaluate What would you say to someone who thinks that conservation is not important?

❺ INQUIRY SKILL: Compare How are land pollution and water pollution alike? How are they different?

✔ TEST PREP
Which is NOT a way to practice conservation?

A. turning off a light when it's not needed

B. recycling plastic bottles

C. setting aside land for wildlife

D. throwing a paint can in a landfill

 Technology
Visit **www.eduplace.com/scp/** to learn more about conservation.

Geologist

Geologists study Earth, how rocks form, and how they change. There are many jobs for geologists. Some geologists advise builders on the construction of skyscrapers, bridges, dams, and tunnels. Certain geologists look for new sources of gas and oil. There are also geologists that study fossils, volcanoes, and earthquakes.

What It Takes!

- A degree in geology, earth science, or geophysics
- Concern for the environment

Land Surveyor

When you see a building, park, or road under construction, you can be sure a land surveyor was there first. Land surveyors measure land to set the boundaries for a piece of property. They prepare maps for legal documents such as deeds and leases.

What It Takes!

- A high-school diploma
- On-the-job training
- Math skills and courses in drafting, drawing, and surveying

EXTREME Science

Trash Bird

Would you believe this 20-ft. tall, 40-ft. long sculpture is made entirely out of trash? An artist found an unusual and humorous way to recycle trash, but trash is a serious problem. Most trash is simply thrown out, dumped, or buried. But we are running out of places to put it. Without recycling, we will be buried in our own trash! You can help by following the three R's: Reduce the amount of trash you throw away. Reuse whatever you can. Recycle the rest.

DID YOU KNOW?

In 1960, the average American family of four discarded about 10 pounds of trash a day. By 2000, that amount had almost doubled to about 18 pounds of trash a day.

Vocabulary

Complete each sentence with a term from the list.

1. A _____ is formed from the remains of plants or animals.

2. A resource that cannot be replaced by nature is a/an _____.

3. Adding harmful materials to an environment causes _____.

4. Wind power and solar energy are each a/an _____.

5. Heat from inside Earth that can be used to make electricity Is _____.

6. A resource that can be replaced by nature is called a/an _____.

7. Material from nature that is useful to people is a/an _____.

8. A rock that contains metal or other useful materials is a/an _____.

9. When people keep natural resources safe, they practice _____.

10. Electricity made from the force of moving water is _____.

alternate energy resource C52
conservation C62
fossil fuel C50
geothermal energy C52
hydroelectric energy C52
natural resource C42
nonrenewable resource C44
ore C42
pollution C60
recycle C62
renewable resource C44

 Test Prep

Write the letter of the best answer choice.

11. Today, the United States gets most of its electricity from _____.

   A. renewable resources.
   B. fossil fuels.
   C. wind power.
   D. alternate energy resources.

12. All of the following are examples of energy resources EXCEPT _____.

   A. oil   C. sand
   B. wind   D. coal

13. One way to practice conservation is to _____.

   A. use nonrenewable resources.
   B. use fossil fuels.
   C. pollute.
   D. recycle.

14. Which of the following is NOT a renewable resource?

   A. wood   C. metal
   B. water   D. air

15. Compare Suppose you can use new wood, a plastic that can be recycled, or used metal to build a doghouse. What are some advantages and disadvantages of using each material?

16. Classify Make a chart like the one shown below. Classify each of the following sources of energy: coal, wind, natural gas, gasoline, solar power, and oil. For each one, place a check mark in the column for *Fossil Fuel* or for *Alternate Energy Source*.

Source of Energy	Fossil Fuel	Alternate Energy Source
coal		

Map the Concept

Choose an object or material that you use every day. Write or draw it in the box in the center of your concept map. Next to each number, list one way that you could reuse the material, recycle the material, and reduce your use of that material.

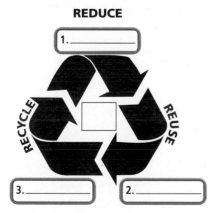

REDUCE

1. _____

RECYCLE

REUSE

3. _____   2. _____

17. Synthesize You can practice conservation before you use a material and after you use it. What things should you consider about the material before you use it? after you use it?

18. Apply List three methods of transportation. Then list the energy resource used for each method. Write whether that energy resource is renewable or nonrenewable.

19. Evaluate Some people say that wind turbines look unattractive and are noisy. What solution could you suggest to address this objection?

20. Analyze Farmers can grow crops in the same soil year after year. But if the soil is blown or washed away, it may take thousands of years to be replaced. Do you think that soil is a renewable resource or a nonrenewable resource? Explain your answer.

Performance Assessment

Write a Conservation Law
Most governments have laws that help people save resources, reduce pollution, and protect the natural world. Use the library or the Internet to research some of these laws. Then think of your own conservation law. Write a paragraph describing your law and how people can obey it.

Write the letter of the best answer choice.

1. Which covers most of Earth's surface?

   A.

   B.

   C.

   D.

2. Which natural resource helps plants grow?

   A. humus

   B. fossil fuels

   C. metal ores

   D. geothermal energy

3. A canyon is a type of _____ .

   A. glacier.

   B. mountain.

   C. plain.

   D. valley.

4. Which energy resource does NOT come from Earth?

   A. fossil fuels

   B. solar energy

   C. geothermal energy

   D. hydroelectric power

5. Most of Earth's fresh water is found in _____ .

   A. glaciers.

   B. lakes.

   C. oceans.

   D. rivers.

6. Which is an example of erosion?

   A. Wind blows sand into rocks.

   B. Plant roots split apart a boulder.

   C. Rain washes soil into a stream.

   D. Water flows into cracks in rocks and freezes.

7. Which represents a nonrenewable resource?

A.

B.

C.

D.

8. Which would cause the most rapid change to rocks on Earth's surface?

A. earthquake

B. glacier

C. waterfall

D. wind

Answer the following in complete sentences.

9. Using the three Rs of conservation can help save natural resources and reduce pollution. This water jug is made from recycled plastic.

For each of the other two Rs, describe a way that you could practice conservation using the jug.

10. Weather conditions on hot, dry summer days can increase air pollution. Some cities offer free bus rides on these days. Explain how free bus rides could reduce air pollution.

Discover!

Building a dam helps some plants and animals but may harm others. When a dam is built, it causes flooding and creates a lake where there used to be dry land. The lake becomes a habitat for fish, birds, and other animals. It may also be a source of water farmers can use for their crops.

The flooding caused by a dam has harmful effects, too. Water may cover land areas that are the homes of plants and animals. Some plants will die, and many animals will have to find new homes.

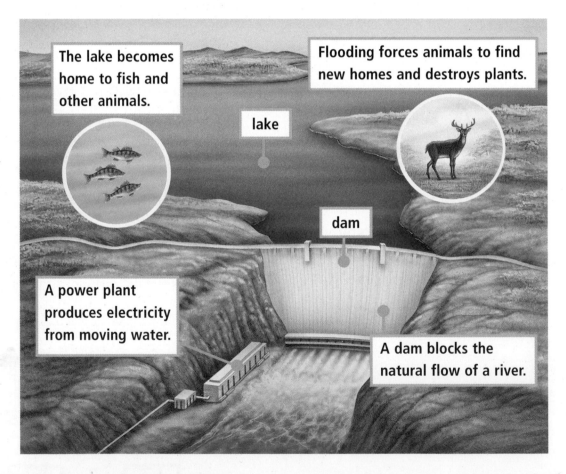

The lake becomes home to fish and other animals.

Flooding forces animals to find new homes and destroys plants.

lake

dam

A power plant produces electricity from moving water.

A dam blocks the natural flow of a river.

See how a dam can change an environment. Go to **www.eduplace.com/scp/** to learn how dam impacts the plants and animals in the area.

The Earth in Space

The Earth in Space

Independent Reading

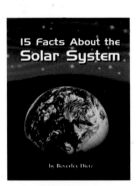

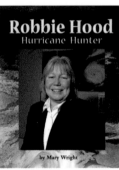

The Man in the Moon

15 Facts About the Solar System

Robbie Hood Hurricane Hunter

Discover!

Each planet has features that make it different from its neighbors in space. Venus is the hottest planet. Jupiter is the largest. Several planets have volcanoes. On which planet is the largest volcano in our solar system? You will have the answer to this question by the end of the unit.

Chapter 8

Patterns
in Earth's
Atmosphere

LESSON 1

A puddle, a cloud, snow on a mountain, water in a bathtub—how are they all connected?

Read about it in Lesson 1.

LESSON 2

Sun, snow, or rain—how do scientists predict the weather?

Read about it in Lesson 2.

LESSON 3

In January, people in Hawaii are surfing while folks in Maine are ice skating—how do weather patterns vary around the world?

Read about it in Lesson 3.

What Is the Water Cycle?

Why It Matters...

Fog covers the shoreline of a rocky coast. A lighthouse sends out a powerful beam to warn ships of danger. Bad weather, such as thick fog or violent storms, is not just a bother. It can be deadly. Understanding how weather occurs can help save lives.

PREPARE TO INVESTIGATE

Inquiry Skill

Predict When you predict, you state what you think will happen based on observations and experiences.

Materials

- 2 plastic bowls
- ice cubes
- warm water and cool water
- clock

Science and Math Toolbox

For step 3, review **Measuring Elapsed Time** on pages H12-H13.

Water and Ice
Procedure

1 **Collaborate** Work with a partner. In your *Science Notebook*, make a chart like the one shown.

2 **Experiment** Fill a plastic bowl halfway with warm water. Fill a second plastic bowl halfway with cool water. Make a label for each bowl.

3 **Use Variables** Place four or five ice cubes in the bowl with the cool water. Set both bowls of water in a warm place for 20 minutes.

4 **Predict** Predict what you think will happen to the bowls of water after 20 minutes. Record your predictions in your chart.

5 **Observe** After 20 minutes, carefully observe both bowls of water. In your chart, record any changes that occurred inside the bowls and on the outside of the bowls.

Conclusion

1. **Hypothesize** Write a hypothesis to explain what happened to the ice cubes in the cool bowl of water.

2. **Compare** Look at your chart. What was different about the outside of the bowls after 20 minutes?

STEP 1

	Warm Water	Cool water and ice
Prediction		
Observation		

STEP 2

warm   cool

STEP 3

warm   cool

Investigate More!

Be an Inventor During some summers, there is not enough rain to grow crops. Based on what you learned in this experiment, invent a way to get water to crops during a dry summer.

Water Moves

VOCABULARY

condensation	p. D7
evaporation	p. D7
precipitation	p. D8
water cycle	p. D8
water vapor	p. D6

READING SKILL

Sequence Use the chart to show events in the water cycle.

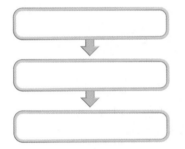

MAIN IDEA In the water cycle, water changes form and moves between the air and Earth's surface.

Changing Water

What do ice, liquid water, and water as a gas have in common? They all are different forms of water. You already know that ice is the solid form and water is the liquid form. **Water vapor** is water in the form of an invisible gas.

Water is one of the few materials on Earth that can be found in all three forms, or states, under normal conditions. You have probably seen or felt water as a solid, a liquid, and a gas in your daily life.

Water Changes State

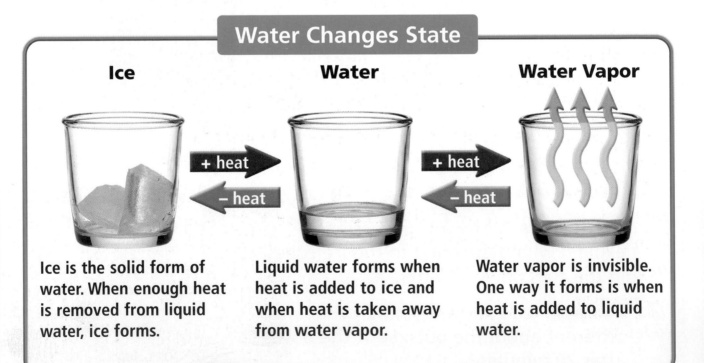

Ice

Ice is the solid form of water. When enough heat is removed from liquid water, ice forms.

Water

Liquid water forms when heat is added to ice and when heat is taken away from water vapor.

Water Vapor

Water vapor is invisible. One way it forms is when heat is added to liquid water.

Why might a puddle evaporate more quickly on a warm day? ▶

Have you ever noticed puddles of water in the street after a rainstorm? Sometimes, in a few hours, the puddles disappear. The liquid water in the puddles changes to the gas water vapor. The change of state from a liquid to a gas is called **evaporation** (ih vap uh RAY shuhn).

On a cool morning, you may have noticed drops of water on leaves or on car windshields. This water is dew. Dew does not fall like rain. It forms on cool surfaces from the condensation (kahn dehn SAY shuhn) of water vapor in air. **Condensation** is the change of state from a gas to a liquid.

Heating or cooling water can change it from one state to another. When heat is added to ice, the ice melts and changes to liquid water. When heat is added to liquid water, the water evaporates. That is why wet clothes on a line dry quickly in sunlight on a warm day.

When heat is taken away from water vapor, it condenses to form liquid water. If enough heat is taken away, the liquid water freezes and becomes ice.

▶ **SEQUENCE** What happens when heat is added to ice?

In some dry areas, animals and plants use dew as a water source. ▶

The Water Cycle

As water changes state, it moves between the air and Earth in a process called the **water cycle**. Water is always moving through the water cycle. This process renews Earth's water supply.

As liquid water on Earth evaporates, it forms water vapor in the air. When the water vapor in air cools, it condenses into tiny droplets. These tiny droplets form clouds. Larger water droplets fall back to Earth as precipitation (prih sihp ih TAY shuhn). **Precipitation** is any form of water that falls from clouds to Earth's surface. Precipitation includes rain, snow, sleet, and hail.

Some of the precipitation soaks into the ground, becoming groundwater. Water that does not soak into the ground flows downhill as runoff. Runoff collects in streams and rivers. Streams and rivers empty into ponds, lakes, and oceans.

▶ **SEQUENCE** What happens after water falls to the ground as precipitation?

Sun

ocean

Condensation This occurs when water vapor in air cools. The water vapor changes to tiny droplets of liquid water. Clouds are made of these tiny droplets.

Precipitation As more water vapor condenses, the droplets in clouds become larger and heavier. These drops of water fall to the ground as precipitation.

water vapor in the air

lake

runoff

Evaporation This occurs when heat from the Sun causes liquid water to change to water vapor, a gas. Water evaporates from oceans, lakes, and rivers.

groundwater

Living Things and the Water Cycle

Living things are part of the water cycle. All living things need water in order to survive. Plants take in water through their roots. Animals drink water.

Living things also return water to the water cycle. Plants give off large amounts of water through their leaves. Animals, including people, give off water as waste. The water cycle renews this water so that it becomes fresh water again. The graph shows some of the many ways that people use water.

▶ **SEQUENCE** How do living things return water to the water cycle?

Water Usage in the United States

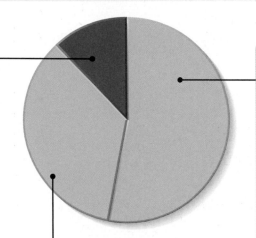

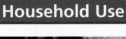
Household Use

People use water in their homes to drink, clean, bathe, and cook.

Agriculture

People use large amounts of water to grow food. Most of this water is used for plant crops.

Industry

Factories, power plants, and other industries use water to cool machines, make products, and produce electricity.

Lesson Wrap-Up

Visual Summary

Water changes state between solid, liquid, and gas when heat is added or taken away.

The water cycle is a process in which water changes state and moves between the air and Earth.

Living things take water from the water cycle and return water to the water cycle.

LINKS for Home and School

MATH **Order Whole Numbers** Write the names of the cities in order. Start with the city with the lowest average yearly snowfall.

City, State	Average Yearly Snowfall
Anchorage, Alaska	71 inches
Boston, Massachusetts	42 inches
Olympia, Washington	17 inches
Syracuse, New York	116 inches

SOCIAL STUDIES Write a Paragraph
In the early 1900s, many families used wooden iceboxes to keep food cold. Write a paragraph about what your life might be like without an electric refrigerator.

Review

1 MAIN IDEA Describe what happens to water as it moves through the water cycle.

2 VOCABULARY Define the term *water vapor*.

3 READING SKILL: Sequence In the water cycle, which event takes place between evaporation and precipitation?

4 CRITICAL THINKING: Synthesize Explain how water you drink today may once have been inside the body of a dinosaur.

5 INQUIRY SKILL: Predict What would happen to the water cycle if the Sun did not provide heat?

 TEST PREP
Precipitation includes all of the following EXCEPT ___.

A. snow.

B. dew.

C. hail.

D. rain.

 Technology
Visit **www.eduplace.com/scp/** to research more about the water cycle.

How Does Weather Change Each Day?

Why It Matters...

What do you think the weather was like when this girl left home? A wet umbrella and puddles are signs that it was raining earlier. Weather affects how you dress and what you do. Having a picnic, playing an outdoor sport, or traveling by airplane are all events that weather can affect.

PREPARE TO INVESTIGATE

Inquiry Skill

Communicate When you communicate, you share information using words, actions, sketches, graphs, tables, and diagrams.

Materials

- thermometer
- rain and snow gauge
- map of local area

Science and Math Toolbox

For step 4, review **Making a Bar Graph** on page H3.

Weather Report

Procedure

STEP 1

① **Collaborate** Work in groups of four. Set a thermometer outside in a shady area. Place a rain and snow gauge in an open area outside.

② **Communicate** In your *Science Notebook*, make a chart like the one shown. Have each group member keep track of one of the weather conditions listed in the chart.

STEP 2

Weather Condition	Day 1	Day 2	Day 3	Day 4	Day 5
Sky					
Wind					
Precipitation					
Temperature					

③ **Observe** Record the weather conditions each day for five days. Observe the kinds of clouds that are in the sky. Note whether they cover more than half or less than half of the sky. Classify the wind as calm, breezy, or strong. Measure and record the temperature and any precipitation.

④ **Communicate** In your *Science Notebook*, make a bar graph like the one shown to show your data for daily temperature.

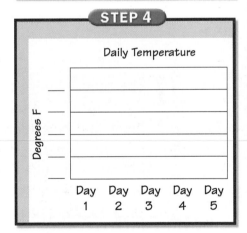
STEP 4

Daily Temperature

Degrees F

Day 1 Day 2 Day 3 Day 4 Day 5

Conclusion

1. **Analyze Data** What was the biggest change in the weather over the week?

2. **Communicate** Use a map of your area to make a weather map for one day. Use symbols such as a sun, a raindrop, or a cloud to stand for the weather conditions.

Investigate More!

Design an Experiment Continue to record the weather data for the rest of the month. At the end of the month, provide a summary of your data for each weather condition.

Weather

VOCABULARY

atmosphere	p. D14
temperature	p. D16
weather	p. D16

READING SKILL

Main Idea and Details
Use the chart to write the main idea and two details for each section of the lesson.

MAIN IDEA Weather is the local condition of Earth's atmosphere. Weather includes temperature, wind, and water in the air.

Earth's Atmosphere

Take a deep breath. The air you just took in is part of Earth's atmosphere (AT muh sfihr). The **atmosphere** is the layers of air that cover Earth's surface. The air in the atmosphere is a mixture of colorless, tasteless gases.

You can think of the atmosphere as a blanket that surrounds Earth. Like a blanket, the atmosphere keeps Earth warm. And like a blanket, the atmosphere has weight, so it presses down on Earth's surface.

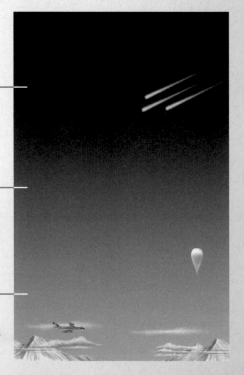

The highest part of the atmosphere extends into space. Satellites orbit in this layer in which there is very little air.

Meteors, chunks of rock from space, burn up where the atmosphere begins to thicken. We see these glowing rocks as "shooting stars."

Some weather balloons can float above the clouds and measure the conditions of the atmosphere. Many jet planes fly just above the clouds.

Weather takes place in the lowest layer of the atmosphere. The atmosphere begins at Earth's surface.

Clouds

Clouds can be many different shapes and sizes. The type of cloud depends on its temperature and height. The table below describes four types of clouds. Many clouds in the sky are two or more cloud types combined.

▶ **MAIN IDEA** Where in the atmosphere does weather take place?

	Clouds and Weather	
Type of Cloud	**Description**	**Likely Weather**
Cumulus	**Cumulus** (KYOOM yuh luhs) clouds are dense white clouds with fluffy tops and flat bottoms.	Small cumulus clouds usually mean good weather.
Stratus	**Stratus** (STRAY tuhs) clouds are flat, layered clouds.	High, thin stratus clouds mean cloudy, dry weather. Low, heavy stratus clouds mean light rain.
Cirrus	**Cirrus** (SEER uhs) clouds are high, thin, and wispy clouds.	These clouds mean good weather.
Cumulonimbus	**Cumulonimbus** (KYOOM yuh loh NIHM bus) clouds are heavy, gray clouds.	These clouds mean bad weather with precipitation. Very tall cumulonimbus clouds can mean thunderstorms.

Changing Weather

Weather is the condition of the atmosphere at a certain place and time. Weather takes place in the lowest layer of the atmosphere.

Weather can change daily, hourly, or even from one minute to the next. The air in the lowest part of the atmosphere is always moving. Moving air, or wind, can bring clouds, changes in temperature, and changes in humidity (hyoo MIHD ih tee) to an area. Humidity is the amount of invisible water vapor in the air.

An important part of the weather is the air temperature (TEHM pur uh chur). **Temperature** is the measure of how hot or cold an object or material is. You use a thermometer (thur MAHM ih tur) to measure temperature in degrees Celsius (SEHL see-uhs) or degrees Fahrenheit (FAHR uhn hyt).

Another part of weather is precipitation. The type of precipitation—rain, sleet, snow, or hail—depends on the temperature of the air. You can measure the amount of precipitation by its depth at the ground.

Wind is an important part of weather. Wind is moving air. It can be measured by its direction and its speed.

Scientists use different tools to measure different parts of weather. Some of these weather tools, or instruments, are shown on the next page.

 **MAIN IDEA** What are two parts of weather?

Thermometer   A thermometer measures the temperature of the air.

Rain Gauge   A rain gauge measures the depth of the precipitation that has fallen.

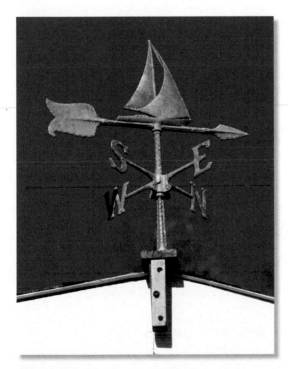

Weathervane   A weathervane shows the direction from which the wind is blowing.

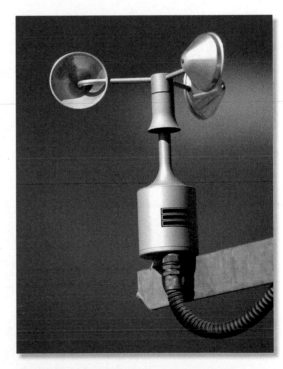

Anemometer   An anemometer measures the wind speed.

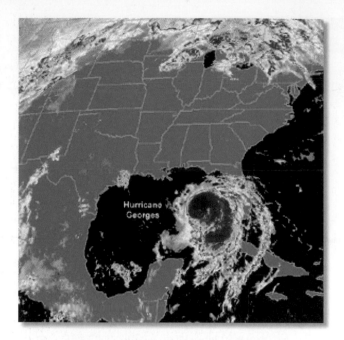

This satellite photo can be used to make a weather map.

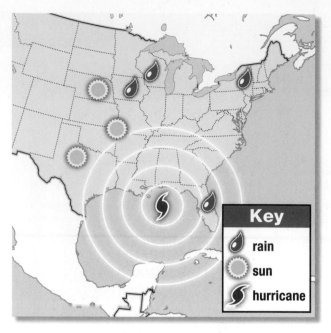

The symbols on this map show information about the weather.

Key
- rain
- sun
- hurricane

Weather Maps

Scientists who study weather are called meteorologists (mee tee uh RAHL uh jihstz). They use many kinds of tools to help them understand and predict weather.

One of the tools used by meteorologists is a weather map. The map uses symbols to show weather patterns. Weather maps can show temperature, wind, and humidity.

Weather maps are put together using information from weather instruments and from satellites. Meteorologists use weather maps to give daily weather forecasts. They also use weather maps and computers to help them predict and track dangerous storms, such as hurricanes.

 **MAIN IDEA** How do meteorologists use weather maps?

Visual Summary

The atmosphere is the blanket of air that covers Earth's surface.

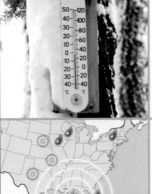

Weather is the condition of the atmosphere at a certain place and time.

Meteorologists study and predict weather using weather maps and computers.

Key
🌢 rain
◯ sun
🌀 hurricane

LINKS for Home and School

MATH **Make a Bar Graph** The rainiest and windiest time of the year in India is called the monsoon season. Use the following information to make a bar graph that shows rainfall in New Delhi, India, during monsoon season. June: 7 inches; July: 9 inches; August: 9 inches; September: 4 inches.

MUSIC **Research Musical Instruments** Woodwind instruments use moving air or "wind" to make musical sounds. Flutes, oboes, and recorders are examples of woodwind instruments. Find the names of six more woodwind instruments.

Review

❶ **MAIN IDEA** What is weather?

❷ **VOCABULARY** Define the term *temperature*.

❸ **READING SKILL: Main Idea and Details** Give three details about parts of weather.

❹ **CRITICAL THINKING: Apply** Identify a type of cloud. Describe the kind of weather this cloud type usually means.

❺ **INQUIRY SKILL: Communicate** Create a chart, sketch, or map to describe the weather outside. Make sure that other students can tell what the weather is like by using the information in your visual.

 TEST PREP
The atmosphere is ___.

A. an instrument that measures wind speed.

B. water that falls from clouds to Earth's surface.

C. the blanket of air that surrounds Earth.

D. a type of cloud that brings heavy rain.

 Technology
Visit **www.eduplace.com/scp/** to find out more about weather.

D19

Where do thunder and lightning come from? The Ibibio (ee BEE bee oh) people of Southern Nigeria (Ny JIHR ee uh) tell a folktale about thunder and lightning. Read part of it below. In the nonfiction selection, *Hurricanes Have Eyes But Can't See,* you'll learn some science facts about thunder and lightning.

How & Why Stories

by Martha Hamilton and Mitch Weiss

Thunder and Lightning

A mother sheep, Thunder, and her son, Lightning, lived in a village. Lightning often misbehaved by burning farmers' crops. Each time he did this his mother grew angry and her booming voice shook the village.

The villagers once again complained to the king. He was so angry that he banished Thunder and Lightning from the earth. He sent them to live in the sky....

And so it is to this very day. Whenever there's a thunderstorm, it's because Lightning has grown angry and thrown his bolts down to the earth. Not long after that, you'll hear his mother, Thunder, angrily scolding him with her booming voice.

Hurricanes Have Eyes But Can't See

by Melvin and Gilda Berger

Lightning is a bright, giant spark of electricity that jumps between a cloud and the ground, between two clouds, or within a cloud.

Inside a thunderhead, powerful winds cause drops of water and ice crystals to rub against one another. This creates an electrical charge that grows bigger and bigger. Soon, it is strong enough to make the electricity jump from one place to another. This makes a giant zigzag spark—a streak of lightning.

Thunder always follows lightning. As lightning flashes through the air, it instantly heats the air to 54,000°F (30,000°C). The heated air explodes. It makes a loud crack of thunder, called a thunderclap.

Sharing Ideas

1. **READING CHECK** In the Ibibio folktale, what causes thunder and lightning?

2. **WRITE ABOUT IT** What new facts did you learn about thunder and lightning after reading the nonfiction selection?

3. **TALK ABOUT IT** Discuss a weather factor you have learned about with your classmates.

What Is Climate?

Why It Matters...

In many places, children enjoy sledding in the winter. In other places, snow never falls. Knowing the average weather conditions over many years helps people plan activities. It also helps them build the right kinds of houses and plant crops that will grow well.

PREPARE TO INVESTIGATE

Inquiry Skill

Research When you do research, you learn more about a subject by looking in books, searching the Internet, or asking science experts.

Materials

- photo cards
- globe
- world map
- research materials

World Weather

Procedure

STEP 2

1. **Collaborate** Work in groups of three. Your teacher will give each student in the group one photo card. Your group will share one world map.

2. **Observe** On a globe, find the location of the place shown on your photo card. Use the world map supplied by your teacher to help you.

STEP 3

3. **Research** Use reference books or the Internet to find the latitude (LAT ih-tood), of your location. Latitude tells how far north or south you are from the midpoint of Earth. When you have found the latitude, write it next to the location on the world map. Also find the average summer temperature and average winter temperature of your location.

STEP 4

Location	Latitude	Average Summer Temperature	Average Winter Temperature
Belem, Brazil			
Tucson, Arizona, USA			
Inuvik, Canada			

4. **Record Data** Work with your group to make a chart like the one shown. Group members should record their data.

Conclusion

1. **Use Numbers** Which location has the greatest difference between its average summer temperature and its average winter temperature?

2. **Infer** How does latitude affect the average summer temperature? How does it affect average winter temperature?

Investigate More!

Research Use books or the Internet to find the places that have had the highest temperature, the lowest temperature, and the lowest yearly precipitation. Label these places on your map.

READING SKILL

Compare and Contrast
As you read, compare and contrast the temperature of different climates.

Climate

MAIN IDEA Climate is the average weather conditions in an area over a long period of time. Climate varies from place to place.

Temperature and Precipitation

Suppose you were going on a trip to Alaska in November. Would you pack shorts and T-shirts? Would you pack a winter coat and mittens if you were headed to Hawaii in June? You probably would not. That's because Alaska has a cold climate (KLY miht), and Hawaii has a warm climate. Knowing the climate of a place can help you pack the right clothing for a trip.

A rainforest has a warm, wet climate. ▼

Greetings from the
RainForest

Climate is the average weather conditions in an area over a long period of time. Climate is not the same as weather. It is cold in Alaska for many months, year after year. So the climate there can be described as cold. But on a day in summer, the weather in Alaska might be warm enough to wear shorts. Climate depends on average temperature and precipitation. In Hawaii, the average temperature is warm. There is usually a lot of precipitation. You could describe Hawaii's climate as warm and wet. Alaska is often cold, and it gets a lot of rain and snowfall. You could say that Alaska's climate is cold and wet.

▶ **COMPARE AND CONTRAST** How are weather and climate alike?

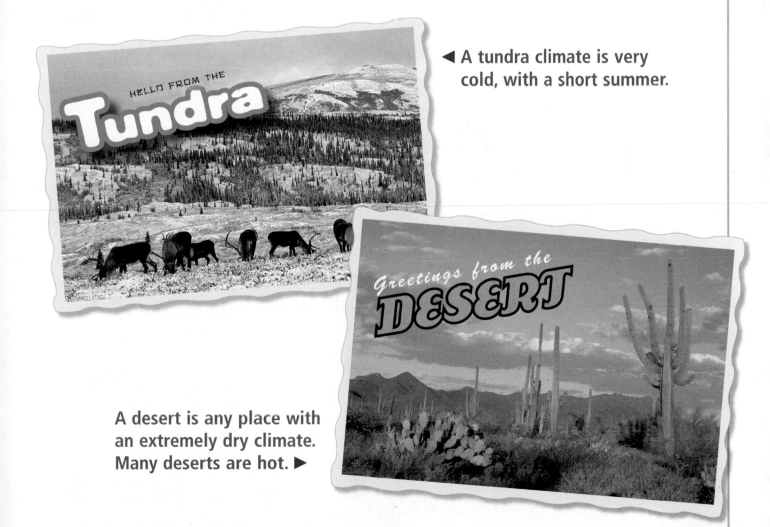

HELLO FROM THE
Tundra

◀ A tundra climate is very cold, with a short summer.

Greetings from the
DESERT

A desert is any place with an extremely dry climate. Many deserts are hot. ▶

Latitude

Climate depends on **latitude** (LAT ih tood), which is the distance north or south of the equator (ih KWAY-tur). The **equator** is an imaginary line around Earth halfway between the North Pole and the South Pole. Places close to the equator are warmer than places that are farther from the equator.

The areas just north and south of the equator have a tropical (TRAHP ih kuhl) climate. A **tropical climate** is very warm and wet for most of or all of the year.

Places that are halfway between the equator and the poles have a **temperate climate**. In these places, summers are warm or hot, and winters are cool or cold.

Two places in the same climate zone can be very different. Mount Shasta and Paris are both in the temperate zone, but Mount Shasta's height above sea level makes it colder.

Mt. Shasta

Climate Zones of the World

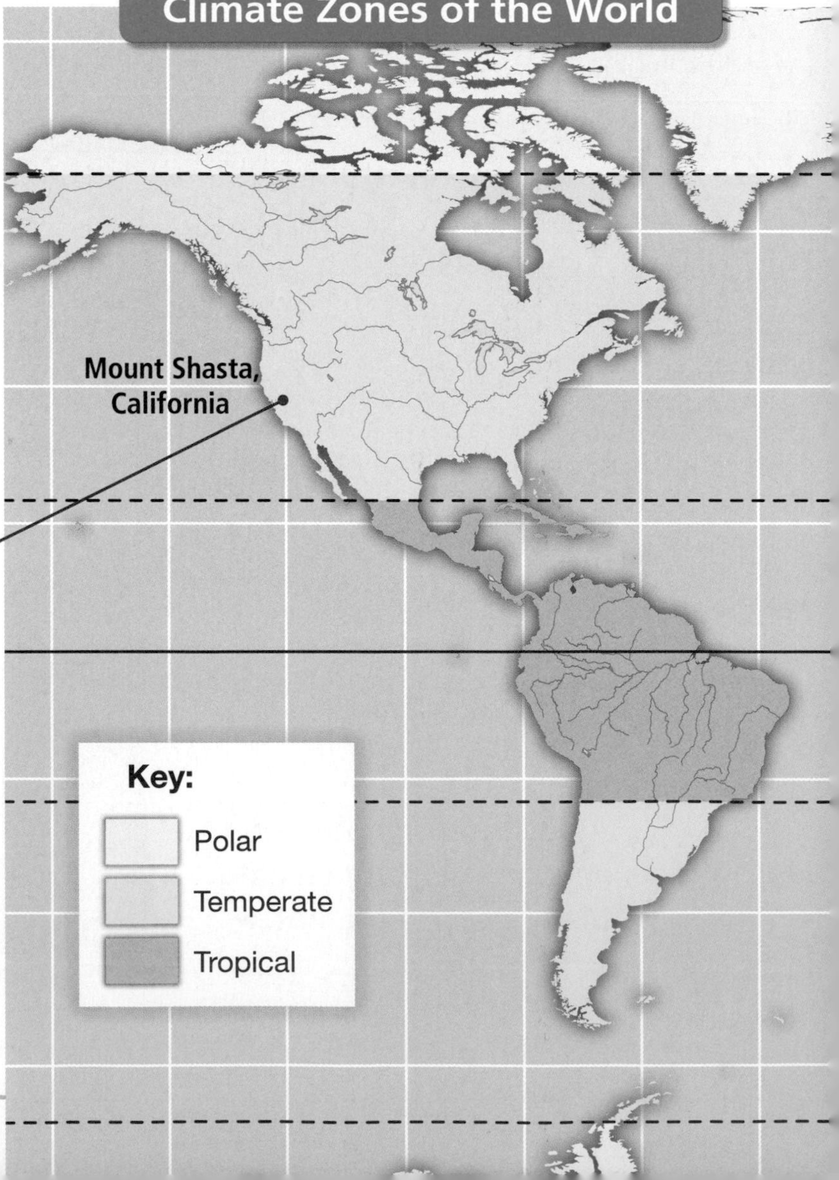

Mount Shasta, California

Key:

Polar

Temperate

Tropical

Closest to the poles, the climate is very cold. It is often quite dry. Places with a **polar climate** have long, cold winters and short, cool summers.

Areas within the climate zones may have different climates. For example, the temperate zone includes both dry climates, such as deserts, and moist climates, such as wetlands. Climates may also differ depending on how high the land is. Mountains have colder climates than do low areas.

▶ **COMPARE AND CONTRAST** **How do summers differ in a temperate climate and a polar climate?**

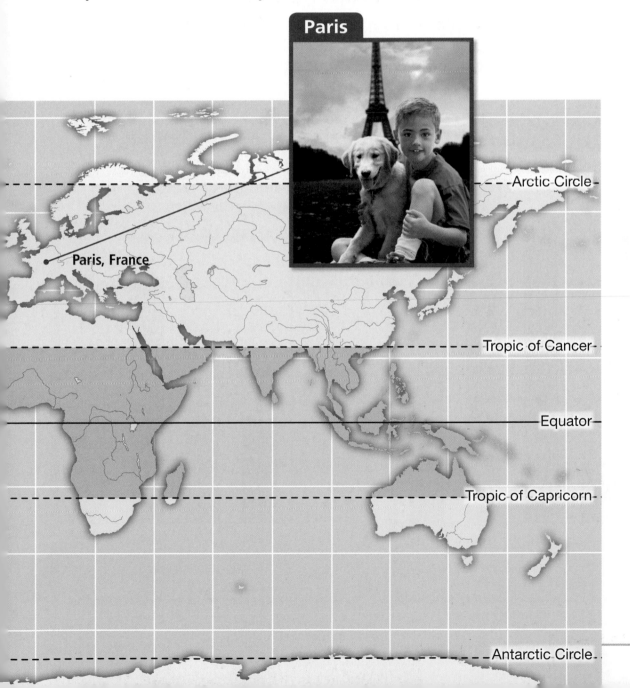

Paris

Paris, France

Arctic Circle

Tropic of Cancer

Equator

Tropic of Capricorn

Antarctic Circle

Weather Patterns and Climate

You cannot tell the climate of a place by observing the weather for one day. Even if you look at the weather for a whole year, you may not know the climate. That year may have been warmer, cooler, drier, or wetter than usual.

Tampa

To learn the climate of a place, scientists look at weather data from many years. The graphs show the average high temperature and average rainfall for Tampa, Florida, during four months. The data was collected over many years.

MAIN IDEA How do scientists learn about the climate of a place?

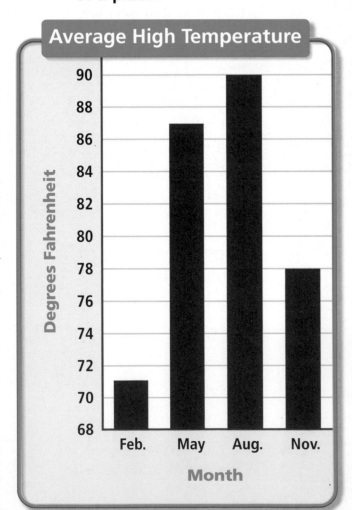

Average High Temperature

Degrees Fahrenheit

Month: Feb., May, Aug., Nov.

Weather data for Tampa, Florida These graphs give a good idea of the climate of Tampa.

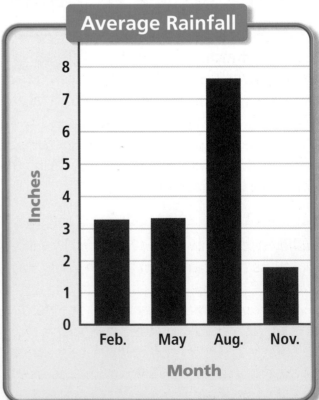

Average Rainfall

Inches

Month: Feb., May, Aug., Nov.

Visual Summary

Climate is the average weather conditions of a place over many years.

Climate zones change with latitude, from tropical to temperate to polar.

Temperatures within a climate zone can vary.

LINKS for Home and School

MATH Find the Difference The 2004 Summer Olympic Games were held in Athens, Greece, in August. The average temperature in Athens during August is 82°F. The 2002 Winter Olympic Games were held in Salt Lake City, Utah, in February. The average temperature in Salt Lake City during February is 37°F. Find the difference in temperature.

WRITING Write a Story The book *Cloudy with a Chance of Meatballs,* by Judi Barrett, is a tall tale about a town with unusual weather. "It rained things like soup and juice. It snowed mashed potatoes and peas. And sometimes the wind blew in storms of hamburgers." Write your own tall tale about a town with unusual weather. Draw a picture to go with your story.

Review

❶ **MAIN IDEA** How are weather and climate different?

❷ **VOCABULARY** What is the equator?

❸ **READING SKILL: Compare and Contrast** Describe how the climates of a hot desert and a tropical rainforest are alike and different.

❹ **CRITICAL THINKING: Analyze** A person has never seen snow. What can you conclude about the climate where she lives?

❺ **INQUIRY SKILL: Research** Find weather data for your area. What are the yearly weather patterns? How would you describe the climate of your area?

✔ TEST PREP

It is usually very warm and wet all year in a ___ climate.

A. temperate

B. desert

C. polar

D. tropical

 Technology
Visit **www.eduplace.com/scp/** to find out more about climate.

Super Storms

Hurricanes are big, powerful windstorms. How big? Look at this photograph of hurricane Ivan taken from space. How large was Ivan? It covered all of Alabama and parts of Georgia and Florida!

When hurricanes roar ashore, they can do terrible damage with wind, rain, surging tides, and huge waves. Fortunately, most hurricanes don't reach land but stay at sea. But 2004 was an exception. Florida got hit with four powerful hurricanes in less than two months. Hurricane Charley was a category 4. Hurricane Frances was a category 2. Hurricane Ivan was a category 3. Hurricane Jeanne was a category 3. What does this chart tell you about each of these storms?

Strength	Damage	Winds	Storm Surge
Category 1	Minimal	74–95 mph	4–5 feet
Category 2	Moderate	96–110 mph	6–8 feet
Category 3	Extensive	111–130 mph	9–12 feet
Category 4	Extreme	131–155 mph	13–18 feet
Category 5	Catastrophic	>155 mph	>18 feet

← Weather scientists divide hurricanes into categories based on wind speed.

The winds in the strongest hurricanes move three times as fast as cars on a freeway!

Vocabulary

Complete each sentence with a term from the list.

1. The blanket of air that surrounds Earth is the _____.

2. The change of state from a liquid to a gas is _____.

3. The condition of the atmosphere at a certain place and time is _____.

4. The _____ is the measure of how hot or cold something is.

5. A place that has long, cold winters and short, cool summers has a/an _____.

6. The change of state from a gas to a liquid is called _____.

7. Water changes state and moves between the atmosphere and Earth in a process called the _____.

8. The imaginary line around Earth halfway between the North Pole and the South Pole is called the _____.

9. Water in the form of an invisible gas is _____.

10. Distance north or south of the equator is _____.

atmosphere D14
climate D25
condensation D7
equator D26
evaporation D7
latitude D26
polar climate D27
precipitation D8
temperate climate D26
temperature D16
tropical climate D26
water cycle D8
water vapor D6
weather D16

Test Prep

Write the letter of the best answer choice.

11. Areas that are close to the equator have a _____.

   A. temperate climate.
   B. dry climate.
   C. tropical climate.
   D. polar climate.

12. The average weather conditions in an area over a period of time is _____.

   A. latitude.   C. climate.
   B. precipitation. D. weather.

13. A place that has warm or hot summers and cool or cold winters has a/an _____.

   A. temperate climate.
   B. tropical climate.
   C. wet climate.
   D. polar climate.

14. Any form of water that falls from clouds to Earth's surface is called _____.

   A. climate.   C. evaporation.
   B. latitude.   D. precipitation.

Inquiry Skills

15. **Research** Many desert climates form in an area called a "rain shadow." Research rain shadows, and explain how they create dry areas.

16. **Predict** Imagine that you are aboard a ship sailing from the equator to the Arctic Circle. How will the weather change along the way? Refer to the diagram below.

Map the Concept

Put the terms below in the correct places on the map. You may use some terms more than once.

temperate climate   equator
polar climate   latitude
tropical climate

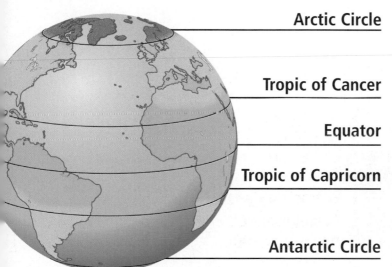

Arctic Circle

Tropic of Cancer

Equator

Tropic of Capricorn

Antarctic Circle

Critical Thinking

17. **Synthesize** Write a paragraph to describe what the weather was like one day this week. Include at least three weather conditions.

18. **Evaluate** Your friend says she lives in a cold, wet climate. During a week you visit, the weather is warm and sunny. Could your friend's statement still be correct? Explain.

19. **Apply** Imagine a group of people starting a settlement in a new place. How could they use information about the climate to help them survive?

20. **Analyze** Suppose you are taking daily weather measurements in a tropical rainforest for a month. You have a thermometer and a rain gauge. How would you expect these measurements to differ from measurements taken in a polar climate?

Performance Assessment

Find Your Role in the Water Cycle
For one day, record each time you use water. Include such activities as bathing, watering plants, cooking, and washing dishes. For each activity, tell how the water you used might return to the water cycle.

Chapter 9

Our Solar System

LESSON 1

They're on mountaintops, in backyards, and there's even one in outer space—what tool makes objects in space easier to see?

Read about it in Lesson 1.

LESSON 2

Nine planets, more than one hundred moons, and thousands of chunks of rock and metal—what do these objects all have in common?

Read about it in Lesson 2.

LESSON 3

Is there life on Mars or water on Venus and Mercury—what do scientists know about the planets closest to the Sun?

Read about it in Lesson 3.

How Do Scientists Use Telescopes?

Why It Matters...

When you look up into the night sky, you can see stars, planets, and the Moon. If you use a telescope, you can see these objects more clearly. Scientists use telescopes to collect information about objects in space.

PREPARE TO INVESTIGATE

Inquiry Skill

Compare When you compare two things, you observe how they are alike and how they are different.

Materials

- 2 cardboard tubes
- transparent tape
- convex lens A (15-cm focal length)
- convex lens B (5-cm focal length)

Making a Telescope
Procedure

STEP 1

1 **Collaborate** Work with a partner to make a telescope. Slip a smaller tube inside a larger tube to make a telescope tube. Tape lens A, the larger, thinner lens, to the larger end of the telescope tube.

2 Tape lens B, the smaller, thicker lens, to the smaller end of the tube.

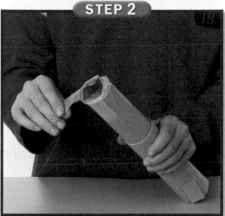
STEP 2

3 **Observe** Without using the telescope, observe three objects that are across the room. In your *Science Notebook*, make a drawing or use words to record how the objects look.

4 Use the telescope to observe the same three objects. Hold the smaller end of the telescope to your eye and look through the lens. Slowly slide the larger tube forward and back until you can see each object clearly.

STEP 4

5 **Record Data** Draw or use words to record how the three objects look through your telescope.

Conclusion

1. **Compare** What differences did you notice when you viewed the objects with just your eyes and then with the aid of a telescope?

2. **Infer** Why do you think telescopes are so useful to scientists who study space?

Investigate More!
Design an Experiment
Predict how the objects you observed in step 4 would look if you held the larger end of the telescope to your eye. Design an experiment to test your prediction.

VOCABULARY

magnify	p. D38
telescope	p. D38

READING SKILL

Problem-Solution Use a diagram like the one below. In the *Problem* column, write "Earth's atmosphere prevents planets from being seen clearly." In the *Solution* column, write a possible solution to the problem.

Problem	Solution

Seeing into Space

MAIN IDEA Telescopes help scientists study stars, planets, and the Moon.

Telescopes

If you look up at the night sky, you can see small points of light. Most of these points of light are stars. How can you see these objects more clearly?

A telescope can help you see details of objects in the sky. A **telescope** is a tool that makes distant objects appear larger and sharper. When you make an object appear larger, you **magnify** it. The number of stars that can be seen through telescopes is much greater than the number that can be seen with just your eyes.

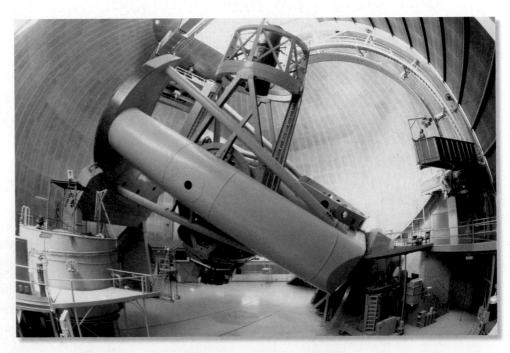

▲ This optical telescope is on Mount Palomar in California.

This radio telescope in Arecibo, Puerto Rico, is the largest in the world. ▲

There are different kinds of telescopes. One kind of telescope magnifies distant objects by collecting light. This is called an optical (AHP tihk-uhl) telescope. Some optical telescopes work like eyeglasses. They use curved pieces of glass called lenses. Other optical telescopes use curved mirrors.

Instead of light, a radio telescope collects radio waves from space. Computers use the radio waves to make pictures of space that scientists can study. As telescopes improve, scientists learn more about objects in space.

▶ **PROBLEM AND SOLUTION** **What tool can you use to see objects in space more clearly?**

The Hubble Space Telescope is an optical telescope. It travels around Earth 569 km (353 mi) above the surface. ▶

A Hubble Scrapbook

The Hubble Space Telescope is different from other telescopes because it is in space. It moves around Earth every 97 minutes. Hubble was launched in 1990 from a space shuttle.

The clouds, dust, and water of Earth's atmosphere blur the view of objects in space. But Hubble helps scientists see space from beyond Earth's atmosphere. It gets a clearer view of distant regions of space.

▶ **PROBLEM AND SOLUTION** **How is the Hubble able to help scientists see space so clearly?**

Pillars of Creation ▼

Gomez's Hamburger ▼

Lagoon Nebula ▼

Visual Summary

Telescopes are tools that make distant objects appear larger and brighter so they can be seen more clearly.

Optical telescopes use lenses or mirrors to collect light from distant objects.

Radio telescopes collect radio waves instead of light.

LINKS for Home and School

MATH **Find the Sum** The Hubble Space Telescope takes 97 minutes to complete 1 orbit around Earth. How long will it take for the Hubble Space Telescope to complete 3 orbits around Earth? Show your work.

ART **Draw a Picture** The night sky inspired Dutch artist Vincent van Gogh to paint *Starry Night* in 1889. Find a copy of this famous painting in an art book, encyclopedia, or on the Internet. Create your own picture of the night sky.

Review

❶ MAIN IDEA What are telescopes used for in science?

❷ VOCABULARY Use the terms *telescope* and *magnify* in a sentence.

❸ READING SKILL: Problem-Solution Suggest a problem that can be solved by using a telescope.

❹ CRITICAL THINKING: Evaluate Why do you think many large telescopes are located on mountaintops?

❺ INQUIRY SKILL: Compare How is a radio telescope different from an optical telescope?

✔ TEST PREP

The Hubble telescope is ___.

A. a radio telescope.

B. above Earth's atmosphere.

C. on a mountaintop.

D. always in the same place.

Technology

Visit **www.eduplace.com/scp/** to research more about telescopes.

What Is the Solar System?

Why It Matters...

A solar flare is an explosion on the Sun. It Is caused by the sudden release of huge amounts of light and gas. How are you affected by something that happens so far away? When energy from the flare reaches Earth's atmosphere, it can disrupt signals from radios, televisions, and cell phones.

PREPARE TO INVESTIGATE

Inquiry Skill

Use Models You can use a model of an object, process, or idea to better understand or describe how it works.

Materials

- drinking straw
- scissors
- metric ruler
- string (1 m long)
- small plastic-foam ball
- metal washer
- tape
- goggles

Science and Math Toolbox

For step 1, review **Using a Tape Measure or Ruler** on page H6.

Planet Movements

Procedure

1 **Measure** Cut a drinking straw so that it is 12 cm long. Thread a piece of string that is 1 m long through the straw.

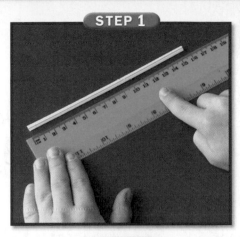
STEP 1

2 Tie one end of the string to a washer. Wrap the other end of the string around a plastic-foam ball and tie it tightly. Then use several pieces of tape to secure the string to the ball.

STEP 2

3 **Use Models** Hold the straw upright with one hand. Rest the washer in your other hand. Stand away from your classmates. Move the straw in a circular motion so the ball swings in a circle around the straw. **Safety:** You and your classmates must wear goggles while the ball is moving.

4 **Record Data** In your *Science Notebook,* describe the motion of the ball.

STEP 3

Conclusion

1. **Infer** What do you think the ball represents in the model?

2. **Use Models** What does the straw represent?

Investigate More!

Research Use the Internet or the library to research the shape of a planet's path. How does it differ from the shape of the path in your model?

Learn by Reading

The Solar System

VOCABULARY

READING SKILL

Compare and Contrast
Use the diagram to compare a moon and a planet.

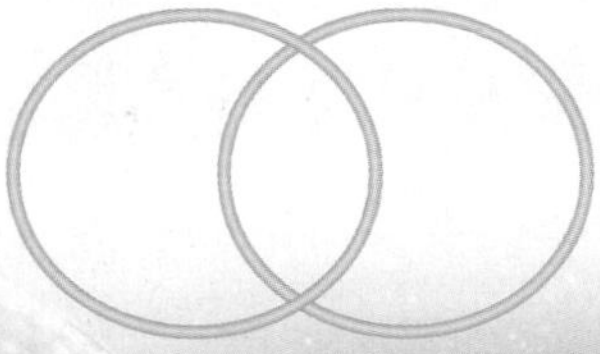

MAIN IDEA The Sun, nine orbiting planets and their moons, and other objects that orbit the Sun make up the solar system.

The Sun and Planets

The **Sun** is the nearest star to Earth. Like all stars, the Sun is a huge sphere of hot gases that gives off heat and light. Earth is one of nine planets that move around the Sun. A **planet** is a large body in space that moves around a star. A planet does not produce light of its own.

Earth and eight other planets each **orbit**, or move in a path, around the Sun. A planet's path around the Sun is an oval.

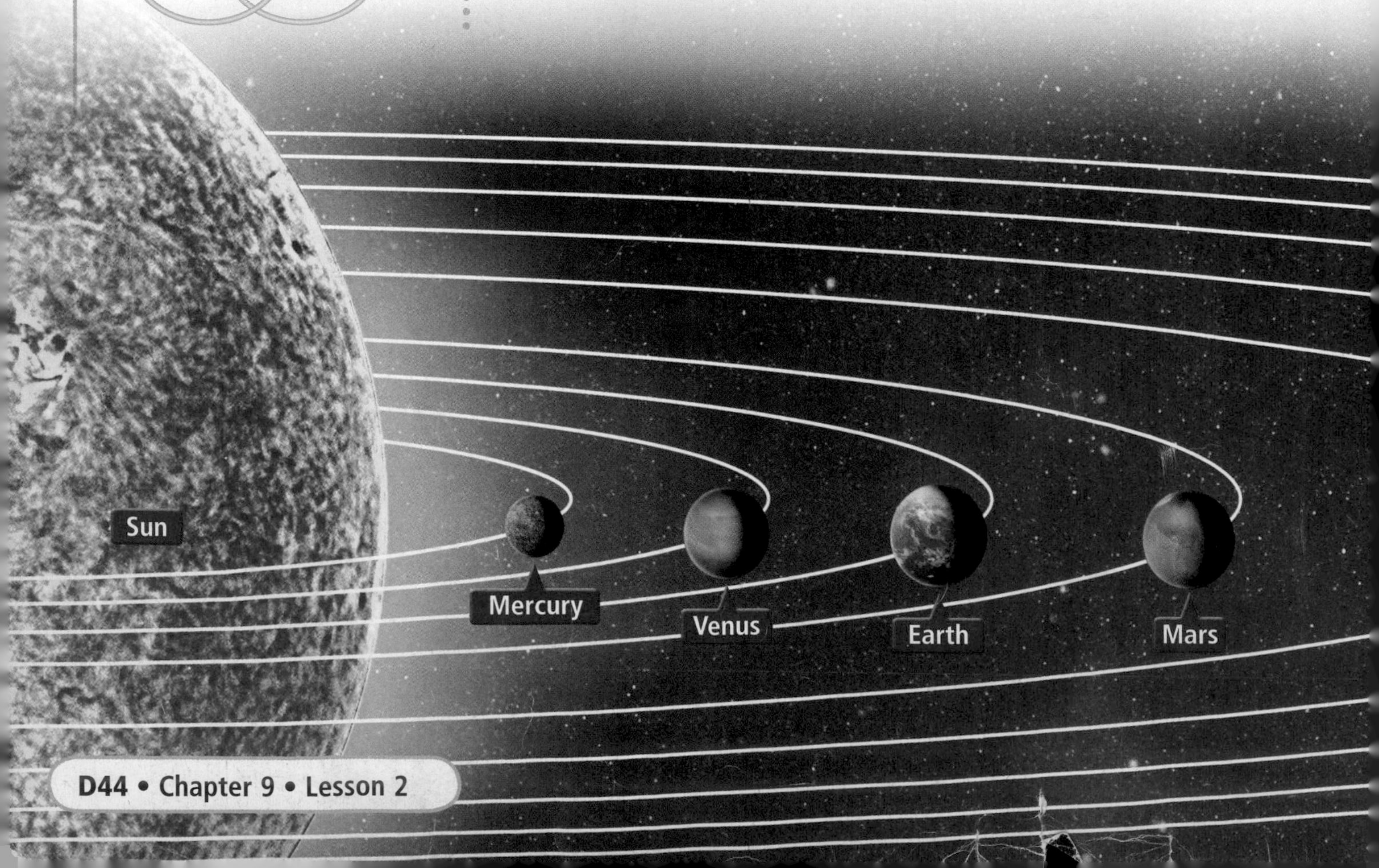

Sun
Mercury
Venus
Earth
Mars

Most planets have one or more moons. A **moon** is a small, rounded body in orbit around a planet. A moon does not produce its own light. The Sun, planets, moons, and other objects that orbit the Sun make up the **solar system** (SOH lur SIHS tuhm).

The farther a planet is from the Sun, the longer it takes to orbit the Sun. The time it takes to complete one trip around the Sun is called a year. Earth's year is about 365 days long. Mercury, the planet closest to the Sun, makes a complete orbit in just 88 Earth days.

As it orbits the Sun, each planet also spins like a top. This spinning causes the cycle of daytime and nighttime. Earth's day, one full turn, is 24-hours long. Some planets spin more slowly than Earth. It takes 243 Earth days for Venus to complete one full turn.

▶ **COMPARE AND CONTRAST** **What is one way that planets and moons are similar?**

Nine planets orbit the Sun in the solar system.

Pluto

Uranus

Neptune

Saturn

Jupiter

The Inner Planets

Mercury, Venus, Earth, and Mars are called the **inner planets**. These planets get a lot of heat and light because they are close to the Sun. The inner planets are small and are made of solid rock materials. Their surfaces have mountains and craters.

Mercury (MUR kyuh ree) is the closest planet to the Sun. Mercury is very hot during the day and very cold at night.

Earth is the third planet from the Sun. It is the only planet known to support life. Earth has an atmosphere. Its temperature range is less extreme than that of other planets.

Venus (VEE nuhs) is the second planet from the Sun. It is covered by thick clouds of gas. The clouds trap heat and make the planet very hot.

Mars (mahrz) is the fourth planet from the Sun. The surface of Mars has many craters, mountains, and volcanoes. Mars is thought to have the largest volcano in the solar system.

The Outer Planets

Jupiter, Saturn, Uranus, Neptune, and Pluto are called the **outer planets**. They are cold and dark because they are far from the Sun. Jupiter, Saturn, Uranus, and Neptune are large. They are made of gases and have many moons. Each of these four planets also has a system of rings. Pluto is small and is made of rocks and frozen gases. It has no rings and only one moon.

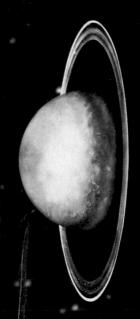

Uranus (YUR uh nuhs) is the seventh planet from the Sun. Unlike any other planet, Uranus spins on its side.

Jupiter (JOO pih tur) is the fifth planet from the Sun and is the largest planet. The Great Red Spot is a large storm.

Neptune (NEHP toon) is the eighth planet from the Sun. Methane in its atmosphere gives Neptune its blue color.

Saturn (SAT urn) is the sixth planet from the Sun. It has beautiful rings made of dust, ice, and rocks.

Pluto (PLOO toh) is the ninth planet from the Sun and is the smallest planet. Because it is so far away, it is the only planet that has not yet been explored by spacecraft.

D47

The Asteroid Belt

The asteroid (AS tuh royd) belt is an area between the inner planets and the outer planets. An **asteroid** is a piece of rock that orbits the Sun. There are thousands of asteroids within the asteroid belt. An asteroid can be as small as a grain of sand or almost as large as the state of California.

Sometimes a piece of an asteroid breaks off and moves close to Earth. As it moves through Earth's atmosphere, it burns up.

▶ **COMPARE AND CONTRAST** Are all asteroids the same size? Explain.

Jupiter

Mars

asteroid belt

This asteroid, named Ida, is about 52 km (32 mi) long.

Visual Summary

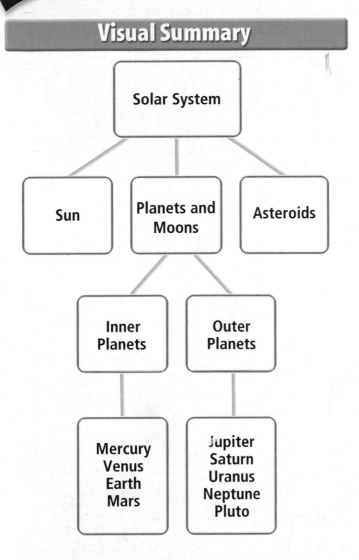

Solar System

Sun | Planets and Moons | Asteroids

Inner Planets | Outer Planets

Mercury
Venus
Earth
Mars

Jupiter
Saturn
Uranus
Neptune
Pluto

 **for Home and School**

MATH **Estimate a Sum** The length of 1 year on Mercury is equal to 88 Earth days. Use rounding to estimate how many Earth days are equal to 2 years on Mercury.

WRITING **Story** In *Peter Pan* by J.M. Barrie, Peter tells Wendy that the way to Neverland is "second (star) to the right and straight on till morning." Write about a fictional place in the sky. Where would it be located? How would you get there?

Review

❶ **MAIN IDEA** Name the nine planets of the solar system in order.

❷ **VOCABULARY** Write a sentence that uses the terms *planet* and *orbit*.

❸ **READING SKILL: Compare and Contrast** Explain one way that inner planets and outer planets are different.

❹ **CRITICAL THINKING: Analyze** A planet has a very long day compared with Earth. What does that tell you about the movement of that planet?

❺ **INQUIRY SKILL: Use Models** Suppose you want to make a model using balls to represent the Sun and planets of the solar system. How many balls would you need?

 TEST PREP
Which statement about the Sun is true?

A. It gives off light.

B. It orbits the planets.

C. It is made of rock.

D. It has one moon.

Technology
Visit **www.eduplace.com/scp/** to find out more about the solar system.

Maria Mitchell
(1818–1889)

She reached for the stars. On a fall night in 1847, Maria Mitchell stood on the rooftop of her parent's house in Nantucket, Massachusetts. She pointed her telescope at the sky and saw a light in a spot where she knew there were no stars. Then she realized what the light was. She was looking at a comet that had never been seen before!

Mitchell's discovery made her famous around the world, when the comet became known as "Mitchell's Comet." At that time, most women were not taught science.

Mitchell's father had encouraged her to learn about the stars when she was a child. By the time she spotted her comet, Mitchell had been studying the Sun, Moon, and stars for many years. She continued to study the Sun and planets throughout her life.

▲ Mitchell (standing) at her Lynn, Massachusetts, observatory. The observatory's telescope was a gift from women across the country.

Mitchell was born in this Nantucket, Massachusetts, house in 1818. The house became a museum in 1902. ▶

Maria Mitchell was working as a librarian during the day and studying the stars at night when she discovered comet 1847 VI, known as "Mitchell's Comet."

Sharing Ideas

1. **READING CHECK** What important discovery did Maria Mitchell make in 1847?

2. **WRITE ABOUT IT** In what way did Mitchell's father help prepare his daughter to become a successful scientist?

3. **TALK ABOUT IT** Discuss how you think Mitchell's work may have helped other women succeed in science.

What Are the Inner Planets?

Why It Matters...

By the time you are an adult, people may be traveling to Mars. Would you like to visit another planet? What you learn about the planets may help you decide whether or not you want to become an astronaut.

Inquiry Skill

Predict When you predict, you state what you think will happen based on observations and experiences.

Materials

- Signs labeled *Sun*, *Mercury*, *Venus*, *Earth*, and *Mars*
- masking tape
- tape measure
- stopwatch

Science and Math Toolbox

For step 4, review **Measuring Elapsed Time** on pages H12–H13.

Orbiting the Sun

Procedure

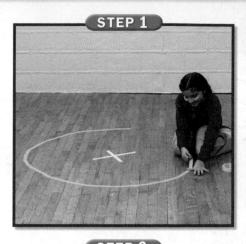

STEP 1

1. **Measure** Make a simple model of the solar system. Use masking tape to make an X on the floor to mark the Sun's position. Mark an orbit around the Sun by placing pieces of tape in a circle 1 m from the X. Make three more orbits with tape, each 1 m farther out from the X.

STEP 2

Distance of Planets from Sun	
Planet	Average distance from Sun (millions of km)
Mercury	58
Venus	108
Earth	150
Mars	228

2. **Collaborate** Five students should hold signs to model the inner planets and the Sun. Use the data in the table to arrange the "planets" in their orbits.

3. **Predict** Predict where each "planet" will be after walking for 5 seconds. Mercury should move most quickly. Venus should move slightly slower. Earth should move more slowly than Venus. Mars should move the slowest.

STEP 2

4. **Use Models** When a timekeeper says to start, the "planets" should walk in their own orbits as described in step 3. After 5 seconds, the timekeeper will tell the "planets" to stop. Draw the position of each "planet."

Conclusion

1. **Compare** Which planet still has the greatest distance to travel to complete its orbit?

2. **Infer** What can you infer about how a planet's distance from the Sun and its speed affects the length of its year?

Investigate More!

Design an Experiment
Extend your model to include Jupiter. How should Jupiter move? Infer how the length of a year on Jupiter and Mars differ.

The Inner Planets

VOCABULARY

space probe   p. D58

READING SKILL

Text Structure Use the diagram below to show how the text in this lesson is arranged.

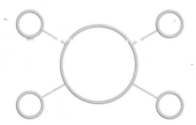

MAIN IDEA The inner planets are Mercury, Venus, Earth, and Mars. They are small, ball-shaped, solid, and rocky.

Mercury

Mercury is the nearest planet to the Sun. It is a tiny rocky planet not much larger than Earth's Moon. As you can see, the surface of Mercury has craters, flat areas, and mountains.

Unlike Earth, Mercury has no water and very little air. There is no blanket of air to keep the temperature steady. Because of this, Mercury gets very hot during the day and very cold at night. You could not live on Mercury.

Mercury's surface looks a bit like the surface of Earth's Moon.

Mercury	
Average temperature	Day: 427°C (800°F); Night: −73°C (−99°F)
Diameter	4,878 km (3,029 mi)
Distance from Sun	58 million km (36 million mi)
Number of moons	none
Length of day	59 Earth days
Length of year	88 Earth days

Venus

Venus is the second planet from the Sun. Venus has been called Earth's twin because it is about the same size as Earth and its orbit is next to Earth's orbit. Venus is a very bright planet in Earth's sky. Often Venus can be seen low in the sky, just after sunset.

Although it looks beautiful from Earth, Venus would not be a very pleasant place to live. It is covered with a thick layer of clouds. The clouds trap heat and make Venus the hottest planet. There is no water on Venus. Its surface is covered with rocks and ash, and there are many volcanoes.

▶ **TEXT STRUCTURE** **How do the charts on pages D54 and D55 help you compare Mercury and Venus?**

Venus	
Average temperature	482°C (900°F)
Diameter	12,104 km (7,519 mi)
Distance from Sun	108 million km (67 million mi)
Number of moons	none
Length of day	243 Earth days
Length of year	225 Earth days

There are many volcanoes on the surface of Venus.

Earth

Earth, the third planet, is your home. It is the only planet in the solar system that is known to support life. Earth has both liquid water and oxygen, which most living things need. In addition, Earth's atmosphere keeps the planet from getting too hot or too cold.

From space, Earth looks like a big blue marble. About three-fourths of Earth's surface is covered by liquid water. Mountains, deserts, valleys, forests, and frozen land areas make up the rest of the surface.

Earth is covered by oceans and clouds.

Earth	
Average temperature	15°C (59°F)
Diameter	12,712 km (7,926 mi)
Distance from Sun	150 million km (93 million mi)
Number of moons	1
Length of day	24 hours
Length of year	about 365 Earth days

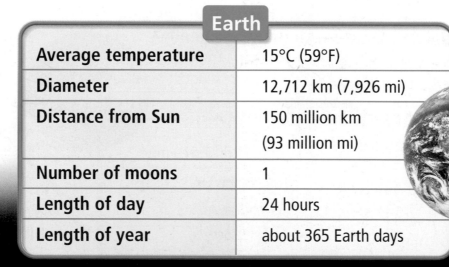

Mars

Mars, the fourth planet, is called the Red Planet. It is covered with red rocks and soil that contain rust. Mars has many volcanoes, including the largest volcano in the solar system. This volcano rises 26 km (16 mi) above the land around it. Canyons, craters, and valleys are features of its surface.

Winds on Mars cause powerful dust storms that sometimes last for months. No liquid water has been found on Mars, but there is ice at the poles. Many scientists think that liquid water and perhaps life may have existed on Mars. But no signs of life have yet been found.

▶ **TEXT STRUCTURE** **In addition to the above text, what else on this page provides information about the surface of Mars?**

Mars	
Average temperature	−63°C (−81°F)
Diameter	6,746 km (4,223 mi)
Distance from Sun	228 million km (141 million mi)
Number of moons	2
Length of day	$24\frac{1}{2}$ hours
Length of year	687 Earth days

Mars has some oxygen in the atmosphere. It also has some frozen water.

Exploring the Inner Planets

If you wanted to learn about a place, you could visit it. But what if the place was too dangerous or too far away to visit? These are reasons why people have not yet visited the planets. Instead, scientists have sent space probes to most of the planets. A **space probe** is a craft that explores outer space carrying instruments, but not people.

Space probes carry cameras, lab equipment, and other tools to take pictures and collect data. They send the information back to Earth to be studied.

▶ **TEXT STRUCTURE** What is a different heading that could be used at the top of this page?

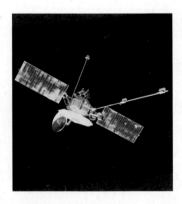

Mariner 10
Mariner 10 was the first space probe ever to collect data about two planets—Mercury and Venus.

Magellan
The Magellan probe was launched in 1989 to map the surface of Venus.

Mars Rovers
Two rovers, Spirit and Opportunity, landed on Mars in 2004. They collected rocks and soil. They also looked for signs that water was once on Mars.

Lesson Wrap-Up

Visual Summary

Mercury is the planet closest to the Sun. It has no water and little air.

Venus is the hottest planet because of its thick cloud layer.

Earth is the only planet known to have liquid water and life.

Mars has red soil and rocks. It has ice at the poles.

LINKS for Home and School

MATH Calculate Elapsed Time On July 20, 1969, astronaut Neil Armstrong became the first human to walk on the Moon. He took the first step at 10:56 P.M. Astronaut Edwin "Buzz" Aldrin joined Armstrong 19 minutes later. At what time did Aldrin take his first step on the Moon?

LITERATURE Research Mythical Characters Many of the planets are named after mythical Roman gods. Venus is named after the Roman goddess of love and beauty. Find out who Jupiter, Mars, Mercury, and Neptune were in Roman mythology.

Review

1 MAIN IDEA What do the inner planets have in common?

2 VOCABULARY What is a space probe?

3 READING SKILL: Text Structure In what order were the inner planets presented in this lesson? What other order could have been used?

4 CRITICAL THINKING: Apply If you were designing a space probe to study a planet, what instruments or tools would you include?

5 INQUIRY SKILL: Predict It takes Earth 365 days and Mars 687 Earth days to complete an orbit around the Sun. When Earth has completed 1 orbit, predict about how far Mars will have traveled on its own orbit.

 TEST PREP
All the following are inner planets EXCEPT ___.

A. Mars.

B. Earth.

C. Saturn.

D. Mercury.

 Technology
Visit **www.eduplace.com/scp/** to learn more about the inner planets.

D59

Eyes on the Skies

Look at those rings! The planet Saturn is a beautiful sight even in a small backyard telescope. How much more exciting would it be to look at Saturn through the biggest telescope in the world?

Compare these two images of Saturn. An amateur astronomer recorded the smaller image with his home telescope. The larger image comes from one of the mighty Keck telescopes on top of Mauna Kea in Hawaii. At the Keck Observatory, astronomers have not one, but two giant eyes on the universe. Each telescope is the largest of its type anywhere.

Here's how Saturn looks through a home telescope. Not bad!

Here's how Saturn looks through the mighty Keck telescope. What a difference!

Each of the twin telescopes at the Keck Observatory has a mirror that is 33 feet across! The Keck telescopes help astronomers see farther and more clearly into outer space than any Earth-based telescope ever has.

Review and Test Prep

Vocabulary

Complete each sentence with a term from the list.

1. When you use a device to make an object look larger, you _____ the object.

2. The Sun and other objects that orbit it make up the _____.

3. When planets move around the Sun, they _____ it.

4. A small, rounded body in orbit around a planet is a/an _____.

5. A craft that explores outer space carrying instruments, but not people, is called a/an _____.

6. Mercury, Venus, Earth, and Mars are called the _____.

7. The nearest star to Earth is the _____.

8. A tool that makes distant objects appear larger is a/an _____.

9. Jupiter, Saturn, Uranus, Neptune, and Pluto are called the _____.

10. A piece of rock that orbits the Sun is a/an _____.

asteroid D48
inner planets D46
magnify D38
moon D45
orbit D44
outer planets D47
planet D44
solar system D45
space probe D58
Sun D44
telescope D38

Test Prep

Write the letter of the best answer choice.

11. The Hubble Space Telescope helps scientists view space from _____.

   A. the surface of Mars.
   B. the atmosphere of Mars.
   C. within Earth's atmosphere.
   D. beyond Earth's atmosphere.

12. The area between the inner planets and outer planets is called the _____.

   A. moon.   C. solar system.
   B. Sun.   D. asteroid belt.

13. Which is true of the inner planets?

   A. They are made of frozen gases.
   B. They are made of rocky materials.
   C. They have no moons.
   D. They orbit the asteroid belt.

14. A large body that orbits a star and does not produce light of its own is a/an _____.

   A. moon.   C. planet.
   B. Sun.   D. asteroid.

15. Use Models You want to make a model of a solar system in which the planets and the moons move. How will the movements of the moons compare with the movements of the planets?

16. Predict Scientists send a space probe to collect and analyze a sample of dust from the surface of Venus. Do you think the dust will contain any bacteria or other tiny living things? Explain.

Map the Concept

Complete the concept map using the following terms:

asteroids   Mars
inner   Mercury
outer   Venus

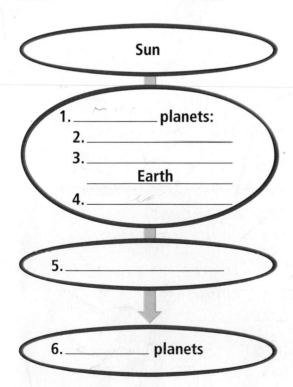

Sun

1. _____ planets:
2. _____
3. _____
    Earth
4. _____

5. _____

6. _____ planets

17. Apply The rovers Spirit and Opportunity landed on Mars in 2004. Why do you think scientists made looking for water such an important part of their mission?

18. Synthesize What advantages might a spacecraft with a crew of astronauts have over a spacecraft with no crew? What advantages might a spacecraft with no crew have?

19. Evaluate Someone tells you that Earth's moon produces its own light. They say that the proof of this is that the Moon is very bright at night. Evaluate this statement.

20. Analyze Venus has a day that is 243 Earth days long. What does this tell you about the speed at which Venus spins compared to Earth?

Performance Assessment

Property for Sale
You have been asked to write an advertisement for land on Mars that is for sale. Describe the land and some of its features. Try to make the land sound attractive so that someone will want to buy it.

Chapter 10

Cycles and Patterns in Space

Lesson Preview

LESSON 1

When it is time for recess in the United States, it is dinnertime on the other side of the world—what causes these differences?

Read about it in Lesson 1.

LESSON 2

From a thin sliver of light to a glowing circle—why does the Moon look different on different nights?

Read about it in Lesson 2.

LESSON 3

The Sun that warms the Earth and the stars we see at night— what do they have in common?

Read about it in Lesson 3.

What Causes Day and Night?

Why It Matters...

Do you like to get up early in the morning? The pattern of day and night affects all living things. Some flowers open in the morning and close at night. Like many other animals, you are active during the day and sleep at night.

PREPARE TO INVESTIGATE

Inquiry Skill

Use Models You can use a model of an object, process, or idea to understand or describe how it works.

Materials

- globe with dot stickers
- flashlight

Science and Math Toolbox

For step 1, review **Making a Chart to Organize Data** on page H10.

A Long Day
Procedure

1. In your *Science Notebook*, make a chart like the one shown.

2. **Use Models** A globe is a model of Earth. Your teacher will show you a globe. Each dot on the globe stands for one hour of time. Record the number of dots there are in all.

3. **Record Data** Use a flashlight to model the Sun. Shine it on the side of Earth where Oregon is. The top of the globe should be tilted toward the Sun. Oregon should just be entering the light. Count the dots that are in the light. Write this number on your chart.

4. **Use Models** Slowly spin the globe until Oregon is just entering the darkness. Count the dots that are in darkness. Write this number on your chart.

Conclusion

1. **Use Numbers** How many dots are on the globe? Why are there that many dots?

2. **Analyze Data** Compare the number of dots in light to the number in darkness.

3. **Use Models** Based on your observations, is daytime always the same length as nighttime? Is daytime or nighttime longer in Oregon when Oregon is tilted toward the Sun?

STEP 1

Number of Dots	
In Light	In Darkness

STEP 3

STEP 4

Investigate More!

Design an Experiment Experiment to find out the length of daylight in Oregon when Oregon is tilted away from the Sun. Predict whether daytime or nighttime will be longer. Test your idea.

VOCABULARY

axis	p. D68
revolve	p. D68
rotate	p. D68

READING SKILL

Cause and Effect

Use the chart below to explain what causes day and night.

Day and Night

MAIN IDEA The pattern of day and night is caused by Earth's rotation.

Rotating Earth

While you are enjoying after-school activities, it is the middle of the night in China. How can this be?

You have learned about one of the ways Earth and the other planets move. They **revolve** (rih VAHLV), or move in a path, around the Sun. While the planets revolve, they also rotate (ROH tayt). To **rotate** is to spin around an axis (AK sihs). An **axis** is an imaginary line through the center of an object. Earth's axis goes through the North and South Poles.

Imagine it is sunrise where you live. As Earth rotates, the side of Earth where you live turns to face the Sun. Only the side of Earth facing the Sun has daylight. Your day begins as the Sun appears to rise in the east.

As the day goes on, the Sun seems to move across the sky. But it is actually not the Sun that is moving. It is the turning of Earth that causes the Sun to look like it is moving. As Earth continues to rotate, your side of Earth turns away from the Sun. The Sun appears to set in the west. Night begins where you live. And now it's daytime on the other side of Earth.

CAUSE AND EFFECT What causes the Sun to appear to move across the sky?

Sun

Day and Night Around the Globe

North America

This part of Earth is facing the Sun, so it is daytime.

Asia

This part of Earth is facing away from the Sun, so it is nighttime.

Africa

This part of Earth has turned away from the Sun, so it is evening.

Length of Day and Night Changes

The length of day and night changes throughout the year. This happens because some parts of Earth face the Sun for more hours than other parts do. The tilt of Earth's axis causes these differences.

As Earth revolves around the Sun, different parts of Earth are tilted toward the Sun. In June, the North Pole is tilted toward the Sun. So places north of the Equator face the Sun for more hours than they face away from it. They have more hours of daylight and fewer hours of darkness.

In December, the North Pole faces away from the Sun. This means that places north of the Equator face away from the Sun for more hours than they face toward it. So, in these places, there are more hours of darkness than daylight.

▶ **CAUSE AND EFFECT** **Why does the length of day and night change throughout the year?**

8:00 P.M. in June

8:00 P.M. in December

Visual Summary

Earth rotates around its axis. This rotation causes the pattern of day and night.

Because Earth's axis is tilted, the number of hours of daylight and darkness change throughout the year.

LINKS for Home and School

MATH **Find Elapsed Time** When it is 5:30 P.M. in Chicago, Illinois, it is 5:30 A.M. in Bangkok, Thailand. How many hours difference is there between the two cities? Draw a picture to show what a child in each city might be doing at these times.

SOCIAL STUDIES Use a Globe

Find Argentina and Sweden on a globe. Which country is in the Northern Hemisphere? Which country is in the Southern Hemisphere? Which country is tilted toward the Sun in December?

Review

❶ **MAIN IDEA** How does Earth's rotation cause day and night?

❷ **VOCABULARY** If you spin a top that stays in one place, are you causing the top to rotate or to revolve? Explain.

❸ **READING SKILL: Cause and Effect** What is one effect of Earth's axis being tilted?

❹ **CRITICAL THINKING: Apply** Sydney, Australia, is south of the equator. In January, the South Pole is tilted toward the Sun. In Sydney, are there more hours of daylight or darkness in January? Explain.

❺ **INQUIRY SKILL: Use Models** Describe how you could make a model of Earth revolving around the Sun.

 TEST PREP
How does Earth move?

A. It only revolves.

B. It only rotates.

C. It rotates and revolves.

D. It rotates in the morning and revolves at night.

 Technology
Visit **www.eduplace.com/scp/** to investigate more about Earth's movements.

D71

What Are the Phases of the Moon?

Why It Matters...

Are those really footprints on the Moon? Yes! People walked on the Moon when they traveled there to study it. On most nights, you can study the Moon from right here on Earth. In fact, you can see something that you won't see if you're on the Moon. You can see the way the Moon appears to change shape.

Inquiry Skill

Communicate When you communicate, you share information using words and sketches.

Materials

- lamp
- plastic-foam ball with craft-stick handle

Moon Motion

Procedure

1. Use a ball with a stick handle to stand for the Moon. Use a lamp or other light to stand for the Sun. You will be an observer on Earth. **Safety:** Do not touch the bulb. It will get hot.

2. **Use Models** Stand in front of the Sun model with your back to it. Hold the Moon model at arm's length in front of you and above your head.

3. **Observe** Slowly make a quarter turn in place and stop, keeping the Moon model in front of you. Look at the shape the light makes on the Moon model.

4. **Record Data** In your *Science Notebook*, draw the pattern of light and dark that you observed on the Moon model in steps 2 and 3.

5. **Use Models** Repeat step 3 two more times. Face a different direction each time. Draw the pattern of light and dark that you observe.

STEP 2

STEP 3

STEP 4

Conclusion

1. **Communicate** Look at your sketches. Are the shapes of light the same or different in each picture? Discuss why.

2. **Infer** If you look at the Moon on several different nights, do you think the Moon will look the same each time? Explain.

Investigate More!

Research Look in books or on the Internet for folklore about the changing shape of the Moon. Find out what the Inuit people of Greenland believed about Anningan, their Moon god.

Moon Phases

MAIN IDEA The Moon goes through a cycle of phases every month.

READING SKILL

Compare and Contrast
Use the chart to compare a full moon and a new moon.

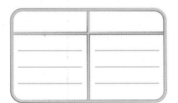

Earth's Moon

You can often see the Moon shining in the night sky. But the Moon does not make its own light. The "moonlight" you see comes from sunlight reflecting, or bouncing, off the Moon's surface. This reflected light makes the side of the Moon that faces the Sun look bright. The side of the Moon that faces away from the Sun is dark.

The Moon is a satellite (SAT l yt) of Earth. A **satellite** is any object that revolves around a planet. As it revolves around Earth, the Moon also rotates on its axis. It takes the Moon $27\frac{1}{3}$ Earth days to revolve once around Earth. It takes the same amount of time for the Moon to rotate once on its axis. As a result, the same side of the Moon always faces Earth.

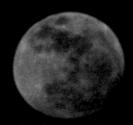

Only one side of the Moon ever faces Earth. Astronauts are the only people who have ever seen the far side of the Moon.

▲ The Moon's surface reflects sunlight, but the Moon does not make its own light.

On some nights, the Moon looks big and round. On other nights, the Moon looks like a thin sliver. The Moon doesn't really change shape. It is always shaped like a ball.

Why does the Moon appear to change shape? As the Moon revolves around Earth, you see different amounts of the Moon's sunlit side. Sometimes you can see a **full moon**, which is all of the Moon's sunlit side. A full moon looks bright and round.

Sometimes you can only see a small part of the Moon's sunlit side. This is when the Moon looks like a thin sliver. Sometimes you can't see any part of the Moon's sunlit side. This is called a **new moon**.

▶ **COMPARE AND CONTRAST** What are two different ways the Moon moves?

The Moon in Motion

The different ways the Moon looks throughout the month are called the **phases of the Moon** (FAYZ ihz). The diagram below shows where the Moon is at each phase. The photos on the next page show how each Moon phase looks as seen from Earth.

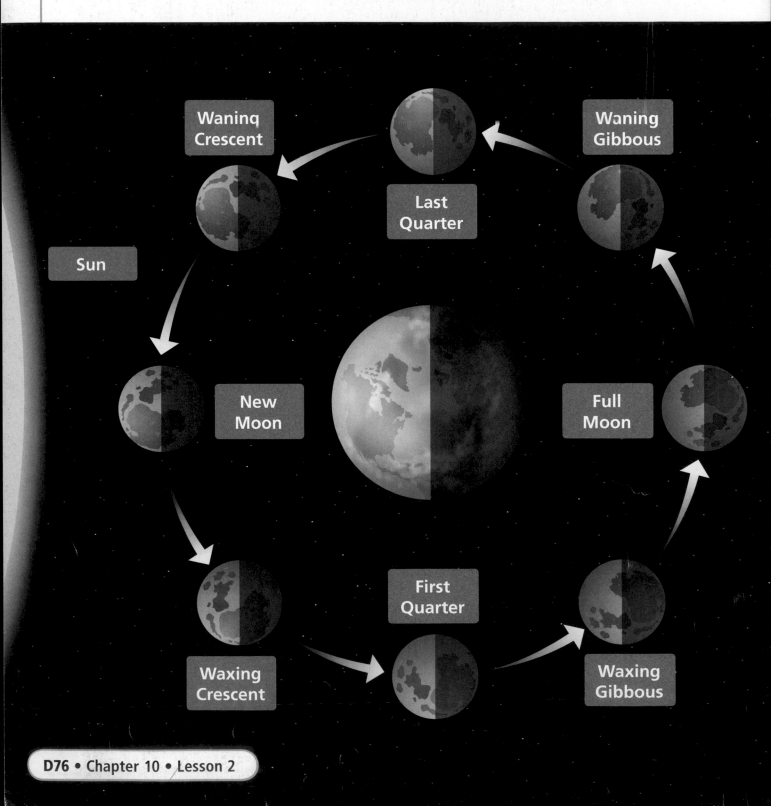

Last Quarter
You can still see about half of the Moon's sunlit side.

Waning Crescent
The Moon looks like a thin sliver.

Waning Gibbous
The Moon looks almost full.

New Moon
You can't see any of the Moon's sunlit side.

Full Moon
All of the Moon's sunlit side is facing Earth.

Waxing Crescent
The Moon looks like a thin sliver.

Waxing Gibbous
The Moon still looks almost full.

First Quarter
About one half of the Moon's sunlit side can be seen.

A Closer Look at the Moon

The rocky surface of the Moon is covered with mountains, flat plains, and craters (KRAY turz). A **crater** is a bowl-shaped dent. It is caused by an object from space striking the surface of a planet or moon. There is no air or liquid water on the Moon, and there are no living things. Daytime temperatures on the moon are much hotter than on Earth. Nighttime temperatures are much colder.

The Moon's diameter is only about one-fourth Earth's diameter. Because the Moon is smaller, its gravity is weaker than Earth's gravity. So things weigh less on the Moon than they do on Earth.

▶ **COMPARE AND CONTRAST** **Compare the daytime temperatures on the Moon to those on Earth.**

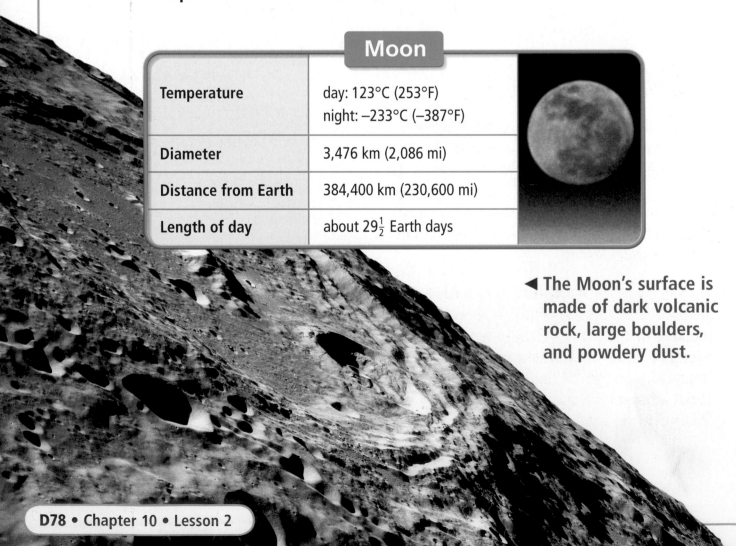

Moon

Temperature	day: 123°C (253°F) night: −233°C (−387°F)
Diameter	3,476 km (2,086 mi)
Distance from Earth	384,400 km (230,600 mi)
Length of day	about $29\frac{1}{2}$ Earth days

◀ The Moon's surface is made of dark volcanic rock, large boulders, and powdery dust.

Visual Summary

Moon

Earth

The Moon reflects light from the Sun.

The phases of the Moon occur as the Moon revolves around Earth.

The Moon's surface is covered with mountains, flat plains, and craters.

LINKS for Home and School

MATH **Use a Calendar** Make a calendar for the current month. Include the month, days of the week, and dates. Use the newspaper, an almanac, or the Internet to research the phases of the Moon for this month. Show when each phase will happen by drawing pictures on the dates on your calendar.

WRITING **Narrative** Throughout history, some Native Americans have used the Moon to measure time. If something happened a long time ago, they often described it as "many Moons ago." Write a narrative story about an event in your life. Begin the story with "Many Moons ago…"

Review

❶ MAIN IDEA Why does the Moon's shape look different on different nights?

❷ VOCABULARY Describe the movement of an object that is a satellite of Jupiter.

❸ READING SKILL: Compare and Contrast How does a full moon compare to a new moon?

❹ CRITICAL THINKING: Evaluate Use what you know about the Moon to explain why there is no life there.

❺ INQUIRY SKILL: Communicate Draw a diagram that would help someone understand why the Moon shines in the night sky.

 TEST PREP
The surface of the Moon has ___.

A. air.

B. liquid water.

C. craters.

D. living things.

 Technology
Visit **www.eduplace.com/scp/** to learn more about the Moon.

Suited for Space!

Have you ever dreamed of traveling through space? It's a lot more complicated than getting into a car and going for a drive. Before humans could travel into space, scientists had to find ways to keep them safe on their journey.

In space, there is no atmosphere to supply astronauts with oxygen. Temperatures are much colder and much hotter than on Earth. The only way for astronauts to travel through space is to take Earth conditions with them. The spacesuit was created to do this.

Each part of the suit has its own purpose. Inside, there is a life-support system that provides oxygen to breathe. A special undergarment inside the suit has tubing sewn right into the fabric. Cool water flows through the tubing, keeping the astronaut's body cool. This allows the astronaut to work and move around as normally as possible.

gloves

Layered gloves and boots had to be sturdy enough to protect astronauts from sharp rocks on Moon missions.

boots

A gold-coated visor shielded against harmful rays from the Sun.

visor   helmet

A communications headset was built into the cap that was worn under the helmet.

cap

The *Apollo 9* spacesuit was the first to contain its own life-support system, called a "backpack."

Sharing Ideas

1. **READING CHECK** Why do astronauts need special spacesuits to survive in outer space?

2. **WRITE ABOUT IT** What is one way that an astronaut's body is kept cool?

3. **TALK ABOUT IT** Discuss how the creation of the spacesuit changed space exploration.

What Is a Star?

Why It Matters...

A star map shows the names of different stars. It also shows where in the sky you can find each star. Suppose you want to learn about one of the stars you see. You can use a star map to find its name. Then you can look up information about that star.

Inquiry Skill

Ask Questions Some questions can be answered by doing an experiment. Others can be answered by asking an expert.

Materials

- cardboard
- black construction paper
- star pattern sheet
- sharp pencil
- cardboard tube
- scissors
- tape

Star Gazing
Procedure

STEP 2

1. Cover your desk with cardboard. Place a sheet of black paper over the cardboard. Place a star pattern sheet on top.

2. **Use Models** Make a star pattern. Use a sharp pencil to poke a small hole through each dot on the star pattern sheet. Push hard enough to make holes in the black paper. Then remove the star pattern sheet.

STEP 3

3. **Use Models** Place one end of a tube over the star pattern you made. Use the tube to trace a circle on the black paper around the star pattern. Make sure that all of the star pattern is within the circle. Cut out a circle that is slightly larger than the one you traced. Tape it onto one end of the tube.

STEP 4

4. **Observe** Look through the open end while holding the tube up to the light. Examine the star pattern. Now look through the tube of a classmate with a different star pattern.

Conclusion

1. **Compare** How were the two patterns similar? How were they different?

2. **Ask Questions** Write two questions that you could ask a scientist who studies stars.

Investigate More!

Be an Inventor Invent a different way to model star patterns. What materials would you use? How would the model work? Use labeled drawings in your description.

READING SKILL

Draw Conclusions
Earth gets heat from the Sun but not from other stars. The Sun looks like the largest star when viewed from Earth. Use the chart to show what conclusions can be drawn from these facts.

Stars

MAIN IDEA The Sun is the closest star to Earth. Other stars are farther away and form patterns in the night sky.

The Night Sky

When you look up at stars in the night sky, they look like tiny dots of light. But really, they are not tiny. They only look that way because they are very far away. A **star** is a ball of hot gases that gives off light and other forms of energy.

Stars come in different sizes. The smallest stars are only about 20 km (about 12 mi) across. White dwarf stars are about the size of Earth. Supergiant stars can be more than 500 million km (about 300 million mi) wide. That is more than 1,000 times the distance from Earth to the Moon!

Stars look small in the night sky because they are far from Earth.

The Sun is the closest star to Earth.

The Sun

The Sun is a star. It is the largest object in the solar system. More than 1 million Earths would fit inside the Sun. Even so, it is just a medium-sized star. The Sun looks much larger than the stars you see at night because it is so much closer to Earth than any other star. Living things on Earth depend on the Sun for heat and light.

Even though the Sun is the closest star to Earth, it is still very far away. The Sun is about 150 million km (about 93 million mi) from Earth.

▶ **DRAW CONCLUSIONS** **Why does the Sun look larger than the other stars you can see?**

Constellations

Have you ever seen a bear in the sky? How about a lion or a dog? Of course not! But if you look closely, you might see a constellation (kahn stuh-LAY shuhn) shaped like one of these animals. A **constellation** is a group of stars that forms a pattern shaped like an animal, person, or object. There are 88 constellations recognized by scientists.

People say that stars "come out" at night. But really, stars are always out. They are always in the sky overhead, even during the day. You just cannot see them during the day because the sky is so bright.

You have learned that the Sun seems to move across the sky each day. Each night, the stars also seem to move across the sky. Like the Sun, the stars do not actually move.

The Big Dipper is part of the Great Bear constellation. ▼

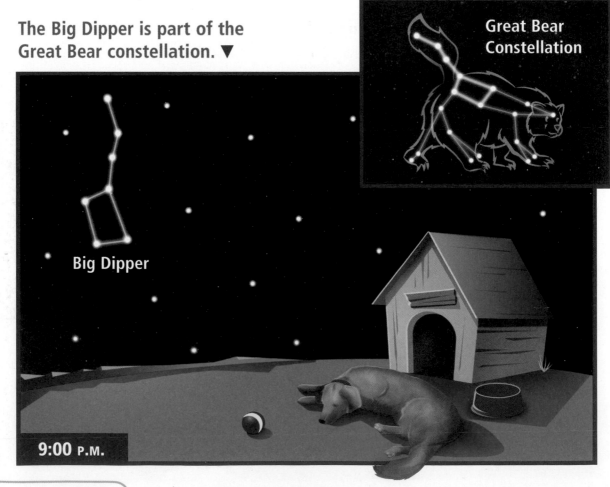

Great Bear Constellation

Big Dipper

9:00 P.M.

The stars appear to move because Earth rotates. As Earth rotates on its axis, the part of the sky you see changes. But the shape of each constellation does not change. The stars in each constellation stay in their fixed places in the pattern.

The night sky also looks different throughout the year. You can see some constellations on a summer night. You can see other constellations on a winter night. This is because Earth revolves around the Sun. As it does, the part of the sky that is overhead at night changes. So you see different constellations.

▶ **DRAW CONCLUSIONS** **Why do you see different constellations at different times of the year?**

Notice how the Big Dipper looks like it has moved. ▼

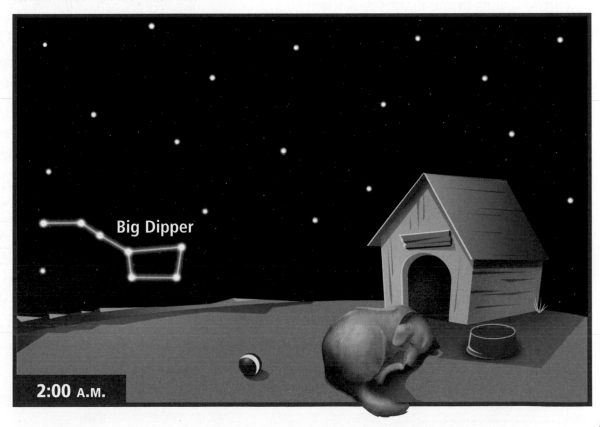

Big Dipper

2:00 A.M.

Visual Summary

Stars

The Sun
The Sun is Earth's closest star. It is a medium-sized star.

Constellations
Constellations are patterns of stars shaped like people, animals, or objects.

 **LINKS** for Home and School

MATH **Find the Difference** There are 88 constellations in the night sky. Ancient people named 48 of them long ago. The other constellations were named in modern times. How many constellations were named in modern times? Show your work.

ART **Make a Mobile** Many of the constellations are named after animals. Find Leo the Lion, Taurus the Bull, and Draco the Dragon on a star map of the northern sky. Make a mobile showing these three animal constellations.

Review

❶ **MAIN IDEA** What is a star?

❷ **VOCABULARY** Use the term *constellation* in a sentence.

❸ **READING SKILL: Draw Conclusions** If Earth did not rotate on its axis, would the stars appear to move across the sky? Explain.

❹ **CRITICAL THINKING: Analyze** You look at two stars in the night sky. One looks brighter than the other. But you learn that they actually have the same brightness. What could you conclude about their distance from Earth?

❺ **INQUIRY SKILL: Ask Questions** Imagine that you and a friend are looking at the night sky. Write two questions about stars that your friend might ask you. Then write answers for those questions.

 TEST PREP
The Sun is ___.

A. the biggest star.

B. made of hot rock.

C. the closest star to Earth.

D. a constellation.

 Technology
Visit **www.eduplace.com/scp/** to learn more about stars.

Planetarium Director

A planetarium is a kind of theater. Instead of showing a movie, a planetarium has a star show. The planetarium director is in charge of the planetarium and the people who work there. One of the best parts of the job is sharing knowledge about stars and planets, and developing shows.

What It Takes!

• A degree in astronomy

• The ability to manage other workers and to make presentations to the public

Satellite Systems Technician

Satellite systems include small home TV satellite dishes and huge communication satellites that orbit Earth. The people who build and take care of this equipment are called satellite systems technicians. Some satellite systems technicians have their own companies. Others work for companies involved in cable television, cellular phones, or broadcasting.

What It Takes!

• A high-school diploma

• Courses in electronics or electrical engineering

Orion's Surprise

Where can you find the awesome, glowing swirl shown here? In the night sky — in the winter constellation called *Orion, the Hunter*. Find the three bright stars of Orion's belt. Now find the stars that make up the sword. Do you see the bright, fuzzy spot in the sword? It's not a star. It's actually a huge collection of gas and dust called a *nebula*.

On a clear night, you can see this nebula with your bare eyes. With binoculars, it looks like a faint, misty cloud. Using a very powerful telescope and special camera, astronomers can see the amazing details and colors shown here.

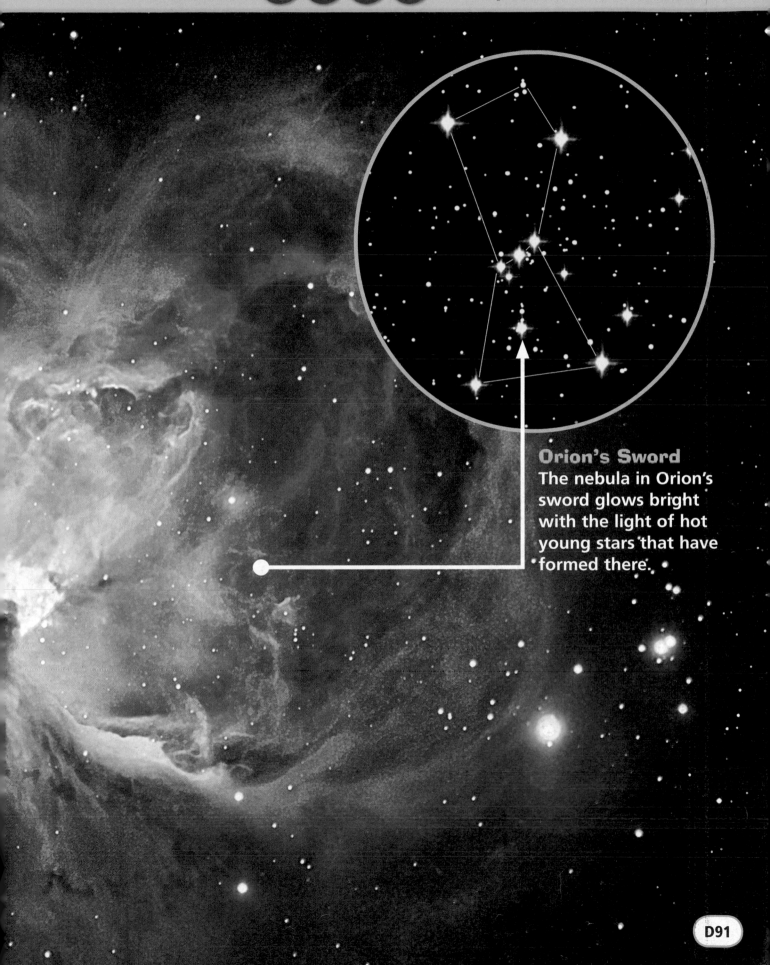

Orion's Sword
The nebula in Orion's sword glows bright with the light of hot young stars that have formed there.

Vocabulary

Complete each sentence with a term from the list.

1. The different ways the Moon looks when seen from Earth are the _____.

2. An imaginary line through the center of an object is called a/an _____.

3. When you can see all of the Moon's sunlit side, it is a/an _____.

4. A ball of hot gases that gives off light and other forms of energy is a/an _____.

5. When none of the Moon's sunlit side is visible, it is a/an _____.

6. To move in a path around another object is to _____.

7. Any object that moves in a path around a planet is a/an _____.

8. A bowl-shaped dent in the surface of a planet or moon is a/an _____.

9. To spin around on an axis is to _____.

10. A group of stars that form a pattern is called a/an _____.

axis D68
constellation D86
crater D78
full moon D75
new moon D75
phases of the Moon D76
revolve D68
rotate D68
satellite D74
star D84

Test Prep

Write the letter of the best answer choice.

11. You can see the Moon in the night sky because _____.

   A. it reflects sunlight.
   B. it is a star.
   C. it makes its own light.
   D. it is made of gas and heat.

12. The pattern of day and night is caused by Earth's _____.

   A. axis.   C. revolution.
   B. gravity.   D. rotation.

13. Stars in the night sky look like tiny dots of light because they are _____.

   A. smaller than Earth.
   B. made of bright rock.
   C. satellites of Earth.
   D. very far away.

14. The Moon is a satellite of _____.

   A. the Sun.   C. a star.
   B. Earth.   D. Venus.

15. **Compare** How is the Sun similar to other stars? How is it different?

16. **Communicate** Draw a diagram that shows the positions of the Sun, the Moon, and Earth during a full moon. Label your diagram so others can understand it.

Map the Concept

Complete the concept map using the following terms:

revolves
rotates
phases of the Moon
pattern of day and night

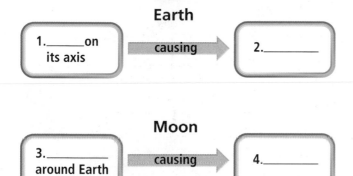

Earth

1._____ on its axis → causing → 2._____

Moon

3._____ around Earth → causing → 4._____

Critical Thinking

17. **Apply** Your family calls a relative who lives in a different country. It is 1:00 in the afternoon where you live. Is it possible that your relative will be in bed for the night? Explain.

18. **Synthesize** The Moon is much smaller than the Sun. But they look about the same size when viewed from Earth. Explain why this is.

19. **Evaluate** You hear someone say that the Sun rises in the morning, moves across the sky, and sets at night. How would you evaluate this statement?

20. **Analyze** How is the movement of the Moon similar to the movement of Earth?

Performance Assessment

Astronaut Report
Imagine that you are an astronaut returning from a walk on the Moon. Write a letter to the local paper about your visit. Describe what you saw and what it felt like to be there.

Write the letter of the best answer choice.

1. Which event happens JUST BEFORE precipitation occurs?

   A. water evaporates

   B. water vapor cools

   C. water vapor in clouds changes into tiny droplets

   D. water droplets in clouds become large and heavy

2. The diagram shows Earth in its orbit around the Sun.

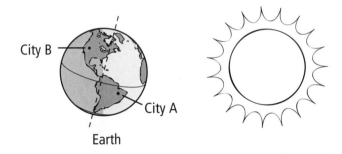

   Which explains why it is day in City A and night in City B?

   A. Earth's axis is tilted.

   B. Earth rotates on its axis.

   C. City A is north of the equator.

   D. Earth revolves around the Sun.

3. Earth is about the same size as _____ .

   A. Mars.

   B. Jupiter.

   C. Pluto.

   D. Venus.

4. A gibbous moon occurs just before and just after a full moon. Which shows a gibbous moon?

   A.

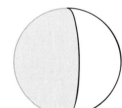

   B.

   C.

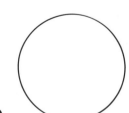

   D.

5. How many stars are there in our solar system?

    A. none

    B. one

    C. nine

    D. hundreds

6. The illustration below MOST likely shows which planet?

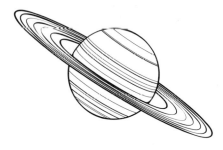

    A. Mars

    B. Pluto

    C. Saturn

    D. Venus

7. The asteroid belt between the inner and outer planets is located between _____ .

    A. Mars and Jupiter.

    B. Venus and Earth.

    C. Jupiter and Saturn.

    D. Saturn and Uranus.

8. Telescopes are tools that make distant objects appear _____ .

    A. dimmer and larger.

    B. larger and sharper.

    C. smaller and brighter.

    D. smaller and dimmer.

Answer the following in complete sentences.

9. Identify each cloud as either cumulus or cumulonimbus. Tell what kind of weather each type of cloud might bring.

Cloud A

Cloud B

10. Explain how a tropical climate and a desert climate are different.

Discover!

The largest volcano in the solar system, Olympus Mons, is on Mars. It rises up from the surface of Mars about 26 km (16 mi). The base of the volcano is about 602 km (374 mi) wide.

Olympus Mons is much bigger than Mauna Loa in Hawaii, one of the largest volcanoes on Earth. Mauna Loa is about 10 km (6 mi) high and about 121 km (75 mi) wide.

Volcanoes on Mars may become so large because the crust of Mars does not move. Lava erupts over and over again in the same place. As the lava builds up, the volcanoes grow higher.

Olympus Mons does not appear to be an active volcano. Scientists believe that it stopped erupting millions of years ago.

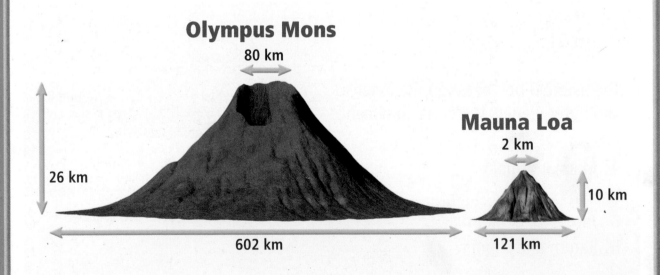

Olympus Mons
80 km
26 km
602 km

Mauna Loa
2 km
10 km
121 km

Explore the planets of the solar system. Go to **www.eduplace.com/scp/** to visit the volcanoes on Mars and other places in the solar system.

PHYSICAL UNIT E SCIENCE

Matter

PHYSICAL SCIENCE

UNIT E

Matter

═══ Independent Reading ═══

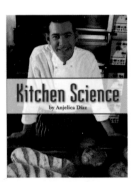

Now You See It, Now You Don't

The Mystery of the Blue Box

Kitchen Science

Discover!

When it was first built over 120 years ago, the Statue of Liberty had a bright, shiny copper surface. Today the surface is no longer shiny and the statue is a light green color. What caused this change? You will have the answer to this question by the end of this unit.

Chapter 11

Matter
Changes

Lesson Preview

LESSON 1

From firefighters' coats that protect from extreme heat to a bouncy basketball—what are some useful properties of matter?

Read about it in Lesson 1.

LESSON 2

A melting ice cube and a paper airplane—do these objects have something in common?

Read about it in Lesson 2.

LESSON 3

Soft clay becomes a shiny vase, a bicycle becomes rusty, and liquid batter turns into cooked pancakes—what causes these changes?

Read about it in Lesson 3.

What Are Physical Properties?

Why It Matters...

Suppose you lost your sweater. How would you describe it? You might say that it's orange. You might also say that it is made of cotton. You might describe the knitted pattern and explain that the size is medium. You can identify sweaters and other objects by describing them.

PREPARE TO INVESTIGATE

Inquiry Skill

Compare When you compare things, you observe how they are different and how they are alike.

Materials

- bag of assorted shells
- metric ruler
- hand lens
- poster board
- markers
- glue or tape

Science and Math Toolbox

For step 2, review **Using a Hand Lens** on page H2.

Sorting Shells
Procedure

STEP 1

1. **Measure** Work with a partner. Open the bag of shells. Spread out the shells on the desk. Use a metric ruler to measure the length of each shell. Record your measurements in your *Science Notebook.*

2. **Compare** Use a hand lens to observe the shells. Notice how the shells are alike and different.

STEP 3

3. **Classify** Choose a physical property (FIHZ ih kuhl PRAHP ur tee) and classify the shells based on that property. A **physical property** is a characteristic that can be observed with the senses. Color, shape, and size are physical properties.

4. **Communicate** Make a poster. Glue or tape the groups of shells on the poster. Write a label for each group. The label should describe the physical properties of the shells in that group.

STEP 4
Classifying Shells
Spiral Shells

Conclusion

1. **Communicate** What physical properties did you use to classify your shells?

2. **Communicate** Which senses did you use to observe the physical properties of the shells?

Investigate More!

Design an Experiment
Think of other ways to describe shells. Does a magnet pull on them? Do they melt in the Sun? Do they float? Can you see through them? List your descriptions.

Physical Properties

MAIN IDEA Matter has properties that can be observed and measured.

VOCABULARY

gas	p. E7
liquid	p. E7
mass	p. E9
matter	p. E6
physical property	p. E7
solid	p. E7
volume	p. E9

READING SKILL

Classify As you read, list examples of solids, liquids, and gases.

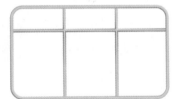

Three States of Matter

What do you like to do in the kitchen? You might like to help with the cooking, or maybe you just like to eat. Whether you're cooking or eating, you're using matter. **Matter** is anything that has mass and takes up space. Everything in this kitchen is matter. And even though you can't see it, the air in the kitchen is matter, too.

Matter is found in different states, or forms. Three states of matter are solid, liquid, and gas. Heating or cooling can cause matter to change from one state to another. Look in this kitchen for matter in different states.

Air is made up of different gases.

Identify five things in this kitchen that are matter.

Water is a liquid.

A **solid** (SAHL ihd) is matter that has a definite shape and takes up a definite amount of space. Ice is a solid. If you heat ice, it becomes liquid (LIHK - wihd) water. A **liquid** takes the shape of its container and takes up a definite amount of space. If you heat water, it becomes water vapor, a gas. A **gas** has no definite shape and does not take up a definite amount of space. A gas will spread out to fill a large space, or it can be squeezed into a small space.

All matter is made up of many tiny particles. These particles are far too small to be seen except with special tools that scientists use. The particles of matter are always moving.

The state of matter is one physical property (FIHZ ih kuhl PRAHP ur tee) of matter. A **physical property** is a characteristic of matter that can be measured or observed with the senses. Shape, size, color, texture, and temperature are some other physical properties.

▶ **CLASSIFY** **What are three states of matter?**

Ice is a solid.

The shape of the sponge is a rectangle.

The melon is larger than each lemon.

The tomato is large, red, and smooth

You can use the physical properties of matter to identify objects.

Observing Matter

Look for the melon in the grocery basket. What physical properties of the melon did you use to find it? You might have looked for its color and shape.

Other physical properties you can observe are texture, temperature, hardness, sound, flavor, and size. You observe the physical properties of matter using your five senses—sight, touch, taste, smell, and hearing. If you could pick up the melon and eat it, you might observe that it is smooth, crisp, sweet, and juicy.

Measuring Matter

How would you describe how heavy a marble or a bowling ball is? You can use a measuring device such as a balance or a scale to find an exact measurement.

How heavy the marble or the bowling ball is depends on its mass. **Mass** is the amount of matter in an object. A balance measures mass. Mass is given in units called grams (g).

Mass is different from weight (wayt). Weight measures the pull of Earth's gravity (GRAV ih tee) on an object. Mass and weight are both physical properties of matter.

The bowling ball and marble have different masses. They also have different volumes (VAHL-yoomz). **Volume** is the amount of space that matter takes up. Look at the containers. The same volume of sand has been put into each container. No matter what the container's shape, the sand takes up the same amount of space in each one.

Volume is also a physical property. The volume of a solid is often measured in cubic centimeters (cm^3). Liquid volume is often measured in liters (L).

▲ The mass of an object equals the sum of the masses of its parts.

 **CLASSIFY** What units describe volume?

◀ Although each container is a different shape and size, the volume of sand in each container is the same.

Useful Properties of Matter

Which would you choose to wear in the rain: a raincoat or a wool sweater? You would probably choose a raincoat because you know raincoats are waterproof. You choose one material over another because of its properties.

The properties of different kinds of matter make them useful for different purposes. You wouldn't cook food on a stove in a plastic pan. A metal pan heats food without melting.

Being magnetic is a useful property of some metals. Some kinds of matter allow electricity to pass through them easily. Glass is a kind of matter that allows light to pass through it.

▶ **CLASSIFY** **What are two useful properties of matter?**

▲ A basketball is made from matter that is unbreakable and springy.

The boaters' raincoats, as well as many parts of the boat, are made from waterproof materials. ▶

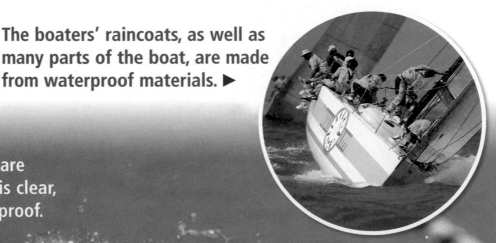

The swimmer's goggles are made from matter that is clear, unbreakable, and waterproof.

Visual Summary

Three states of matter are solid, liquid, and gas.

You can describe physical properties of matter by using your five senses and by measuring.

The properties of matter make matter useful for different purposes.

LINKS for Home and School

SOCIAL STUDIES **Describe Matter** In the Middle Ages, people understood matter differently from the way we understand it now. They thought that matter was made up of only earth, fire, air, and water. Use these four "elements" to describe three everyday objects.

LITERATURE **Write Descriptions** Choose two common objects, one from nature and one made by people. Write a paragraph that describes each object as if you had never seen it before. Be sure to use at least four of your five senses. Read the descriptions to the class. Can students guess the objects?

Review

❶ **MAIN IDEA** List four physical properties of an apple.

❷ **VOCABULARY** Using your own words, describe what matter is.

❸ **READING SKILL: Classify** Would you classify vinegar as a solid, a liquid, or a gas? Explain.

❹ **CRITICAL THINKING: Synthesize** Water is in the solid state when it is below 0°C. It is a gas above 100°C. In what state is it at 50°C?

❺ **INQUIRY SKILL: Compare** How are mass and volume different?

✔ **TEST PREP**
Mass is measured with a ___.

A. measuring cup.

B. ruler.

C. balance.

D. thermometer.

 Technology
Visit **www.eduplace.com/scp/** to find out more about the physical properties of matter.

What Is a Physical Change in Matter?

Why It Matters...

This sculptor used a chain saw to cut the wood and make it look like a man. The shape of the wood is being changed. Wood that was cut from the block is now wood chips on the floor. The sculptor has not changed the kind of matter from which the block is made.

PREPARE TO INVESTIGATE

Inquiry Skill

Observe When you observe, you gather information about the environment using your five senses: seeing, hearing, smelling, touching and tasting.

Materials

- plastic bowl
- metal spoon
- ice cube
- 2 sugar cubes
- waxed paper
- aluminum foil
- clock or watch

Science and Math Toolbox

For step 1, review **Measuring Elapsed Time** on page H12.

Investigate

Change It
Procedure

1. **Collaborate** Work with a partner. Place an ice cube in a plastic bowl. Observe the ice cube after 10 minutes. Record your observations in your *Science Notebook*.

2. **Compare** Use a metal spoon to crush a sugar cube wrapped in waxed paper. Unwrap the crushed cube and compare it to an uncrushed one. Record how they are alike and different.

3. **Observe** Record how a sheet of aluminum foil looks. Then gently crumple the foil into a loose ball. Again record how the foil looks.

4. **Compare** Now carefully pull apart the crumpled foil ball. Flatten and smooth it. Record how the foil was changed in steps 3 and 4.

STEP 1

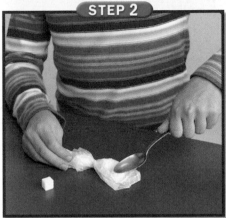
STEP 2

STEP 4

Conclusion

1. **Infer** What caused the ice cube to change in step 1?

2. **Compare** How are the changes in the ice cube and the sugar cube alike? How are they different?

3. **Compare** How are the changes in the aluminum foil and the sugar cube alike? How are they different?

Investigate More!

Design an Experiment
How would the melted ice cube change if you put it in a freezer? Design and carry out an experiment to find out. Then, compare your results to the original ice cube.

Physical Changes

VOCABULARY

condense   p. E15
evaporate   p. E15
freeze   p. E15
melt   p. E15
physical change   p. E14

READING SKILL

Cause and Effect Use
a chart to show how
heating causes matter to
change state.

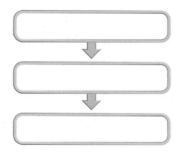

MAIN IDEA A physical change is a change in the way matter looks.

Energy and Changing States

What happens to ice cubes left in a glass in a warm room? They become liquid water. Water has changed state from a solid to a liquid. In either state, water is still water. A change in state is a physical change. A **physical change** is a change in the size, shape, or state of matter. A physical change does not change the makeup of the matter.

Why do you have to eat a frozen juice bar quickly on a hot day? The juice bar melts because energy, in the form of heat, causes it to change state.

Solid
The particles of a solid are very close together. They move back and forth in fixed positions.

Matter heats up when energy is added to it. Adding energy causes the particles of matter to move faster. Adding enough heat to a solid causes it to **melt**, or change state from a solid to a liquid. When a liquid is heated enough, it will boil, or change state from a liquid to a gas. When liquids **evaporate** (ih VAP uh rayt), they change state slowly from a liquid to a gas. You can think of boiling as a liquid evaporating rapidly.

Matter cools when energy is taken away. Taking away energy causes the particles of matter to move more slowly. When a gas is cooled, it will **condense** (kuhn-DEHNS), or change state from a gas to a liquid. When a liquid is cooled enough it will **freeze**, or change state from a liquid to a solid.

▶ **CAUSE AND EFFECT** What causes matter to change state?

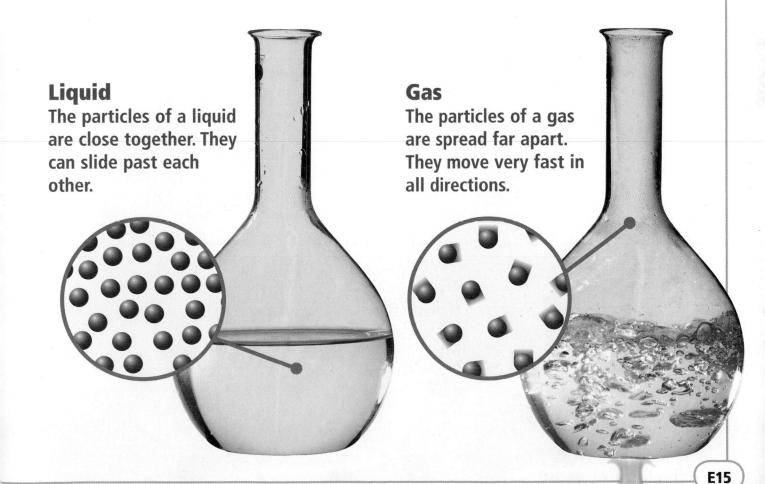

Liquid
The particles of a liquid are close together. They can slide past each other.

Gas
The particles of a gas are spread far apart. They move very fast in all directions.

Useful Physical Changes

How do you make a paper airplane? You fold a sheet of paper in a certain way. You can also use scissors to cut notches in the wings of the plane. In both cases, you are changing the shape of the paper. These physical changes are useful because they allow the paper to glide through the air.

Every day you make physical changes to matter so that the matter is useful to you. Sharpening pencils and tying shoelaces are physical changes. Mixing chopped celery into tuna fish is a physical change. You can taste both the celery and the tuna. That's because mixing does not change the celery or the tuna into new kinds of matter.

▶ **CAUSE AND EFFECT** **What are two ways that you can make a useful physical change?**

Molding clay and folding paper are useful physical changes.

Visual Summary

A physical change is a change in the size, shape, or state of matter. Energy must be added or removed to change state.

Cutting, folding, molding, and mixing are physical changes that make matter useful.

LINKS for Home and School

MATH **Compare Temperatures** Do research to find the melting temperatures of aluminum, gold, lead, and water. Draw a long thermometer and mark the melting point of each material on it.

WRITING **Narrative** Think about a time in your life when you have experienced matter changing states. Write a paragraph that explains what you were doing, what kind of matter changed state, and how the matter changed. Be sure to use a topic sentence in your paragraph.

Review

❶ **MAIN IDEA** What happens to matter during a physical change?

❷ **VOCABULARY** Explain what happens when matter freezes.

❸ **READING SKILL: Cause and Effect** What causes ice on a pond to melt?

❹ **CRITICAL THINKING: Predict** Suppose you blow up a balloon and put it in a freezer. Predict what the balloon will look like when you take it out an hour later.

❺ **INQUIRY SKILL: Observe** Describe a physical change that you observe every day. Explain how this physical change is useful.

✓ TEST PREP

Which is an example of water evaporating?

A. Drops of water form on the outside of a cold glass.

B. Water in a pond turns to ice.

C. Rain falls during a storm.

D. Wet socks on a clothesline become dry.

 Technology
Visit **www.eduplace.com/scp/** to investigate more about physical changes in matter.

High-Tech Hang Gliding

Get a bird's-eye view. A hang glider is like a kite that a person can hang from and ride through the air without an engine. Today's hang gliders are faster, lighter, and easier to use than ever before. The V-shaped gliders are made from new materials and have high-tech designs.

Hang glider designers use computers to design better wings. Some of the fastest hang gliders have wings covered with a type of polyester film. This material is light and strong.

Many hang gliders have parts made from carbon fiber—a material that is strong, lightweight, and flexible. Flexible material can bend without breaking. Hang gliders made with carbon fiber are faster and easier to control than older models.

This balloon is made of the type of polyester film used to make glider wings.

Hang glider wings made from polyester film are light and strong.

Carbon fiber crossbars are strong, light and flexible.

Sharing Ideas

1. **READING CHECK** What high-tech materials are used to make hang gliders?

2. **WRITE ABOUT IT** How are today's hang gliders different from previous hang gliders?

3. **TALK ABOUT IT** Discuss what hang glider designers are trying to make hang gliders do and be.

What Is a Chemical Change in Matter?

Why It Matters...

This sculpture of a dog was once a shiny, silver-colored metal. Over time the metal parts have rusted. When metal rusts, it looks different from the original metal. Rusting is another way that matter changes. But rusting is not a physical change.

PREPARE TO INVESTIGATE

Inquiry Skill

Infer When you infer, you use facts you know and observations you have made to draw a conclusion.

Materials

- 2 pieces of steel wool
- 2 white paper plates
- plastic bag, self-sealing
- water
- toothpicks
- small plastic bowl
- scissors
- hand lens
- magnet
- goggles
- disposable gloves

Science and Math Toolbox

For step 3, review **Using a Hand Lens** on page H2.

A Rusty Change
Procedure

STEP 1

Material	Color	Feel	Magnetic
Fibers (dry)			
Fibers (wet)			

1. In your *Science Notebook*, make a chart like the one shown. Place a dry piece of steel wool in a plastic bag and seal the bag. Dip another piece of steel wool in water and place it in a plastic bowl. Leave them overnight. **Safety:** Wear goggles and disposable gloves.

2. **Observe** The next day, remove the dry steel wool from the bag. Use scissors to snip some of its fibers onto a paper plate. Use a toothpick to tap on parts of the wet steel wool. Tap until you have a pile of colored pieces.

STEP 2

3. **Record Data** Use a hand lens to carefully observe the dry fibers and colored pieces from the steel wool. Record the properties of each.

4. **Compare** Hold a magnet close to the fibers and colored pieces from the steel wool. Compare and record what happens.

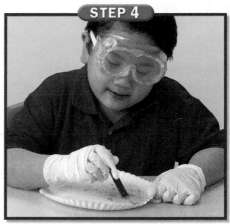

STEP 4

Conclusion

1. **Compare** The color change is due to rust. How is the rust similar to the original steel wool? How is it different?

2. **Infer** Are rust and steel wool the same material? What observations support your conclusion?

Investigate More!

Solve a Problem When metal rusts, its properties change. The metal object may no longer be useful. Make a list of ways to keep metal from rusting.

Chemical Changes

VOCABULARY

chemical change p. E23
chemical   p. E22
  property

READING SKILL

Sequence List the properties of a wooden match before it has burned. Then, list the properties of the match after it has burned.

MAIN IDEA In a chemical change, a new kind of matter with different properties is formed.

Chemical Changes

Compare the tarnished silver candleholder with the candleholder after it was cleaned. Before cleaning, the silver is dull and has a dark coating. After cleaning, the silver is bright and shiny.

Silver reacts with sulfur, a chemical in air. A new kind of matter is formed that has different properties from the original silver. The ability to react with sulfur to form new matter is a chemical (KEHM ih kuhl) property of silver. A **chemical property** is a property that describes how matter can react with other kinds of matter. Some other chemical properties of matter are the ability to burn, rust, and explode.

Before

When sulfur in air combines with silver, a new kind of matter forms.

After

Cleaning the tarnished silver removes the new matter.

Liquid A + Liquid B = New Matter

A piece of wood cannot rust, but it can burn. The ability to burn is a chemical property of wood, paper, and some other kinds of matter. Compare the wooden match before and after it has burned. You probably notice a difference. Burning has changed the chemical properties of the wood.

The burned part of the match is no longer wood. It is a different kind of matter. A chemical change has taken place. A **chemical change** is a change in matter in which one or more new kinds of matter form. A chemical change is different from a physical change. In a chemical change, the original matter and the new matter have different properties. Rusting is a chemical change. Iron rusts when it comes in contact with air and water. The new matter that forms is softer than iron and is orange-colored.

▲ The properties of the yellow matter differ from the properties of the two clear liquids that formed it.

▲ When a wooden match burns, new matter forms. It has different properties than wood.

▶ SEQUENCE What happens to a wooden match after it has burned?

Before heating

After heating

▲ Heating clay causes a chemical change. After heating, the vase is strong, shiny, and waterproof.

During cooking, pancake batter undergoes a chemical change. The cooked pancakes have properties that are different than the properties of the batter. ▶

Useful Chemical Changes

Chemical changes are an important part of life. Many take place in your body. You could not stay alive without them. For example, when you eat, a series of chemical changes begins. Inside your body, food is changed chemically into new matter that your body can use for energy and growth. Cooking food also causes chemical changes.

A series of chemical changes in plants uses energy from sunlight to make food. Chemical changes that take place in a battery are used to produce electricity. Cars and buses move because of chemical changes. When gasoline is burned in the engine, chemical changes release energy. Colorful displays of exploding fireworks also come from chemical changes.

▶ **CAUSE AND EFFECT** **What are two things people do that cause chemical changes?**

Lesson Wrap-Up

Visual Summary

A chemical property describes how matter can react with other kinds of matter.

In a chemical change, the makeup of matter changes and a different kind of matter forms.

Useful chemical changes include burning fuel and cooking.

LINKS for Home and School

MATH Work With Fractions A father cooks 12 pancakes. John eats 5 pancakes. His brother, Bill, eats the rest of the pancakes. What fractions tell how many pancakes each boy ate?

HEALTH Observe Chemical Changes
Your stomach produces acid to break down food. Sometimes it makes too much acid, which can harm the stomach. Antacid medicines reduce stomach acid by changing it to water and a salt. You can show this chemical change by adding some baking soda (antacid) to vinegar (an acid). Observe what happens. How do you know this is a chemical change?

Review

❶ **MAIN IDEA** What happens during a chemical change?

❷ **VOCABULARY** Write a sentence using the term *chemical property*.

❸ **READING SKILL: Sequence**
Write the steps of the chemical change in the correct order.
A. A nail falls in water.
B. A nail is orange and brittle.
C. A nail is gray and hard.

❹ **CRITICAL THINKING: Generalize** What chemical property is shared by paper, wood, and oil?

❺ **INQUIRY SKILL: Infer**
Think about how an egg changes when it is cooked. Is this a physical change or a chemical change? Explain.

 TEST PREP
Which is NOT an example of a chemical change?

A. food cooking

B. water freezing

C. a match burning

D. iron rusting

Technology
Visit **www.eduplace.com/scp/** to find out more about chemical changes.

Sand to Glass

What can you do with sand? You can dig a hole in it. You can build a sand castle with it. And if you have enough heat, you can actually change it into glass! Here's how. Glassmakers put sand and other minerals into a super-hot oven called a furnace. The sand mixture melts into a stretchy goo, like taffy candy. Glassmakers can then shape and mold it. They have to work fast, though. As the goo cools, it quickly turns into solid, smooth glass!

Many beautiful works of art begin as ordinary sand like this.

Artist Dale Chihuly made these beautiful glass balls. He adds minerals such as iron, copper, and cobalt to produce physical changes that create these colors.

Vocabulary

Complete each sentence with a term from the list.

1. When solids change state to become liquids, they _____.

2. The amount of matter in an object is the _____ of that object.

3. A/an _____ describes how matter can react with other kinds of matter.

4. Solid, _____, and gas are three states of matter.

5. When gases change state to become liquids, they _____.

6. Matter that has a definite shape and takes up a definite amount of space is a/an _____.

7. When liquids slowly change to a gas, they _____.

8. Matter that has no definite shape and does not take up a definite amount of space is a/an _____.

9. When liquids change state to become solids, they _____.

10. Anything that has mass and takes up space is _____.

chemical change E23
chemical property E22
condense E15
evaporate E15
freeze E15
gas E7
liquid F7
mass E9
matter E6
melt E15
physical change E14
physical property E7
solid E7
volume E9

Test Prep

Write the letter of the best answer choice.

11. A trait of matter that can be measured or observed is called a _____.

   A. chemical property
   B. chemical change
   C. physical property
   D. physical change

12. The amount of space an object takes up is called its _____.

   A. mass C. length
   B. weight D. volume

13. Cutting is a _____ because it only changes the way matter looks.

   A. chemical change
   B. physical change
   C. chemical property
   D. state of matter

14. Which of the following is an example of a chemical change?

   A. burning wood C. molding clay
   B. boiling water D melting ice

15. **Compare** You place a large block of ice in a pan and observe it melting. Then you heat the water, and observe it boiling. Describe how the shape of the water changed each time the water changed state.

16. **Infer** A sculptor is finishing work on an iron statue. The sculptor applies a clear liquid to all parts of the statue. When the coating dries, the statue is placed outdoors. Years later, the statue looks as it did when it was new. What might explain the fact that no rust formed?

Map the Concept

The chart shows physical changes and chemical changes. Place each item in the list into the correct category.

melting ice	evaporating water
rusting iron	cooking food
burning wood	chopping wood

Physical Change	Chemical Change

17. **Apply** Write a paragraph that describes your favorite shirt. Include three physical properties.

18. **Synthesize** Plants take in water and a gas called carbon dioxide. Experiments show that plants make sugar and give off oxygen gas. What can you conclude about the kinds of changes that take place inside a plant to produce sugar and oxygen? Explain your answer.

19. **Evaluate** Steel is made from carbon mixed with iron. Which statement would support the idea that steel is a result of a physical change? Explain your answer.
    Steel is made up of carbon particles and iron particles.
    Steel particles are neither carbon particles nor iron particles.

20. **Analyze** When you arrive at school on a rainy day, your rain hat is covered with water drops. At the end of the day, your hat is dry. What kind of change has taken place? Explain.

Performance Assessment

Bake Pumpkin Bread
Find a simple recipe for pumpkin bread. List the steps needed to make the bread. Identify each step as a physical or chemical change.

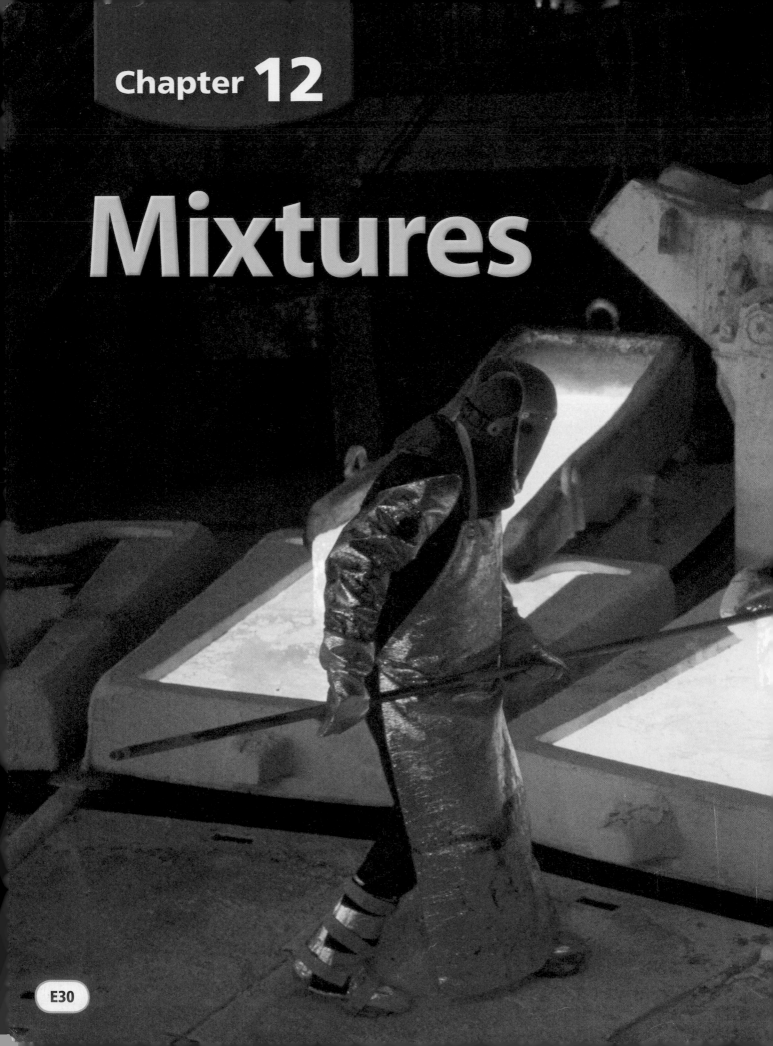

Chapter **12**

Mixtures

LESSON 1

A bowl of soup, a puffy cloud, and a block of concrete— what do they all have in common?

Read about it in Lesson 1.

LESSON 2

Dirt, water, and a shallow pan—how can they help you find gold?

Read about it in Lesson 2.

LESSON 3

Seawater and drinking water—how could you get one from the other?

Read about it in Lesson 3.

How Are Mixtures Made?

Why It Matters...

You gather milk, strawberries, and ice to make a fruit smoothie. You mix the items in a blender. The items used to make the smoothie look very different now. Like a smoothie, many useful things are made by mixing together two or more kinds of matter.

PREPARE TO INVESTIGATE

Inquiry Skill

Observe When you observe, you gather information using your five senses: sight, smell, touch, taste, and hearing.

Materials

- paper clips
- toothpicks
- dry beans
- rice
- water
- salt
- plastic spoon
- 6 small plastic bowls

Science and Math Toolbox

For step 1, review **Making a Chart to Organize Data** on page H10.

The Great Mix-Up
Procedure

1. **Collaborate** Work in a small group. In your *Science Notebook*, make a chart like the one shown.

Material	Properties before mixing	Properties after mixing
paper clips		
toothpicks		
beans		
rice		
salt		
water		

2. Fill each of five small plastic bowls halfway with one of the following materials: paper clips, toothpicks, dry beans, rice, and water. Put a spoonful of salt into a sixth bowl.

3. **Observe** Look at the material in each bowl. Smell and touch it. Record your observations in your chart. **Safety:** Do not taste any materials.

STEP 4

4. **Record Data** Pour the paper clips into the bowl of toothpicks and stir them together. Observe and record the properties of the mixed materials.

5. **Record Data** Repeat step 4, pouring the beans into the rice.

STEP 5

6. **Observe** Repeat step 4, pouring the salt into the water.

Conclusion

1. **Analyze Data** Which materials changed when you mixed them together? How did they change?

2. **Predict** What will happen if you mix beans and paper clips?

Investigate More!

Design an Experiment
Mix together three or more of the materials. Have the properties of the materials changed after being mixed together? Give reasons for your answer.

Making Mixtures

READING SKILL

Compare and Contrast
Use a chart to tell how a substance and a mixture are the same and how they are different.

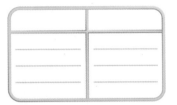

MAIN IDEA A mixture is made up of two or more substances that are physically combined.

Substances

You've learned that everything pictured here—the food, the plate, the bowls—is matter. Some things are made up of only one kind of matter. The salt in the shaker is one example. Salt is made only of salt. It does not contain any other kind of matter. Salt is a substance (SUHB stuhns). A **substance** is a single kind of matter with certain properties. Every part of a substance is the same throughout. Some other substances are sugar, water, and gold.

▲ Salt and water are both substances. They each have different properties.

▼ These materials can be combined to make a tasty mixture for nachos.

Mixing It Up

Most kinds of matter are not substances. Most kinds of matter are mixtures (MIHKS churz). A **mixture** is matter that is made up of two or more substances, or materials, that are physically combined, or mixed. The plate of nachos is a mixture. It is made up of corn chips, beans, olives, tomatoes, and cheese.

Making a mixture is a physical change. Mixing together two or more substances often changes the form, color, or texture of those substances. But the properties of each substance in the mixture do not change. You can pick the tomatoes out of the nachos, and they are still tomatoes. If you mix salt and water, you can still taste the salt in the water.

▶ **COMPARE AND CONTRAST** What do nachos and salt water have in common?

Each kind of matter in the nachos has the same properties as it did before it became a part of the mixture. ▼

Solid-Liquid Mixtures

Have you ever made mud pies? If so, you know that they are made by mixing together soil and water. Many mixtures are made by combining solids and liquids.

Salt water is a solid-liquid mixture. You cannot see the salt, so the mixture appears to be a liquid. A damp sponge is a solid-liquid mixture. You cannot see the water, so the mixture appears to be a solid. When water and clothes are mixed unevenly in a washing machine, you can easily see both the solid and liquid parts.

▲ You can see both solids and liquid in this mixture of soapy water.

Some mixtures are made by blending two or more materials. Soil is a mixture. Water is a substance. Mud is a mixture of soil and water. ▼

Liquid-Gas Mixtures

What do clouds and soft drinks have in common? Both are mixtures of liquids and gases. A soft drink appears to be a liquid. But when you pour a soft drink, you can see bubbles rising through the liquid. Each tiny bubble contains carbon dioxide (KAHR-buhn dy AHK syd) gas that was mixed with the liquid to make it fizzy.

Puffy white clouds may appear to be solid, but in fact they are made of tiny droplets of liquid water mixed with air. Sometimes droplets of water mix so completely with air that you cannot see them. But they are still there. You can feel water in the air on humid days.

▲ Clouds are a mixture of water droplets and air.

▶ **COMPARE AND CONTRAST**   **How are mud and clouds different?**

You can make a liquid-gas mixture by spraying water into the air. As in all mixtures, the properties of the air and the water are not changed. ▶

Solid-Gas Mixtures

You have probably seen smoke rising from a barbecue grill. Smoke is a mixture made up of air, other gases, and tiny solid particles of ash. Dust is another solid that mixes with air. These solid-gas mixtures act like gases. Other solid-gas mixtures, such as soil and concrete, appear to be solids. These mixtures have pockets of air trapped inside them.

▶ **COMPARE AND CONTRAST** What do ash and dust have in common?

▲ A smoking barbecue grill releases tiny solid particles into the air.

Particles of dust hang in the air of this forest. The dusty air is a solid-gas mixture. ▼

Lesson Wrap-Up

Visual Summary

	A substance is a single kind of matter with certain properties.
	A mixture is a combination of two or more substances. Making a mixture is a physical change.
	Mixtures can be any combination of solids, liquids, and gases.

LINKS for Home and School

MATH Write a Word Problem Find a soup recipe. Write a word problem that uses information from the recipe. Exchange word problems with a partner. Challenge your partner to solve your word problem.

SOCIAL STUDIES Write a Story People come from other countries to live in the United States. Just as materials in a mixture keep their properties, immigrants often hold on to their culture, including languages, recipes, and beliefs. Write a story about an immigrant coming to America. How can his or her culture be preserved? How can it be shared?

Review

❶ **MAIN IDEA** Why is mud a mixture?

❷ **VOCABULARY** Write a sentence using the term *substance*.

❸ **READING SKILL: Compare and Contrast** How is a mixture different from a substance?

❹ **CRITICAL THINKING: Draw Conclusions** Suppose you allow a glass of clear liquid to dry up. A white solid is left at the bottom of the glass. The solid has a sweet taste. What can you conclude about the liquid that was in the glass?

❺ **INQUIRY SKILL: Observe** How would you decide whether strawberry yogurt is a mixture or a substance?

 TEST PREP
When substances are combined in a mixture, they ____.

A. become new kinds of matter.

B. keep their properties.

C. cannot be separated.

D. undergo a chemical change.

 Technology
Visit **www.eduplace.com/scp/** to find out more about how mixtures are made.

How Can Mixtures Be Separated?

Why It Matters...

Some people still pan for gold in the American West. They scoop up sand and water into a shallow pan. Then they swirl the mixture around. Gold dust is heavier than the rest of the sand. As the pan is swirled, the gold dust sinks to the bottom. Panning is one way to separate a mixture.

PREPARE TO INVESTIGATE

Inquiry Skill

Record Data When you record data, you write measurements, predictions, and observations about an experiment.

Materials

- mixtures from Lesson 1
- magnet
- strainer
- clock or watch with second hand

Science and Math Toolbox

For steps 2 and 3, review **Measuring Elapsed Time** on pages H12–H13.

Un-mixing Mixtures
Procedure

1. **Collaborate** Work with a partner. In your *Science Notebook*, make a chart like the one shown.

2. **Record Data** Separate a mixture of paper clips and toothpicks by hand. Have your partner time you. Record the time in your chart.

3. **Measure** Mix the toothpicks and paper clips together again. Keep time as your partner uses a magnet to separate the mixture. Record the time in your chart.

4. **Measure** Repeat steps 2 and 3 with a mixture of beans and rice. For step 3, use a strainer instead of the magnet.

5. **Observe** Put two spoonfuls of water in a dish. Mix in one spoonful of salt. Leave the mixture in a sunny spot until the water evaporates. Record how long it takes for the water to dry up.

Conclusion

1. **Analyze Data** In steps 2–5, which method of separating mixtures was fastest?

2. **Communicate** What property was used to separate the paper clips from the toothpicks in step 3?

3. **Infer** How do you know the properties of the salt and water did not change when they were mixed?

STEP 1

Mixture	By Hand	Using a Tool
Paper clips and toothpicks		
Beans and rice		

STEP 2

STEP 4

Investigate More!

Design an Experiment
How could you speed up the separation of the salt and water? Plan an experiment and ask your teacher to help you conduct it.

READING SKILL

Problem-Solution
Use the chart to list one type of mixture and to describe how it could be separated.

You can separate the beads by color.

Separating Mixtures

MAIN IDEA The properties of matter can be used to separate the substances that make up a mixture.

Picking by Hand

If you're making a necklace, how do you choose which beads to use? You might look for beads with a certain color, shape, or size. Or maybe you want to use only beads made of wood or glass.

You have learned that color, shape, and size are physical properties. Wood has physical properties that make it different from metal, glass, or plastic. You can use the physical properties of substances in a mixture to choose the ones you want to take out, or separate, from the mixture.

You can separate the beads by size.

Sometimes the properties of substances in a mixture are easy to see and easy to handle. You can separate those substances by hand. You can easily pick out all the red beads or all the wooden beads. But suppose the beads were tiny, like grains of sand, or as large as boulders. Then it would be quite difficult to separate them by hand.

Mixtures made of solids are often easy to separate by hand. You can also separate some liquid mixtures and liquid-solid mixtures by hand. For a mixture of oil and water, you can skim most of the oil from the top of the water. You can pick out the rocks in a mixture of water and gravel. You can also pour the water off carefully.

▶ **PROBLEM AND SOLUTION** **What makes beads easy to separate by hand?**

Using Tools

If you've ever sifted sand to find shells at the beach, then you've used a tool to separate a mixture. If the parts of a mixture are hard to see or to hold, you use tools to separate them. Using tools also saves time. At the beach, you can use a strainer to find shells. A strainer is a container that has many holes of the same size. When you put a mixture in a strainer, anything smaller than the holes falls through them. Anything larger stays in the strainer.

A strainer is a kind of filter (FIHL tur). A **filter** is a device or material that traps some substances and allows others to pass through. Water can pass through a coffee filter, but the coffee grounds cannot.

It would take a long time to dig through all the sand and shell mixture in the pail to find each shell. The strainer quickly separates the sand from the shells.

A magnet can be used to quickly separate the paper clips from this mixture.

Strainers and filters separate a mixture by the size of its parts. Other tools separate mixtures by other properties of the materials in the mixture. A magnet is a tool that attracts, or pulls on, objects that contain iron. A magnet can be used to pick up only the objects in a mixture that contain iron. Other objects that do not contain iron are left behind.

The temperature at which a substance melts is another property that can be used to separate substances in a mixture. Most metals are found mixed with rock in the Earth. To separate the metal from the rock, the rock is heated until the metal melts and flows away. The rock melts at a higher temperature than the metal, so the rock stays solid.

▶ **PROBLEM AND SOLUTION** **Identify two tools that are used to separate mixtures.**

Using Water

Water is another tool that can be used to separate mixtures. Some objects float in water. Other objects sink. You can use water to easily separate a mixture of corks and marbles in a container. If you pour water into the container, the corks float to the top and the marbles sink.

Some materials will mix completely and evenly with water. Other materials will not. You can separate a mixture of sand and salt by mixing it with water. The salt will mix completely with the water, seeming to disappear. The sand can be removed by filtering it from the salty water. How can you remove the salt from the water? If you allow the water to evaporate, the salt will be left behind.

▶ **PROBLEM AND SOLUTION** **How can water be used to separate a mixture?**

Corks and marbles have different properties. You can use water to separate a mixture of corks and marbles.

Visual Summary

A mixture can be separated by using the properties of the substances in the mixture.

Some mixtures can be easily separated by hand. Other mixtures can be separated by using tools.

Water is another tool that is used to separate mixtures.

LINKS for Home and School

MATH Write Decimals as Fractions
In a bowl of 100 mixed nuts, 0.46 of the nuts are almonds, 0.23 of the nuts are cashews, and 0.31 of the nuts are walnuts. Write each decimal as a fraction to represent each kind of nut in the bowl.

WRITING Expository Window screens are a kind of filter. The small holes allow fresh air to pass through, while keeping insects and animals out. Imagine that you are the inventor of the window screen. Write an advertisement for your invention. Explain how it works.

Review

❶ MAIN IDEA How can substances in a mixture be separated?

❷ VOCABULARY What is a filter?

❸ READING SKILL: Problem-Solution How can a mixture of rocks and sand be separated?

❹ CRITICAL THINKING: Apply How could you quickly separate a mixture of steel thumbtacks and erasers without pricking your fingers on the sharp thumbtacks?

❺ INQUIRY SKILL: Record Data Count up the different mixtures mentioned in this lesson. Determine how many can be separated by each of these methods: by hand, using tools, by evaporation, and using water. Record the data in a table.

 TEST PREP
To separate parts of a mixture by size, you would use a ___.

A. magnet

B. cup of water

C. pan

D. strainer

 Technology
Visit **www.eduplace.com/scp/** to find out more about how mixtures can be separated.

Freckle Juice

by Judy Blume

Is there a secret recipe for freckles?
In *Freckle Juice*, by Judy Blume, a boy named
Andrew wants freckles more than anything
else. He even spends his entire allowance on
a secret recipe.

The way Andrew sees it, there are two great
reasons to have freckles—you get to look like
Nicky Lane, a cool boy in your class. And two,
your mother won't be able to see that you
haven't washed behind your ears—after all,
you can't tell freckles from dirty skin, can you?
When a girl named Sharon sells Andrew a
secret recipe, he thinks all his problems are
solved. Andrew carefully begins to mix the
strange combination of ingredients.

"Now, first the grape juice,"
Andrew thought. He filled the
glass halfway and added an ice
cube. All drinks tasted better
cold and he was sure this one
would too.

Then he added the other ingredients one by one. His mother had two kinds of vinegars—wine vinegar and plain vinegar. Andrew picked the wine one. He put in some hot mustard, one spoonful of mayonnaise and plenty of pepper and salt. Then some ketchup…that was hard to pour. But what about olive oil? His mother had vegetable oil, but no olive oil. Maybe the stuff that looked like water in the olive jar was what Sharon meant. He put in a few spoonfuls of that. Now for the lemon. Andrew cut one in half and squeezed. Oh no! A seed dropped in by mistake. He picked it out with his spoon. He hated pits in his juice. Now all he needed was that speck of onion and he was all set. He stirred up the drink and smelled it.

OH! IT SMELLED AWFUL! JUST PLAIN AWFUL! He'd have to hold his nose while he drank it. He stuck his tongue into the glass to taste it. Ick! Terrible! He didn't know how he would ever manage to get it down . . . and fast too. It said to drink it very fast! That old Sharon! She probably thought he wouldn't be able to drink it. Well, he'd show her. He'd drink it all right!

Read *Freckle Juice* to find out if Andrew's plan works!

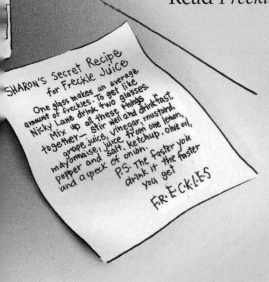

Sharing Ideas

1. **READING CHECK** List the items Andrew combined to make the freckle juice mixture.

2. **WRITE ABOUT IT** Write the next paragraph in the story. Describe how Andrew reacts after drinking the freckle juice mixture.

3. **TALK ABOUT IT** Discuss how the properties of the ingredients did not change after Andrew mixed them.

What Are Solutions?

Why It Matters...

When you mix together powdered fabric dye and water, they combine completely and evenly. You cannot see the dye or the water separately. When you dip a piece of cloth in the mixture, the colors on the cloth come out looking even. The dye and water form a special kind of mixture.

PREPARE TO INVESTIGATE

Inquiry Skill

Analyze Data When you analyze data, you look for patterns that can help you make predictions, hypotheses, and generalizations.

Materials

- sand
- salt
- food coloring
- vegetable or salad oil
- water
- 4 clear plastic containers with lids
- marking pen
- plastic spoon
- clock or watch

Shake It Up!
Procedure

STEP 1

1. **Collaborate** Work in a group. Label each of four containers *Salt*, *Sand*, *Food Coloring*, and *Oil*. Fill each container halfway with water. **Safety:** Wear goggles.

STEP 2

2. **Observe** Add a spoonful of sand to the *Sand* container. Close the lid and hold it on as you shake the container. Observe the mixture. Record your observations in your *Science Notebook*.

3. **Record Data** Repeat step 2, adding a spoonful of salt to the container labeled *Salt*. Repeat step 2 again, adding 3 drops of food coloring to the *Food Coloring* container. Record all observations.

STEP 4

4. **Observe** Add a small amount of oil to the *Oil* container. Close the lid and shake it well for about 1 minute. Record your observations. Let the mixture stand for 3 minutes. Record your observations.

5. **Compare** Look carefully at each mixture. Observe how they are alike and how they are different. Record your observations.

Conclusion

1. **Analyze Data** Which materials appear to mix evenly with water?

2. **Communicate** Draw a diagram to show the oil and water mixture after it stood.

Investigate More!

Research Salt water is a common mixture. Do research to find out some important uses of salt water, also called saline. Look for medical uses, as well as uses in manufacturing.

► **VOCABULARY**

alloy	p. E55
dissolve	p. E52
solution	p. E52

► **READING SKILL**

Classify Use the chart to list types of solutions.

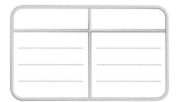

Solutions at a Swimming Pool

Solutions

MAIN IDEA A solution is a special mixture in which two or more kinds of matter are evenly mixed.

Common Solutions

When you swim in a pool, you can often smell and taste chlorine in the water. But you cannot see chlorine. Pool water is a solution (suh LOO shuhn). A **solution** is a special kind of mixture in which two or more substances are so evenly mixed that the separate parts cannot be seen. Each kind of matter in a solution keeps its own properties. That is why you can smell and taste the chlorine in the water in a swimming pool.

In pool water, the chlorine has dissolved (dih ZAHLVD) in the water. To **dissolve** means to mix completely with another substance to form a solution.

Gas and Gas

Air is a solution made up of several gases. Air contains nitrogen, oxygen, and carbon dioxide.

Some Types of Solutions

Type	Example	Parts
gas dissolved in gas	air	oxygen, nitrogen, other gases
solid dissolved in solid	steel	iron, nickel, chromium
solid dissolved in liquid	ocean water	salt, minerals, water
gas dissolved in liquid	soda water	carbon dioxide, water

The substances in a solution are evenly mixed. Dissolving is a physical change. The properties of the substances that form the solution have not changed.

Not all solutions are made by mixing a solid substance with water. Many solutions are mixtures of matter in other states.

 **CLASSIFY** What type of a solution is air?

Liquid and Solid

Pool water is a solution made by dissolving solid chemicals, including chlorine, in water.

Solid and Solid

The brass in this lifeguard's whistle is an alloy. An alloy is a solid solution made of at least one metal.

Making and Separating a Solution

The powdered grape drink mix is a purple solid. The water is a clear liquid.

When the drink mix is added to water, the solid dissolves completely.

Separating Solutions

It is easy to make grape drink with drink mix and water. You stir the solid powder into the water. As you stir, you notice that the water becomes evenly colored. It is purple throughout. No solid particles of drink mix can be seen in the solution. Now think about trying to separate a solution of grape drink into its parts—water and solid drink mix.

Solutions, such as the grape drink, are mixtures that cannot be separated by hand. The parts of the solution are too small to hold. They are too small to be separated by a filter. If you cannot see the parts of a solution, then how can you separate them?

Recall that each part of a solution is the same kind of matter it was before it became part of the mixture. You can separate the parts of a solution by using some of the properties of that matter. One of these properties is the ability to change state.

This solution can be separated using the properties of its parts. Heating causes the water to evaporate.

When the water evaporates, a purple solid remains. The substances in the solution have been separated.

You can separate some solutions by using evaporation. Recall that when a liquid evaporates, it changes state from a liquid to a gas. You can separate a solution of salt and water by using evaporation. When the water evaporates, it leaves the salt behind.

Not all solutions can be separated using evaporation. An **alloy** is a solid solution made of at least one metal. An alloy, such as brass, is a solid dissolved in a solid. Evaporation would not work to separate parts of this solution. It also could not be used to separate the substances that make up air. They are all gases!

▶ CLASSIFY What type of solution is steel?

When ocean water evaporates, it leaves behind a coating of salt.

Visual Summary

Solutions are special mixtures in which two or more kinds of matter are evenly mixed.

Some solutions can be separated by evaporation.

LINKS for Home and School

LITERATURE **Write a Science Fiction Story** Science fiction stories tell about real or imaginary science and how it affects people's lives. Write a science fiction story about a person who combines substances to create a special mixture or solution. Explain what happens when the different substances are mixed together. Describe what the solution is used for. Identify any special properties of the solution.

MUSIC **Draw a Picture** Many musical instruments are made of brass, which is an alloy. Use the Internet, the library, or another resource to find examples of brass instruments. Choose one instrument and draw a picture of someone playing it.

Review

❶ **MAIN IDEA** What is a solution?

❷ **VOCABULARY** Use your own words to explain what the term *dissolve* means.

❸ **READING SKILL: Classify** Explain why alloys are classified as solutions.

❹ **CRITICAL THINKING: Analyze** Which machine would separate salt from ocean water: one that filters water through a strainer or one that evaporates water? Explain.

❺ **INQUIRY SKILL: Analyze Data** Suppose you heat a piece of metal over a burner. After 5 minutes, the metal starts to drip liquid metal. After 10 minutes, the metal stops dripping, and it is half its original size. What does the data tell you about the metal?

✔ **TEST PREP**
When salt water evaporates, salt ___.

A. dissolves.

B. changes to a gas.

C. is left behind.

D. passes through a filter.

 Technology
Visit **www.eduplace.com/scp/** to investigate more about solutions.

Metallurgists

What do bicycles, toasters, and cars have in common? They are all made with metal. Metallurgists are scientists who work with metals, usually at companies that make metal products. They know how to get metals out of rocks and minerals and how to create and use alloys.

What It Takes!

- A degree in metallurgical engineering, materials science, or materials engineering
- Strong problem-solving skills

Jewelry Designer

Creating jewelry is part art and part science. Jewelry designers use artistic abilities to craft pieces that will attract customers' attention. They use science knowledge to work with all sorts of precious metals and gems. For example, to shape rings into different sizes, jewelry designers must have an understanding of the properties of metals like gold and silver.

What It Takes!

- A high-school diploma
- Courses in gemology, jewelry manufacturing, and jewelry design

Bubble Solution

How do you make a bubble this big?
First, you need a really big bubble-blowing ring. But that's not enough. The solution is in the *solution*— the special bubble solution!

The bubble solution is mostly water, but water alone won't form big bubbles. Adding soap helps, but soap bubbles tend to dry out and pop before they get very big. So what's the secret to making extreme bubbles? Read the next page!

Soft drinks are a solution of water, sugar, and flavoring. The bubbles created in soft drinks are very small and pop instantly in the air. Why do you think that is?

Secret Ingredient

The secret ingredient is glycerin. Glycerin is a clear, colorless, syrupy liquid that keeps bubbles from drying out as they stretch and expand. That way, bubbles have a chance to grow jumbo-sized before they pop!

Vocabulary

Complete each sentence with a term from the list.

1. A single kind of matter that has certain properties and is always the same throughout is a/an _____.

2. When substances mix completely to form a solution, one substance is said to _____ in the other.

3. Matter made of two or more substances that are physically combined, or mixed together, is a/an _____.

4. A device or material that traps some substances and allows others to pass through is a/an _____.

5. A mixture in which two or more kinds of matter are so evenly mixed that separate parts cannot be seen is called a/an _____.

6. A solid solution made of at least one metal is called a/an _____.

alloy E53
dissolve E52
filter E44
mixture E35
solution E52
substance E34

Test Prep

Write the letter of the best answer choice.

7. The parts of a mixture _____.

   A. cannot be separated.
   B. have new properties.
   C. keep their original properties.
   D. are always spread out evenly.

8. A filter separates substances by _____.

   A. temperature.
   B. size.
   C. color.
   D. age.

9. Unlike a mixture, the parts of a solution _____.

   A. cannot be seen.
   B. cannot be separated.
   C. have new properties.
   D. can be separated by hand.

10. Dissolving salt in water is an example of _____.

   A. a chemical change.
   B. melting.
   C. a physical change.
   D. evaporating.

Inquiry Skills

11. Observe Suppose the labels have fallen off two jars of clear liquid. The labels are *Water* and *Salt Water*. The liquids look and smell exactly alike. What are two ways that you could find out which label belongs to which jar?

12. Analyze Data Suppose you mix together a spoonful of salt and a spoonful of sugar. You cannot tell the two substances apart without a hand lens. Is this mixture a solution? Explain how you know

Map the Concept

Use the following terms to fill in the concept map below.

alloy
mixture
solution

_____	_____	_____
two substances physically combined	two substances physically combined	two substances physically combined
	separate parts cannot be seen	separate parts cannot be seen
		solid solution that includes at least one metal

Critical Thinking

13. Evaluate A gold ring is made of a solution of gold and other metals, such as nickel. What kind of mixture is the ring?

14. Analyze Is air a mixture? Explain why or why not.

15. Synthesize Describe how a metal could be removed from rock. What would have to be done for the metal to become an alloy in a finished piece of jewelry?

16. Apply Explain how you could separate a mixture of gravel, iron filings, and salt.

17. Evaluate A certain salad dressing is made by mixing vinegar with a pinch of salt. This clear liquid is then mixed with oil and spices. The oil floats to the top of the clear liquid. The spices settle to the bottom. Is the salad dressing a mixture? A solution? Give evidence to support your answers.

Performance Assessment

Make a Mixture

Choose four substances or materials that you could mix together. Describe how you could use a magnet, strainer, and water to separate the materials in your mixture.

Write the letter of the best answer choice.

1. Which kind of solution can be separated by evaporation?

   A. gas-gas
   B. gas-solid
   C. liquid-solid
   D. solid-solid

2. Which is an example of a physical change?

   A.

   B.

   C.

   D.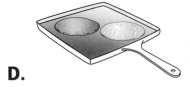

3. Which change happens when energy is taken away from a gas?

   A. boiling
   B. condensation
   C. evaporation
   D. melting

4. You can measure the MASS of an object with a _____ .

   A. balance.
   B. metric ruler.
   C. liter.
   D. thermometer.

5. Breaking a bowling ball into pieces would affect which of its physical properties?

   A. color
   B. shape
   C. mass
   D. weight

6. Which is a CHEMICAL property of matter?

   A. texture
   B. ability to change state
   C. ability to burn
   D. temperature

7. Which is a mixture of a liquid in a gas?

A.

B.

C.

D.

8. The parts of a mixture _____ .

A. cannot be separated.

B. blend into one substance.

C. keep their original properties.

D. are always spread out evenly.

Answer the following in complete sentences.

9. Name the three states of matter. Explain the differences among the three states using water as an example.

10. Alex needs to separate a mixture that contains marbles, paper clips, and corks. She cannot do it by hand. Describe how Alex could separate the objects in the mixture.

Discover!

The Statue of Liberty has welcomed people to the United States for more than 115 years. In that time, the statue has been exposed to precipitation, pollution, and salty ocean air. Substances in the environment, especially in air, have caused changes to the statue's copper surface.

When the copper combined with oxygen in air, chemical changes turned the new copper surface dark brown. Over many years, more chemical changes produced a layer of a new substance on the statue's surface. This new substance changed the dark surface to the light green it is today.

The statue had a bright copper surface when it was built in France in the early 1880s. Copper is a pinkish-brown metal.

The statue was put on an island in New York Harbor in 1886. By that time, the shiny copper surface had turned dark brown.

Substances in the environment caused more chemical changes. The dark brown copper started to turn green.

Today, the statue is light green. The new substance that coats the surface of the copper is called a patina.

See the Statue of Liberty change. Go to **www.eduplace.com/scp/** to play a timeline of important events in the statue's history.

PHYSICAL SCIENCE

UNIT F

Energy and Change

PHYSICAL UNIT F SCIENCE

Energy and Change

Independent Reading

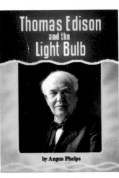

Thomas Edison and the Light Bulb

Tsunami!

Seeing with Heat

Discover!

To score in soccer you must kick the ball into the other team's goal. A kick can make the ball move straight forward or curve to one side. How does a soccer player kick the ball to make it move in these different ways? You will find the answer to this question by the end of this unit.

Chapter 13

Forms of Energy

LESSON

1

Hold, dribble, pass—how does the energy of a basketball change during a game?

Read about it in Lesson 1.

LESSON

2

From music traveling through the air to echoes bouncing off walls—what is sound and how does it move?

Read about it in Lesson 2.

LESSON

3

An electric light bulb and your beating heart—what do these two things have in common?

Read about it in Lesson 3.

How Is Energy Stored and Released?

Why It Matters...

A swimmer jumps into the water and hits the surface with a loud splash! Water sprays everywhere! The sound and motion caused by the swimmer's jump are forms of energy. Everything you do, see, or hear involves energy.

PREPARE TO INVESTIGATE

Inquiry Skill

Measure When you measure, you use tools to find distance, mass, or other information about an object.

Materials

- thin dowel
- plastic-foam ball
- spring
- tape
- metric tape measure
- goggles

Science and Math Toolbox

For steps 3 and 4, review **Using a Tape Measure or Ruler** on page H6.

Launch It!
Procedure

STEP 2

1. **Collaborate** Work with a partner. Tape one end of a thin dowel to the surface of a table as shown. Half of the dowel should stick out past the edge of the table. Slide a spring onto that end of the dowel. **Safety:** Wear goggles.

2. Push a plastic-foam ball onto the same end of the dowel. Slide the ball back and forth until it can move freely.

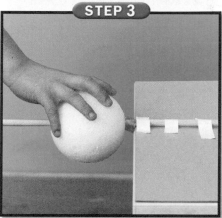

STEP 3

3. **Measure** Push the ball toward the desk until the coils of the spring are squeezed tightly together. Let go of the ball. After the ball stops rolling, use a tape measure to find out how far the ball traveled. Record the distance in your *Science Notebook*. **Safety:** Make sure the ball is always aimed away from people.

4. **Use Variables** Repeat step 3, but squeeze the spring only halfway. Predict how far the ball will travel. Release the ball. Then measure and record the distance.

STEP 4

Conclusion

1. **Infer** The spring stored energy when you squeezed it. What happened to this stored energy when you let go of ball?

2. **Hypothesize** Explain why squeezing the spring less affects the distance the ball travels.

Investigate More!

Be an Inventor Invent a tool, toy, or machine that uses the stored energy of a spring to make another object move. Draw a picture of your invention. Describe how it might be useful or fun.

▶ **READING SKILL**

Classify Look around your classroom for ways that energy is being used. Use a chart to classify the energy as kinetic or potential.

Energy and Motion

MAIN IDEA Energy is the ability to cause motion or other changes in matter. There are many forms of energy.

Forms of Energy

You use energy to ride a bike. A stove uses energy to cook food. A car uses energy to travel. How can energy do all these things? Energy is the ability to cause movement or to cause matter to change in other ways.

There are many forms of energy. Each form of energy changes matter, but in a different way. For example, a bike is matter. The energy you use to ride a bike causes that matter to move. Food is matter. The energy used to cook food causes that matter to heat up.

Which form of energy are these children using to play leapfrog? Look at the chart on the next page.

Forms of Energy

Electrical Energy Electrical (ih LEHK-trih kuhl) energy is the energy of charged particles. It is used to run appliances and other machines.

Mechanical Energy Mechanical (mih-KAN ih kuhl) energy is the energy of moving objects. It is used to move people and objects from place to place.

Sound Energy Sound energy is energy you can hear. It moves as waves through air or other matter. It is used to hear music.

Light Energy Light energy is energy you can see. It moves as waves through space or clear matter. It allows you to see books and other objects.

Thermal Energy Thermal energy is the energy of tiny moving particles of matter. It is used to heat food and warm homes.

Chemical Energy Chemical energy is energy that is stored in substances. It is found in food, fuel, and batteries.

 **CLASSIFY** What form of energy does a guitar produce?

Kinetic and Potential Energy

Some energy involves motion. For example, a bowling ball rolling down an alley has energy of motion. Energy of motion is also called **kinetic energy** (kuh NEHT ihk EHN ur jee).

Other energy does not involve motion. For example, chemical energy is a form of stored energy. Stored energy is also called **potential energy** (puh-TEHN shuhl EHN ur jee).

Objects can have potential energy because of their position. A diver standing on a diving board above a pool has potential energy because of his or her position. Objects can also have potential energy because of the substances they contain. For example, a battery has potential energy because of the chemicals inside it.

potential energy

The children at the top of the hill have potential energy because of their position. As the boy slides down the hill, he has kinetic energy because of his motion.

kinetic energy

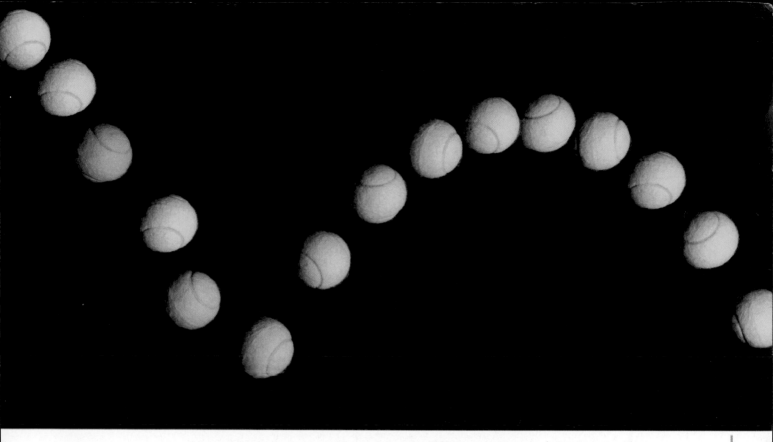

When the ball is at its highest point, it has the most potential energy. As the ball falls, it loses potential energy and gains kinetic energy.

Energy Changes

Potential energy can change to kinetic energy. When you hold a ball above the ground, it has potential energy because of its position. When you drop the ball, it falls to the ground because of gravity. As the ball falls, its potential energy changes to kinetic energy.

Kinetic energy can also change to potential energy. As the ball falls, it has kinetic energy. When it bounces off the ground, it still has kinetic energy. As the ball moves upward, it slows down because its kinetic energy is changing back to potential energy.

▶ **CLASSIFY** A diver stands at the end of a diving board above the water. Does the diver have kinetic energy or potential energy?

Using Energy

You have learned that kinetic and potential energy can change back and forth. Energy can also change from one form to another. For example, when you move around, the chemical energy stored in the food you ate is changed to mechanical energy and heat energy. When a car engine runs, chemical energy in gasoline is changed to mechanical and heat energy.

Whenever you use energy, it almost always changes form. When you switch on a light to do your homework, electrical energy is changed to light energy. When you use a calculator to do math, chemical energy stored in the calculator's battery is changed to electrical energy.

▶ **CLASSIFY** **What energy change takes place when you plug in a toaster and turn it on?**

Gasoline in the cans contains stored chemical energy that is released when the gasoline burns inside the car engine. ▶

◀ Food contains stored chemical energy. Cells in your body change some of this energy to mechanical energy and heat energy.

Visual Summary

Energy is the ability to cause motion or other changes in matter.

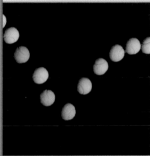

Kinetic energy is energy of motion. Potential energy is stored energy.

Energy can change from one form to another.

LINKS for Home and School

MATH **Multiply With 9** Mrs. Wagner plans to take 9 students on an evening hike to watch fireflies. Each student will have a flashlight that uses chemical energy from batteries. Each flashlight requires 4 batteries. How many batteries does Mrs. Wagner need in all? Show your work.

ART **Identify Forms of Energy** Use library resources or the Internet to find a copy of the famous painting *Washington Crossing the Delaware*, by Emanuel Gottlieb Leutze. Identify and describe one example of potential energy and one example of kinetic energy shown in the painting.

Review

❶ **MAIN IDEA** What is energy?

❷ **VOCABULARY** Define the term *kinetic energy*.

❸ **READING SKILL: Classify** Classify chemical energy as either kinetic or potential energy.

❹ **CRITICAL THINKING: Analyze** You wind up a rubber band on the propeller of a toy airplane. When you let go of the rubber band, the propeller turns and the airplane flies. What energy changes occurred?

❺ **INQUIRY SKILL: Measure** The amount of chemical energy in gasoline affects how far a car can travel. What measurement could you use to evaluate the chemical energy stored in 5 L of gasoline?

✔ **TEST PREP**
A bouncing ball has ___.

A. mechanical energy.

B. light energy.

C. electrical energy.

D. chemical energy.

 Technology
Visit **www.eduplace.com/scp/** to find out more about energy.

Lesson 2

What Are Waves?

Why It Matters...

You may have made waves in a parachute in gym class. You have probably made waves on water. Waves are a way energy moves from one place to another. Many familiar forms of energy, including light and sound, move in waves.

PREPARE TO INVESTIGATE

Inquiry Skill

Observe When you observe, you gather information about the environment using your five senses: seeing, hearing, smelling, touching, and tasting.

Materials

- empty coffee can
- metal spoon
- large washer
- string
- hand lens
- sand
- goggles

Science and Math Toolbox

For step 2, review **Using a Hand Lens** on page H2.

Seeing Sounds
Procedure

STEP 1

1. **Collaborate** Work with a partner. Turn an empty coffee can upside down. Have your partner tap the bottom of the can with the spoon. In your *Science Notebook*, record what happens. **Safety**: Wear goggles.

STEP 2

2. **Observe** Place a few grains of sand on the bottom of the can. As your partner taps the can with the spoon, use a hand lens to observe the grains of sand. Record your observations.

3. **Record Data** Hold a metal washer by the edge. Use the spoon to tap the washer. Record your observations.

STEP 4

4. **Observe** Now tie one end of a string to the washer. Have your partner hold the other end of the string so that the washer hangs. Tap the washer with the spoon. Record your observations.

Conclusion

1. **Observe** What happened to the sand grains in step 2? What do you think caused this?

2. **Compare** How did the noise the washer made differ in steps 3 and 4?

3. **Hypothesize** What might explain the difference in the sounds?

Investigate More!

Research Use the Internet or library to find information about musical instruments made from common objects, unusual materials, or junk. Describe how musicians use the objects to make music.

▶ READING SKILL

Draw Conclusions Use a chart to record what you can tell about a sound wave from the pitch and volume of the sound.

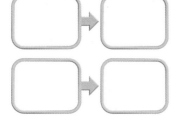

Waves

MAIN IDEA Waves carry energy from place to place.

How Energy Travels

Suddenly the side of a mountain slides into the ocean. It's a landslide! The energy of the moving rocks and soil creates waves in the ocean. These waves reach a distant island, where they push water onto the shore. How did the energy of the landslide move through the water? It traveled in waves. A **wave** is a movement that carries energy from one place to another.

Many forms of energy can travel in waves. Mechanical energy, heat energy, light energy, and sound energy can all travel in waves.

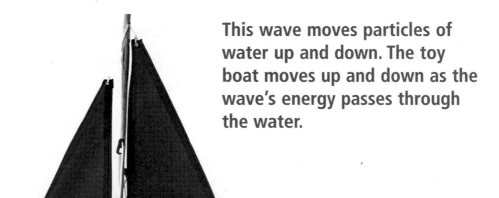

This wave moves particles of water up and down. The toy boat moves up and down as the wave's energy passes through the water.

water particles

wave energy

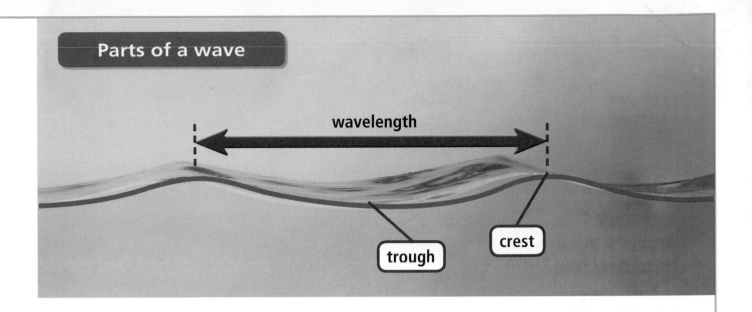

Parts of a wave

wavelength

trough

crest

Measuring Waves

All waves have traits that can be measured. The **crest** of a wave is its highest point. The **trough** (trawf) of a wave is its lowest point. Waves with more energy have higher crests and deeper troughs.

The wavelength of a wave is the distance between one crest and the next crest or one trough and the next trough. Waves with shorter wavelengths have crests and troughs that are closer together. When crests (or troughs) are close together, each crest is followed quickly by the next. You can count how many crests pass by in a given time. This is the frequency (FREE kwuhn see) of the wave.

▶ **DRAW CONCLUSIONS** If a wave has high crests and deep troughs, what can you conclude about how much energy the wave has?

Sound Waves

Sound is a form of energy that travels in waves. Sound is produced when particles of matter **vibrate** (VY brayt), or move back and forth quickly.

A guitar string vibrates when you pluck it. The string moves back and forth so quickly that it looks like a blur. The movement of the string creates sound waves in the air around it. The sound waves move out in all directions from the vibrating string. You hear the waves as sounds.

When a guitar string is plucked, it vibrates. The energy of the vibrations travels through the air as sound waves.

A sound wave moves particles of matter back and forth. It is like a spring that is squeezed and then released. As the sound wave travels through matter, particles of matter squeeze together and then spread apart. This happens over and over again as the wave moves away from its source. A crest is where particles of matter are bunched close together. A trough is where particles are spread far apart. This happens over and over again as the wave moves away from the source.

When a sound wave travels from its source, the particles that carry the wave do not travel with the wave. The particles move back and forth, but stay in the same general location. For this reason, a sound wave can travel only through matter. It cannot travel through empty space.

▶ **DRAW CONCLUSIONS** **Can noise from Earth travel to other planets in the solar system? Why or why not?**

A sound wave moves particles of matter back and forth. Particles of air squeeze together and then spread apart as a sound wave passes through.

High and Low Sounds

There is a big difference between the tweet of a songbird and the growl of a lion. Vibrating matter produces both sounds. But one sound is much higher than the other. How high or low a sound seems is called **pitch** (pihch).

Pitch depends on the frequency of sound waves. High-pitched sounds have high frequency sound waves. Low-pitched sounds have low frequency sound waves. Small objects vibrate more quickly and make high-pitched sounds. Large objects vibrate more slowly and make low-pitched sounds.

▲ Which bars on the xylophone make higher-pitched sounds, the small bars or the large bars?

◄ When you blow across the openings, these bottles produce sounds of different pitch. The pitch depends on the amount of air that can vibrate in the bottles.

Loud and Soft Sounds

How loud or soft a sound seems is called **volume** (VAHL yoom). Volume depends on the size of the crests and troughs of sound waves. A sound with high volume, such as a siren, has waves with high crests and deep troughs. A sound with low volume, such as a whisper, has low crests and shallow troughs. Waves with high crests and deep troughs have more energy than waves with low crests and shallow troughs. You hear this difference in energy as a difference in volume.

▶ **DRAW CONCLUSIONS** **What can you conclude about sound waves that produce a high-pitched sound?**

▲ A mouse makes soft, high-pitched sounds.

A jackhammer produces very loud sounds. High-volume sounds can hurt your ears. Ear protectors reduce the amount of sound that reaches the ears. ▶

Dolphins use sound to communicate. Dolphins can communicate over long distances because sound waves travel a long way through water.

Sound Moves Through Matter

Most of the time, you hear sound waves that travel through the air, which is a gas. Sound waves can also travel through liquids. Dolphins use sound waves to communicate with each other under water. Sounds can also travel through solids, such as a wooden door. Sound waves travel faster through solids than liquids. They travel faster through liquids than gases.

Sound waves can reflect (rih FLEHKT), or bounce, off of objects. Reflected sound waves are called echoes (EHK ohz). You can hear echoes when sound waves bounce off the face of a large building or the walls of a gym.

▶ **DRAW CONCLUSIONS** Will a sound wave travel fastest through air, water, or wood?

Visual Summary

Waves are up-and-down or back-and-forth movements that carry energy.

Sound is the energy of vibrating matter. Sound travels in waves through matter.

Pitch depends on the frequency of sound waves. Volume depends on the size of the crests and troughs.

LINKS for Home and School

MATH **Make a Number Line** The volume of a sound is measured in a unit called *decibels*. A whisper is about 30 decibels. A baby crying is about 110 decibels. Use the library or Internet to find the decibel measurements of five sounds. Show the data on a number line.

MUSIC **Model Sound Waves** Some composers use sounds to represent people, animals, ideas, feelings, or events. For example, in the symphony *Peter and the Wolf*, by Sergei Prokofiev, characters are represented by different instruments. Flutes represent the bird, French horns are the wolf, and oboes are the duck. Think of a story and write the instrument you would use to represent each character.

Review

❶ MAIN IDEA How does sound travel?

❷ VOCABULARY What is the pitch of a sound?

❸ READING SKILL: Draw Conclusions A jet engine produces a loud sound. What can you conclude about how much energy the engine produces?

❹ CRITICAL THINKING: Evaluate In a movie, a spaceship flies through outer space, where there is no matter. Its engines make a loud roaring sound. Why is this not correct?

❺ INQUIRY SKILL: Observe An organ has small and large pipes. Describe the pitch of the sounds produced by the different pipes.

 TEST PREP

The size of crests and troughs determine the ___ of a sound.

A. pitch

B. notes

C. volume

D. beauty

 Technology
Visit **www.eduplace.com/scp/** to learn more about waves.

Sound Safari

What happens in a sound studio?
The setting is a classroom. A group of students is about to make its own sound studio. The students need to produce all kinds of sounds—growls, chirps, thunder, rattles, and echoes. How will they do it? Let's listen in!

Characters

Mr. Lee: teacher

Elaine
Rena } students
Rico
David

Sound Studio

Elaine: I have a question. Who decided we should put on a play called *Lost in the Jungle Cave*? I mean, couldn't we just do something simple? How about *Lost in the Library*? You don't need monkey sounds for that.

Rena: True, but you don't need a sound-effects team for that either. Libraries are pretty silent, remember?

Mr. Lee: All right, everybody, let's focus on the jungle, not the library. Rena, tell about the play, *Lost in the Jungle Cave*.

Rena: Okay. In the play, MuMu the Monkey runs into a cave after a thunderstorm. Her friend LuLu the Lion looks for her in the jungle. That means we need a monkey, a thunderstorm, a lion, and other jungle noises.

Rico: This is going to be great! I can make just about any animal sound. Squeak! Chirrrrrrp! GROWWWWL!

Rena: Is that supposed to be a lion? Lions don't GROWWWWL. They ROARRRR.

David: Does anybody know what a monkey sounds like? I read someplace that monkeys are really loud. Let me give it a try. I-I-I-I-EEEK-EEEK!

Rena: The script says that MuMu the monkey calls to LuLu from inside that cave. But all she can hear is her own echo! How can we make an echo?

Mr. Lee: We can make an echo in the gym later. Now, let's take a look in this bag of tricks [*pulls out a bag*]. I've got coconut shells, copper sheets, bits of tinfoil....

Rena: These are for sound effects?

Mr. Lee: Think about sounds you might hear in the jungle.

David: What about bees? BUZZZZZZZZ. How's that?

Mr. Lee: Nice try, but not all animals make sounds the way we do. Bees wings move so fast that the air vibrates—and you hear a buzzing sound. Thunder works in a similar way.

Rena: *[confused]* But thunder doesn't buzz!

Mr. Lee: When lightning heats air, it makes the air vibrate. That creates sound waves and makes a loud boom.

Rico: So how can we make a thunder sound for the play?

Mr. Lee: In the 1700s, a fellow named John Dennis hung a large sheet of thin copper from the ceiling by wires. When he rattled it, it sounded like thunder. When someone copied Dennis's idea, he accused the man of "stealing my thunder!" It's a famous saying now.

Rena: I have an idea for the coconut shells. Listen. The lion is running to find MuMu. *[knocks coconut shell halves on table]*

David: Umm, that sounds like a horse running. There are no horses in the play.

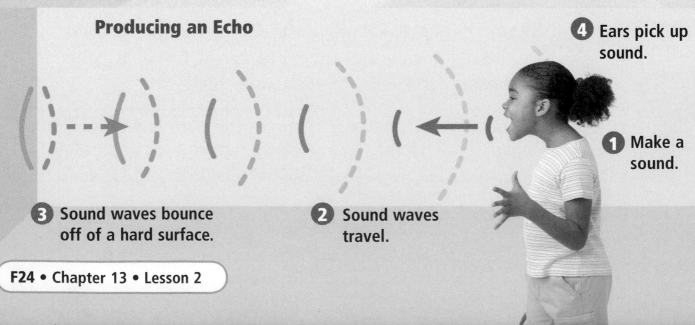

Producing an Echo

4 Ears pick up sound.

1 Make a sound.

3 Sound waves bounce off of a hard surface.

2 Sound waves travel.

Elaine: Hey, if I rustle these bits of tinfoil, it sounds like animals running through leaves.

Rena: OK. MuMu is in the cave. From a distance, she hears Lulu. ROAR!

Elaine: When she is far away, the sound is soft. But she follows the sound. *[stirs the tinfoil]* As she gets closer...

David: The roar gets louder. ROOOOOOARRR! Finally, LuLu finds MuMu!!!!! ROOOOOOOOOAAAARRRRR! I-I-I-I-EEEK-EEEK!

Mr. Lee: Good job, team. Now all we need is the echo!

David: We need a big area with a flat wall that sound waves can bounce off, like the gymnasium.

[MR. LEE and STUDENTS walk to the gymnasium.]

David: Okay. This is the part where MuMu runs into the dark, scary cave. *[dramatically]* She cries out, but all she hears is her own echo!

David: *[shouts toward the wall]* I-I-I-I-EEEK-EEEK, I-I-I-I-EEEK-EEEK!

[They hear the echo: I-I-I-I-EEEK-EEEK, I-I-I-I-EEEK-EEEK.]

Mr. Lee: Congratulations kids, I think we're ready for the play!

Sharing Ideas

1. **READING CHECK** What makes an echo?

2. **WRITE ABOUT IT** Compare the way that a lion produces sound to the way that a bee produces sound.

3. **TALK ABOUT IT** Discuss new ways to create sound effects using everyday objects.

What Is Electrical Energy?

Why It Matters...

What forms of energy do you notice in this parade? If you were there, you would probably notice energy in the forms of light, motion, and sound. Although you may not notice electrical energy, it powers the whole parade. Electrical energy also powers most of the appliances and lights you use every day.

PREPARE TO INVESTIGATE

Inquiry Skill

Research When you do research, you learn more about a subject by looking in books, searching the Internet, or asking science experts.

Materials

- 2 dry cells (size D)
- 2 dry-cell holders
- buzzer
- insulated wires, with stripped ends

Circuit Search
Procedure

STEP 1

1. **Research** Use the Internet, library, or other resources to find out how to make a simple electric circuit (SUR kiht). The circuit should include one or more dry cells. Have your teacher check the instructions before you follow them.

STEP 2

2. Using the materials provided, follow the instructions to set up a circuit. Do not connect the last wire to the dry cell yet. **Safety:** The wires may be sharp.

3. **Predict** Predict what will happen when you make the last connection and complete the circuit. Record your prediction in your *Science Notebook*.

STEP 3

4. **Experiment** Complete the circuit by connecting the last wire to the dry-cell holder. Observe and record what happens.

Conclusion

1. **Analyze Data** What form of energy does a dry cell contain? What form of energy does the buzzer produce?

2. **Research** Use science resources to find out what form of energy travels through the wires of the circuit.

3. **Hypothesize** Use your results to hypothesize how a doorbell works.

Investigate More!

Solve a Problem People who are hearing impaired may not be able to hear a doorbell ringing. How could you use a circuit to create a signal that a hearing-impaired person could sense?

▶ **READING SKILL**

Cause and Effect
Use a graphic
organizer to list
some possible effects
of electrical energy.

Electrical Energy

MAIN IDEA Electrical energy is the energy of
charged particles.

Flow of Electric Charges

Most people take electricity for granted
until there is a power blackout. That's when
they realize that electrical energy is an
important part of everyday life. Electrical
energy is the energy of charged particles of
matter. For electricity to run lamps and TVs,
some of these charged particles must move.

Charged particles of matter carry either
a positive or a negative electric charge.
Positively charged particles and negatively
charged particles attract each other.
Negatively charged particles tend to flow, or
move, toward positively charged particles.
This flow of charged particles is an **electric
current** (KUR uhnt).

**Electric current moves
through a complete circuit,
causing the bulb to light.** ▶

Electric current flows through a path called an **electric circuit** (SUR kiht). A circuit is made up of wires and electrical devices. It has a source of electricity, such as a battery. Electric current can flow through a circuit only if the circuit is complete. There cannot be any gap in the circuit.

▶ **CAUSE AND EFFECT** What causes negative charges to flow?

When a lamp is unplugged, there is a gap in the circuit. The lamp can be turned on only when it is plugged in and the circuit is complete. ▶

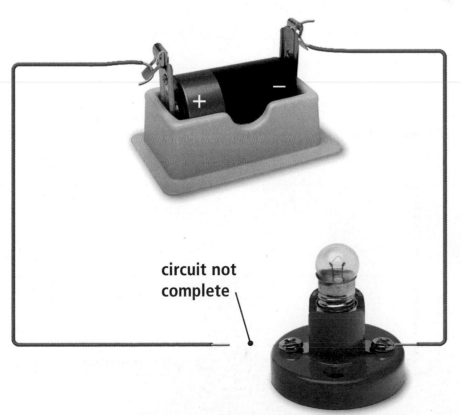

circuit not complete

◀ Any gap in a circuit stops electric current, so the bulb does not light.

Using Electric Current

Electric current powers many devices. Most of these devices change electrical energy into other forms of energy. When a radio is in use, electrical energy is changed into sound energy. When a lamp is turned on, electrical energy is changed into light energy. The turning blades of a fan have mechanical energy that comes from electrical energy.

Most electrical devices have cords and plugs. Electric current flows from an outlet, through a plug to a cord. The cord is attached to the electrical device, such as a fan.

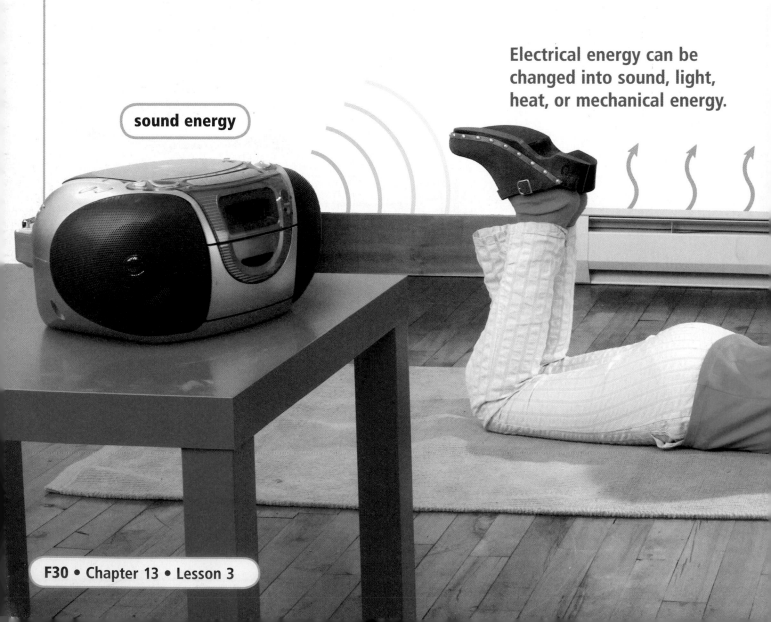

Electrical energy can be changed into sound, light, heat, or mechanical energy.

sound energy

The current flows from the device back through the cord. From the cord, it flows to the plug and then to the outlet. This makes a complete circuit.

A switch on a device opens or closes a gap in the circuit. When a switch is turned on, the gap in the circuit is closed. Electricity flows through the device, so it runs. When the switch is turned off, the gap in the circuit is open. The device cannot run. Even if a lamp is plugged in, it works only when its switch is turned on.

▶ **CAUSE AND EFFECT** **Why does an electrical device work only when its switch is turned on?**

light and heat energy

electrical energy

heat energy

mechanical energy

▲ Warning signs like this can protect people from dangerous electric charges.

Electrical Energy and Your Body

Look around you. Each person in your class is using electrical energy right now. The human body uses electrical energy to function. Electrical signals in the heart keep it beating at the right pace. Electrical signals also carry messages from the brain to other parts of the body.

Where do the heart and brain get electrical energy? It comes from the chemical energy in food. The body changes some of the chemical energy in food into electrical energy.

Electric current from a source outside the body can be very dangerous. If a large amount of electricity passes through the body, it can stop the heart from beating. It can also change to heat energy and cause burns.

▶ **CAUSE AND EFFECT** **How does the brain use electrical energy?**

A pacemaker is an electrical device that helps keep the heart beating at the right rate. ▶

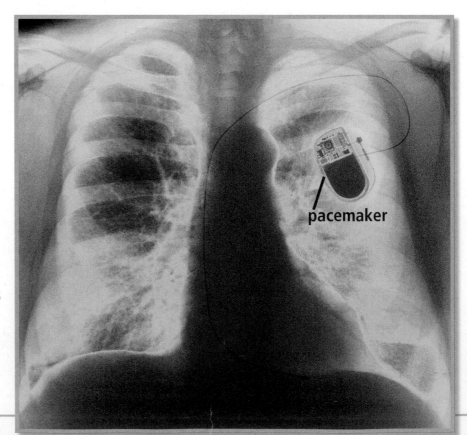

pacemaker

Visual Summary

The flow of charged particles is an electric current. Electric current moves through a complete circuit.

Electrical devices change electrical energy into sound, light, heat, or motion.

DANGER HIGH VOLTAGE

Electricity can be dangerous to the human body.

LINKS for Home and School

WRITING Narrative Can you remember a time when the power went out in your home or school? Write a narrative story about how you and others dealt with the "blackout." If you have not experienced a blackout, use your imagination.

SOCIAL STUDIES Write a Dialogue Which electrical device is the most important to human lives today? Is it the light bulb? The dishwasher? The television? Choose two electrical appliances. Write a dialogue in which two characters debate which of those appliances is more important to humankind.

Review

❶ **MAIN IDEA** What is electrical energy?

❷ **VOCABULARY** Write a definition of *electric current*.

❸ **READING SKILL: Cause and Effect** What might happen to someone who touches a strong electric current?

❹ **CRITICAL THINKING: Apply** In many homes, there are devices called circuit breakers. A circuit breaker is similar to an on-off switch. It breaks, or turns off, if too much electric current flows through the wires. Explain how a circuit breaker works.

❺ **INQUIRY SKILL: Research** Use the Internet or library to learn what a generator does. Write a brief paragraph explaining what you learned.

 TEST PREP
The path an electric current flows through is a(n) ___.

A. plug

B. outlet

C. machine

D. circuit

 Technology
Visit **www.eduplace.com/scp/** to learn more about electrical energy.

Echoes in the Dark

Dark forms flutter and dive across the night sky. Bats! You can barely see them. But they can see you ... as clearly as if it were daylight. How?

Bats send out powerful, high-pitched calls that human ears can't hear. The sound waves reflect off objects — tree branches, rooftops, even an insect in flight. The bat's huge, sensitive ears pick up the echo. The reflected sound waves tell the bat where objects are, how big they are, and even how they are moving.

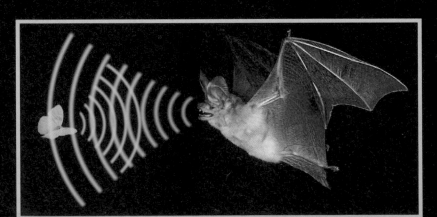

◀ Using reflected sound to locate objects is called echolocation.

Hello! If you shout in a canyon you may hear your own voice coming back at you. The echo will slowly fade as the sound waves lose energy to the air and rocks.

▲ **Blind as a bat?** Actually, many species have very good vision.

Vocabulary

Complete each sentence with a term from the list.

1. To move back and forth quickly is to _____.

2. The energy that an object has because of its motion is called _____.

3. A movement that carries energy from place to place is a/an _____.

4. Electric current can flow only through a complete _____.

5. The lowest point of a wave is the _____.

6. The energy stored in an object because of its position or the substances it is made of is _____.

7. The highest point of a wave is the _____.

8. How loud or soft a sound seems is its _____.

9. The flow of charged particles is called _____.

10. How high or low a sound seems is its _____.

crest F15
electric circuit F29
electric current F28
kinetic energy F8
pitch F18
potential energy F8
trough F15
vibrate F16
volume F19
wave F14

Test Prep

Write the letter of the best answer choice.

11. High-frequency sound waves produce sounds that are high in _____.

   A. pitch
   B. wavelength
   C. volume
   D. energy

12. Moving charges produce a/an _____.

   A. wave
   B. vibration
   C. electric current
   D. complete circuit

13. When objects vibrate, they produce _____.

   A. chemical energy
   B. potential energy
   C. sound energy
   D. light energy

14. Chemical energy is a form of _____.

   A. sound energy
   B. kinetic energy
   C. light energy
   D. potential energy

15. **Observe** You see an amusement park ride with a car on a track. The car climbs up a hill, sits at the top of the hill for a moment, and then moves quickly back to the bottom of the hill. Describe the changes of energy in this amusement park ride.

16. **Research** Humans can sense the frequency of sound waves as pitch. Light also travels in waves. Humans can sense the wavelengths of light waves. Use science resources to find out how humans sense different wavelengths of light. Share what you learn with your classmates.

Map the Concept

Label the diagram using the terms below:

trough	1. _____.
wavelength	2. _____.
vibrate	3. _____.
crest	4. _____.

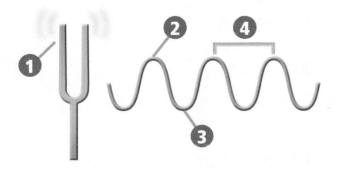

17. **Synthesize** Many musical instruments, such as pianos, have wires or strings that are strung very tightly. What type of energy do the strung wires have? What type of energy do the wires have after you strike or pluck them to make a sound?

18. **Apply** Choose an electrical machine or appliance in your home. What type of energy does that machine or appliance change electrical energy into?

19. **Analyze** The noise of an engine suddenly increases in both volume and pitch. What has happened to the crests, troughs, and frequency of the sound waves made by the engine?

20. **Evaluate** Support the following statement: A car with a full tank of gas that is parked on a hill has energy.

Performance Assessment

Switch It Up

Use a dry cell to build an electric circuit that contains a switch and a buzzer or bulb. Draw a diagram of your circuit. Your diagram should explain how the switch turns the buzzer or bulb on and off.

Chapter 14

Heat, Temperature, and Light

LESSON

1

A cup of hot cocoa or rubbing your hands together on a cold day—where does heat come from?

Read about it in Lesson 1.

LESSON

2

It might be a day for baseball or a day for ice skating—how can you measure temperature to find out?

Read about it in Lesson 2.

LESSON

3

Whether it strikes the Moon, a mirror, or a bicycle—what is light, and how does it behave?

Read about it in Lesson 3.

What Is Heat?

Why It Matters...

It can get cold at night when you are camping. One way to stay warm is to build a campfire. The campfire produces heat. Understanding how heat is produced can help you stay warm.

PREPARE TO INVESTIGATE

Inquiry Skill

Compare When you compare two things, you observe how they are alike and how they are different.

Materials

- clock or watch
- measuring cup
- small bowl
- vinegar
- steel wool pad
- plastic gloves
- goggles

Science and Math Toolbox

For steps 2 and 4, review **Measuring Elapsed Time** on pages H12–H13.

Feel the Heat
Procedure

1 **Observe** Hold your hands together. Do they feel cool or warm? Record your observations in your *Science Notebook*.

2 **Compare** Rub your hands together very quickly for 10 seconds. Notice whether they feel cooler or warmer than they did before. Record your observations.

3 **Observe** Pick up a steel wool pad and hold it in your hands. Does it feel cool or warm? Record your observations.

4 **Measure** Pour $\frac{1}{4}$ cup of vinegar into a bowl. Place the steel wool pad in the bowl for 2 minutes. Then remove the pad and squeeze it out over the bowl. Place the pad on a paper towel to dry for 5 minutes. **Safety:** Wear plastic gloves and goggles.

5 **Compare** Remove the gloves and pick up the steel wool pad. Does it feel cooler or warmer than it did before? Record your observations.

STEP 2

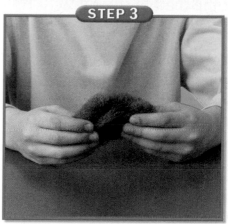
STEP 3

STEP 4

Conclusion

1. **Infer** What type of energy did you use when you rubbed your hands together? What type of energy did it change into?

2. **Infer** What type of energy was in the steel wool pad and the vinegar? What type of energy did it change into?

Investigate More!

Design an Experiment
What happens when coins are rubbed against other materials? Choose some materials to try. Make a prediction about each material. Carry out your plan. Present your results.

Heat

VOCABULARY

friction	p. F45
heat	p. F42
thermal energy	p. F42

READING SKILL

Cause and Effect Use the chart to show how thermal energy moves from a warmer object to a cooler object.

MAIN IDEA Thermal energy moves from warmer objects to cooler objects. You feel the movement of thermal energy as heat.

Thermal Energy

You have learned that matter is made up of tiny particles that are always in motion. The energy of moving particles in matter is called **thermal energy** (THUR muhl). The more thermal energy an object has, the faster its particles move. You feel thermal energy as heat. **Heat** is the flow of thermal energy from warmer objects to cooler objects. Thermal energy is sometimes called heat energy.

A welder uses heat to melt metal. The thermal energy from the hot flames moves to the cooler metal object.

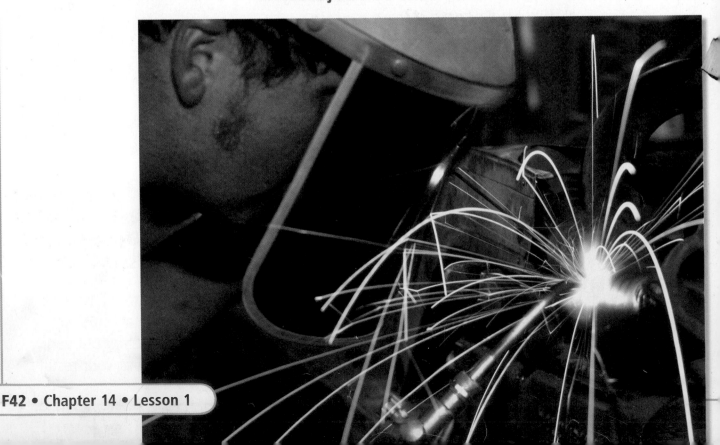

Why does your hand feel cold when you hold an ice cube? Thermal energy from your hand moves to the ice cube. The ice melts because its particles have gained thermal energy. A warm mug of hot chocolate heats your hands because thermal energy from the mug moves to your cooler hands.

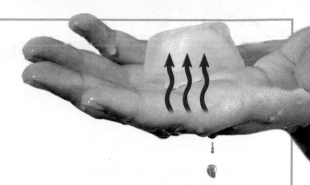

▲ When you hold an ice cube, thermal energy from your warm hand moves to the cold ice. Your hand feels cold because it has lost thermal energy.

Look below to see how thermal energy moves from the hot cereal. After a few minutes, the cereal is cooler and the spoon is warmer. If you held your hand over the cereal, you would feel the heat. The spoon and air have gained thermal energy, so they have become warmer. The cereal has lost thermal energy, so it has become cooler. This flow of thermal energy will continue until the cereal, the air, and the spoon are all equally warm.

▶ CAUSE AND EFFECT What causes an object to feel warm when you touch it?

◀ Thermal energy moves from the hot cereal to the cooler spoon and cooler surrounding air.

▲ The heat lamp changes electrical energy into thermal energy that keeps these chicks warm. The lamp also gives off light energy.

Producing Thermal Energy

There are many forms of energy. You have learned about light energy, electrical energy, mechanical energy, sound energy, and chemical energy. Each of these forms of energy can change into thermal energy. This is how thermal energy is produced. Electrical appliances such as toasters, electric stoves, and hair dryers all use electrical energy to produce thermal energy.

You have probably noticed that you feel warm when you stand in the sunlight. That is because the Sun gives off energy that becomes thermal energy and light energy.

Did you know that you can also produce thermal energy? You have probably noticed that when you rub your hands together, they get warm. This happens because friction (FRIHK shuhn) produces thermal energy. **Friction** is a force that occurs when one object rubs against another object. Friction slows down and stops motion between two surfaces that touch.

Another way to produce thermal energy is by changing chemical energy to thermal energy. Why do you feel heat from a campfire? When wood is burned, the chemical energy stored in the wood changes to thermal energy. Your body is warm because it changes the chemical energy stored in the food you eat to thermal energy. When you squeeze a thermal pack, chemicals inside it combine to produce thermal energy. The chemical energy stored inside the pack changes to thermal energy.

▲ How does this thermal pack get warm?

▶ **CAUSE AND EFFECT** What causes your hands to get warm when you rub them together?

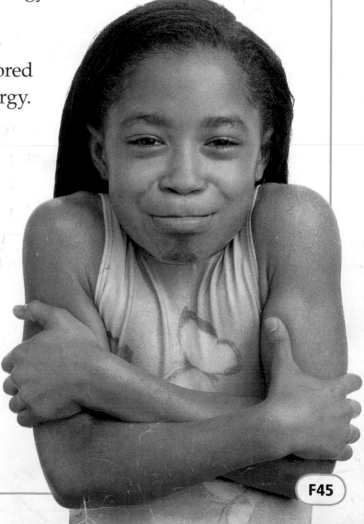

Quickly rubbing your arms can make you feel warmer when you are cold. Friction between your moving hands and your arms produces thermal energy. ▶

Thermal energy can be used to cook a pizza.

Using Thermal Energy

People use thermal energy for many things. People who live in cold climates use thermal energy to heat their homes. In factories, thermal energy is used to melt steel so that it can be shaped to build cars, refrigerators, and other useful things. People use thermal energy to cook food. What are some ways you use thermal energy?

 **CAUSE AND EFFECT** **What is the effect of thermal energy on steel?**

Visual Summary

Heat is the flow of thermal energy from warmer objects to cooler objects.

Other forms of energy can be changed into thermal energy.

Thermal energy has many uses, including heating homes and cooking food.

LINKS for Home and School

TECHNOLOGY Write an Explanatory Paragraph

An insulator is a material that prevents the transfer of heat, electricity, or sound. What is the best insulator for heat? The best insulator is nothing at all. Research how a vacuum flask works. Write a paragraph that explains how a vacuum can be used to keep a drink hot or cold.

SOCIAL STUDIES Role-Play an Interview

Most mammals have fur coats that keep them warm. Birds have feathers to do the job. With a partner, role-play an imaginary interview between a human reporter and a mammal or bird. Discuss the advantages and disadvantages of having fur or feathers.

Review

❶ **MAIN IDEA** How does thermal energy move?

❷ **VOCABULARY** What is friction?

❸ **READING SKILL: Cause and Effect** What is the effect of rubbing your hands together?

❹ **CRITICAL THINKING: Evaluate** You hold a cup of ice water, and your hand becomes cold. A friend says that it is cold because the cold from the cup moved to your hand. Is your friend's statement correct? Explain.

❺ **INQUIRY SKILL: Compare** How is the way a toaster produces thermal energy different from the way a thermal pack produces thermal energy?

 TEST PREP
Heat is the flow of ___.

A. chemical energy.

B. thermal energy.

C. electrical energy.

D. kinetic energy.

 Technology
Visit **www.eduplace.com/scp/** to learn more about thermal energy.

What Is Temperature?

Why It Matters...

What is the temperature outside? Is it hot or cold? You can measure to find out. Knowing what this measurement means can help you plan your day. On a cold day, you might wear a jacket. On a very hot day, you might go to the beach and have a cold drink.

PREPARE TO INVESTIGATE

Inquiry Skill

Predict When you predict, you state what you think will happen based on observations and experiences.

Materials

- metal spoon
- strip thermometer
- bowl
- warm water
- thermometer
- clock or watch

Science and Math Toolbox

For steps 2 through 5, review **Using a Thermometer** on page H8.

Track Temperature

Procedure

1. In your *Science Notebook*, make a chart like the one shown.

2. **Measure** Attach a strip thermometer to a metal spoon. Read the strip thermometer and record the temperature on your chart.

3. **Measure** Fill a bowl halfway with warm water. Use a regular thermometer to measure the water temperature. Record the temperature on your chart.

4. **Predict** Place the spoon in the bowl. Make sure the strip thermometer does not touch the water. Predict whether the temperatures of the spoon and the water will change over time. Record your prediction.

5. **Record Data** Record the temperatures of the spoon and the water after 5 minutes, and again after 10 minutes.

Conclusion

1. **Communicate** Use your data to make two bar graphs. One should show how the temperature of the spoon changed. The other graph should show how the temperature of the water changed.

2. **Analyze Data** Describe how the temperatures of the spoon and the water changed over time.

STEP 1

| | Temperature | | |
	Start	5 Minutes	10 Minutes
Spoon			
Water			

STEP 2

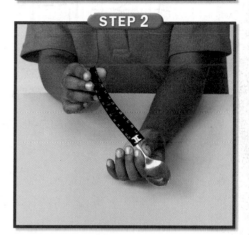

STEP 4

Investigate More!

Design an Experiment
Predict what will happen to the temperature of the cold spoon and the warm water after 1 hour. Design and conduct an experiment to find out.

▶ **READING SKILL**

Compare and Contrast
Use a chart to list the degrees Fahrenheit and degrees Celsius at which water freezes and boils.

Measuring Temperature

MAIN IDEA Temperature is measured using a thermometer. Temperature can be measured in degrees Fahrenheit or in degrees Celsius.

Measuring Temperature

When weather announcers tell if it is hot or cold out, they report the air temperature (TEHM pur uh chur). **Temperature** is a measure of how hot or cold something is. The tool that is used to measure temperature is a **thermometer** (thur MAHM ih tur). There are several kinds of thermometers. Some thermometers measure the temperature in an oven. Some thermometers measure the temperature of the air indoors or outdoors. And if you have ever had a fever, you know that some thermometers measure the temperature of your body.

A meat thermometer is used to tell when meat has cooked long enough.

Temperature is measured in units called degrees. Just as a ruler shows inches and centimeters, a thermometer shows degrees Fahrenheit (FAR-uhn hyt) and degrees Celsius (SEHL-see uhs). Fahrenheit and Celsius are two different scales for measuring temperature. For example, boiling water in a pan on the stove would be described as 212°F or 100°C.

▶ **COMPARE AND CONTRAST** **Compare the temperature at which water boils on the Fahrenheit scale and the Celsius scale.**

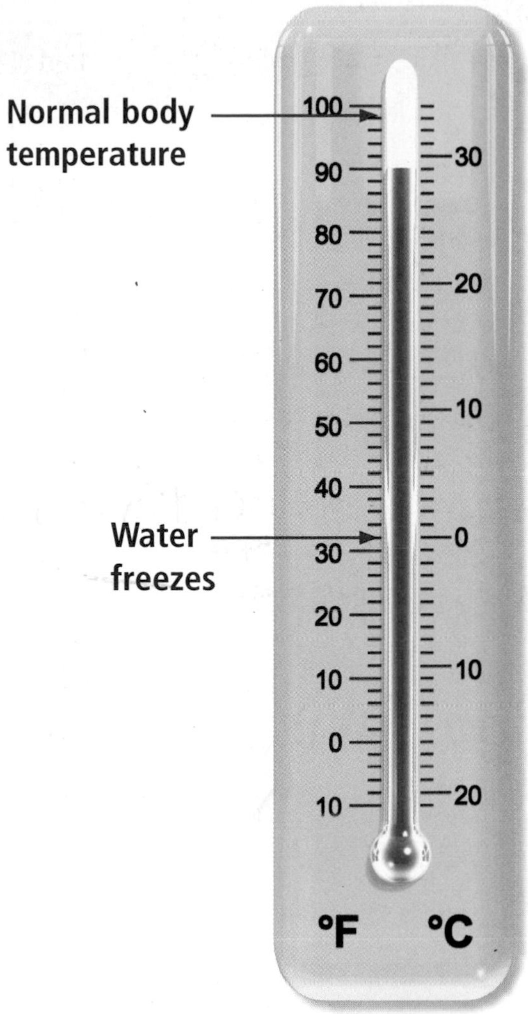

Normal body temperature is 98.6°F (37.0°C). An ear thermometer is one way to measure body temperature. ▼

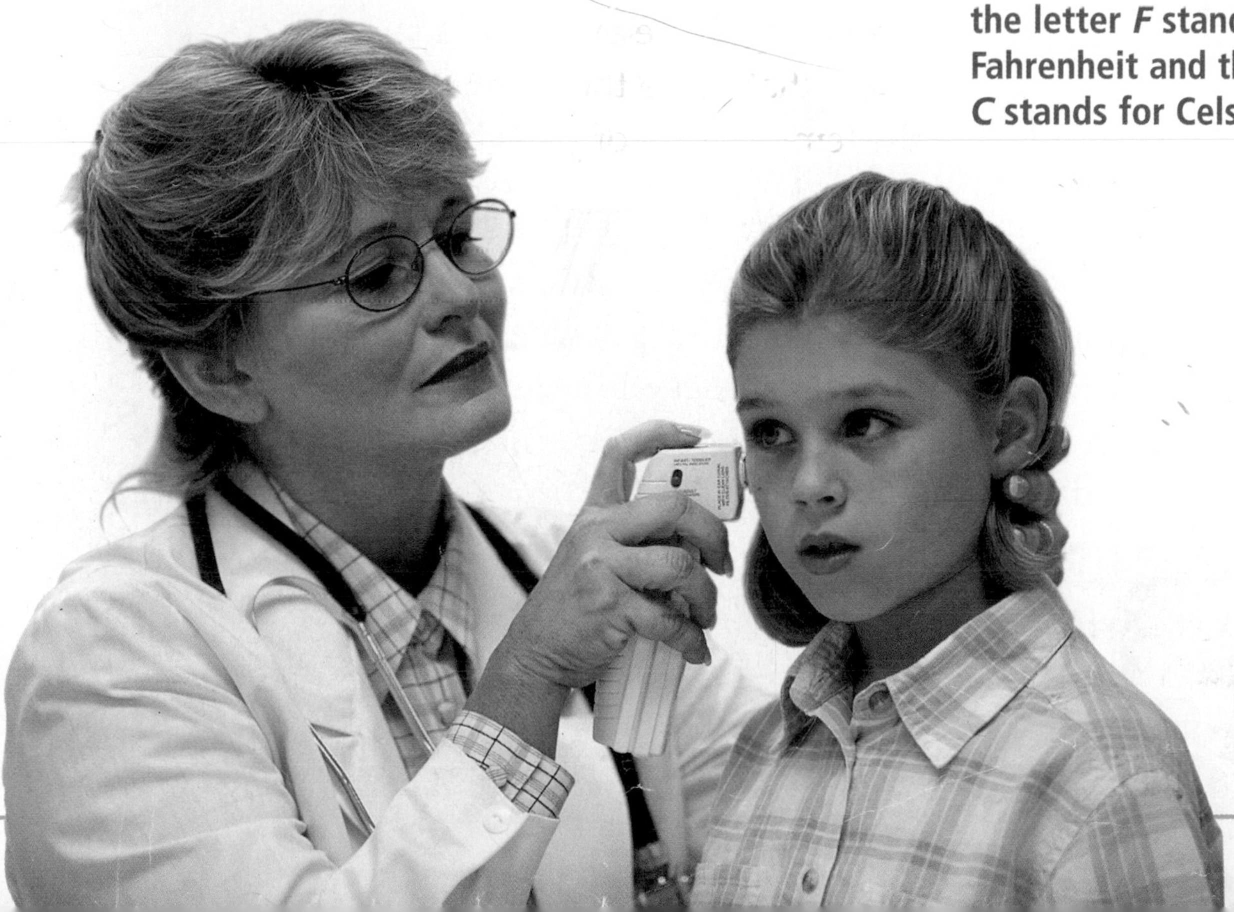

Normal body temperature

Water freezes

°F   °C

▲ On this thermometer, the letter *F* stands for Fahrenheit and the letter *C* stands for Celsius.

On a warm day, the particles of the liquid in the outdoor thermometer move faster and spread out.

On a cold day, the particles of the liquid move slower and take up less space.

How a Thermometer Works

Compare the thermometers shown above. You can see that the liquid in the warmer thermometer is higher in the tube. As temperature increases, the particles of the liquid move faster and spread out. This causes the liquid to take up more space and rise up the tube. As temperature decreases, the particles of liquid slow down and move closer together. The liquid takes up less space and moves down the tube.

▶ **COMPARE AND CONTRAST** Describe how the motion of the particles of a warm liquid is different than the motion of the particles of a cool liquid.

Visual Summary

Temperature is a measure of how hot or cold something is.

°F
Temperature can be measured in degrees Fahrenheit.

°C
Temperature can be measured in degrees Celsius.

 **for Home and School**

MATH Using Negative Numbers In 1922, a temperature of 58°C was recorded in Libya. The space probe Voyager 2 recorded a temperature of −235°C on Triton, a moon of Neptune, in 1989. And on January 5, 1974, the temperature in Hope Bay, Antarctica, was 15°C. Write the temperatures 58°C, −235°C, and 15°C in order, from coldest to warmest.

WRITING Story People often use exaggeration or similes when they talk about temperature. On a hot summer day, you might say, "It's boiling outside!" In an air-conditioned room, you might think, "I'm as cool as a cucumber." Write a short story about temperature using at least four examples of exaggeration and simile.

Review

❶ **MAIN IDEA** What is temperature?

❷ **VOCABULARY** Use the term *thermometer* in a sentence.

❸ **READING SKILL: Compare and Contrast** Compare what happens to the particles of liquid in a thermometer when the temperature increases and when it decreases.

❹ **CRITICAL THINKING: Apply** Your thermometer reads 85 degrees. Your friend's thermometer reads 30 degrees. It is very hot in both places. Explain how this can be true.

❺ **INQUIRY SKILL: Predict** Two thermometers are placed outdoors 1 m apart. One is in shade, and the other is in direct sunlight. Predict which will show a higher temperature after 20 minutes.

 TEST PREP
A thermometer can be used in an oven to measure ___.

A. mass.

B. length.

C. volume.

D. temperature.

 Technology
Visit **www.eduplace.com/scp/** to learn more about temperature.

Thermometers Through Time

How can heat be measured? In the late 1500s, the Italian scientist Galileo Galilei discussed this question with his friends in Padua, Italy.

Galileo built a thermoscope. He placed a glass bottle with a narrow neck upside down in water. Water in the neck trapped air in the bottle. As the room got warmer, the air in the bottle expanded. The air pushed down the water level. As the room cooled, the air contracted. The water level rose. The thermoscope showed changes in air temperature.

▼ Anders Celsius

Anders Celsius invents the centigrade scale. Later it is renamed the Celsius scale.

1592 A.D. | **1714** | **1742** | **1848**

Galileo Galilei invents the thermoscope.

Galileo Gallilei ▶

Daniel Gabriel Fahrenheit invents the first reliable mercury thermometer.

Lord Kelvin of Scotland proposes a new temperature scale. On the Kelvin scale, 0° represents the coldest temperature possible, and is called "absolute zero."

Later scientists used Galileo's idea to build thermometers that measure temperature according to a scale. The Fahrenheit, Celsius, and Kelvin scales are still in use today.

The metal tag on the lowest floating bubble tells the temperature. ▼

Galileo thermometer
These thermometers have glass bubbles floating in water. As the temperature of the air changes the bubbles rise and fall. ▶

2006

Modern thermometers use electricity, infrared energy, and even fiber optics.

Sharing Ideas

1. **READING CHECK** What problem was Galileo trying to solve when he invented the thermoscope?

2. **WRITE ABOUT IT** Write a lab manual entry that Fahrenheit might have made to describe his thermometer.

3. **TALK ABOUT IT** Discuss an example of how another scientist improved on Galileo's invention.

What Is Light?

Why It Matters...

You would probably notice the flashing lights on a sign at an amusement park. But do you notice the light that surrounds you every day? Light shines from the Sun. It also shines from colored light bulbs like the ones below. Right now, you are using light to read this book. Without light, you could not see the world around you.

Inquiry Skill

Observe When you observe, you gather information about the environment using your five senses: sight, smell, touch, taste, and hearing.

Materials

- flashlight
- sheet of paper
- mirror
- piece of clear plastic wrap

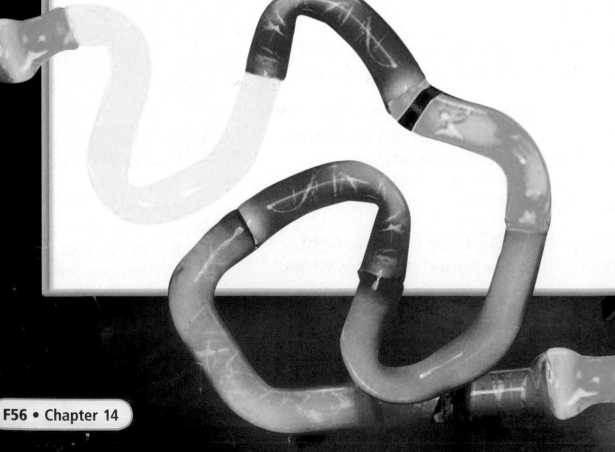

Shining Light
Procedure

STEP 1

1. **Collaborate** Work with a partner. Hold a sheet of paper about 10 cm above a table. Ask your partner to shine a flashlight straight down onto the paper.

2. **Observe** Observe the light on the paper. See if light from the flashlight is shining anywhere else. Write your observations in your *Science Notebook*.

STEP 3

3. Hold a mirror above the table. Again, have your partner shine the flashlight straight down onto the mirror.

4. **Record Data** Observe the light on the mirror. Look to see if the light shines anywhere else. Record your observations.

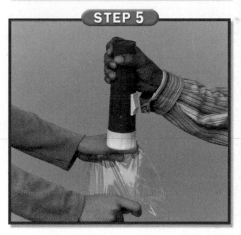
STEP 5

5. Hold a piece of clear plastic wrap while your partner shines a flashlight over it.

6. **Observe** Observe the light on the plastic wrap. See if the light shines anywhere else. Record your observations.

Conclusion

1. **Analyze Data** Describe how the light acted when you shined it on the paper, on the mirror, and on the plastic wrap.

2. **Hypothesize** Write a hypothesis to explain why the light acted differently each time.

Investigate More!

Design an Experiment Predict how the light would look if you shined the flashlight on wax paper, aluminum foil, and a glass of water. Test your predictions.

Light

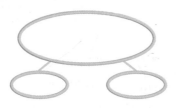
MAIN IDEA Light travels as waves. When light waves hit an object, they are absorbed or change direction.

Energy You Can See

Did you see your shadow today? You probably did if the Sun was shining. The Sun is a source of light. **Light** is a form of energy that you can see. Like sound, light travels as waves. Light waves move in one direction, away from their source. Unlike sound, light does not need matter to carry it. Light can travel through empty space. This is how light from the Sun reaches Earth and other planets.

You can see several shadows around this astronaut. Light waves travel through empty space, but are blocked by some materials.

You see shadows on sunny days because some matter blocks light waves. Wood, metal, and brick all block light. So does your body. Other matter, such as air, water, and glass, lets light pass through. This is why you can see under water.

You may have been warned not to touch light bulbs because they are hot. Many light sources give off heat in addition to light. You can probably name some other examples, such as the Sun and fire.

Most objects, however, do not give off their own light. You see most objects because light from another source bounces off them and into your eyes. You see the Moon from Earth because light from the Sun bounces off the surface of the Moon. This is also how you see your pencil, a desk, or any other object that does not give off its own light.

▲ Powerful lights in this stadium make night seem like day

When electricity passes through the thin wire inside the bulb, the wire gets very hot and begins to glow. ▼

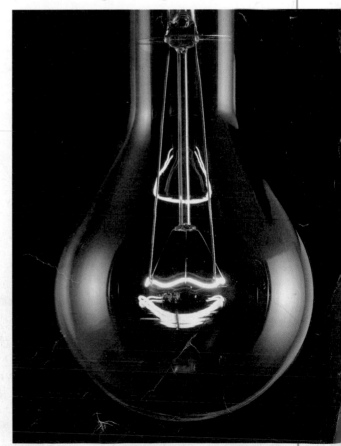

▶ **MAIN IDEA** **How does light travel?**

Bouncing Light

Light waves travel in straight lines. What they do when they hit an object depends on the object's surface. Light waves **reflect** (rih FLEHKT) from, or bounce off, objects that have a smooth, shiny surface. When light waves reflect off a mirror, for example, the waves bounce back toward you. You see yourself in the mirror because light waves bounce directly back to your eye.

Most objects do not have such smooth, shiny surfaces. When light waves hit most objects, like the Moon or a pencil, they bounce back in many different directions. You do not see your face reflected by the object. You just see the object.

▲ Mirrors make this one girl appear like a whole group of girls.

Sometimes the surface of water is very smooth. When it is, water reflects light like a mirror. ▼

◀ Light waves are bent as they move from the air into the water. This causes the pencil to look like it is in two pieces.

Bending Light

Light waves can pass through some materials, but their straight path is changed. Light waves refract (rih FRAKT) when they move from air to water. To **refract** is to bend. Refracted light makes objects look bent, broken, or wavy. The pencil above looks like it is broken in two pieces because light is bent by the water.

Glass is another material that refracts light. The lenses in eyeglasses are curved to bend light. This helps people who wear glasses see better. A hand lens, which is also curved, refracts light to make an object look larger.

▶ **MAIN IDEA** What happens to light when it moves from one material to another?

Light is refracted by this lens. How is this useful? ▼

Colors and Light

Look at the bands of color that appear as light shines through the glass crystals. This shows that light is made up of all the colors of the rainbow.

When white light shines on a colored object, the surface of the object absorbs (uhb SAWRBZ), or takes in, some of the light waves that strike it. So the object absorbs some colors. The object reflects other colors. You see the reflected colors but not the absorbed colors. Bananas look yellow because they reflect yellow light. They absorb other colors.

MAIN IDEA **Why does a banana look yellow?**

▲ When white sunlight passes through a prism, each color of light bends differently and separates to form a rainbow.

A lime looks green because it reflects green light and absorbs the other colors of light. ▶

Visual Summary

Light travels in waves and can pass through empty space.

When light hits an object, the light changes direction. It can reflect, refract, or be absorbed.

When white light hits an object, you see only the reflected colors. The other colors are absorbed.

LINKS for Home and School

MATH **Use Plane Figures** Cut three different shapes from cardboard or heavy paper. Use a light source and the cutouts to cast shadows against a wall. How does the shape and size of each shadow compare with the shape and size of its cutout? Change the angle and distance of the light source. Describe any differences.

LITERATURE **Write a Poem** Read the poems about light in *Flicker Flash* by Joan Bransfield Graham. Write an original poem about light in the same style. Arrange the lines of your poem so that they resemble a shape or object related to light.

Review

1 MAIN IDEA What is light and how does it travel?

2 VOCABULARY Use the term *reflect* in a sentence.

3 READING SKILL: Main Idea and Details List some details that support the following main idea: *When light travels, it is blocked by some materials.*

4 CRITICAL THINKING: Evaluate Your friend tells you that red apples have only red light in them. How would you evaluate this statement?

5 INQUIRY SKILL: Observe A spoon in a glass of water looks bent. Is the spoon really bent? Explain.

TEST PREP
All of the following give off their own light except ___.

A. the Moon

B. the Sun

C. a fire

D. a light bulb

 Technology
Visit **www.eduplace.com/scp/** to find out more about light.

EXTREME Science

Mighty Mirrors

What do all these mirrors do? They collect sunlight over a huge area. Then they reflect all that energy into a very small area. The place where all this sunlight comes together gets extremely hot. How hot? Would you believe $4,000^\circ$ C, or $7,200^\circ$ F? That's so hot you could actually melt a diamond, the hardest substance on Earth!

This huge sunlight collection and concentration system is called a solar furnace. Scientists can use the extreme thermal energy of a solar furnace to test the effects of high temperatures on various materials.

The Odeillo solar furnace in the Pyrenees Mountains of France is the world's biggest. The curved face of the collector is over 120 feet high and has 1,830 individual mirrors.

People can use thermal energy collected in small solar ovens like this to cook food.

Vocabulary

Complete each sentence with a term from the list.

1. A force that slows down and stops motion between two surfaces that touch is called _____.

2. When light waves bounce off an object, they _____.

3. A tool used to measure temperature is a _____.

4. The energy of moving particles of matter is called _____.

5. The measure of the hotness or coldness of something is called _____.

6. To bend light is to _____.

7. The flow of thermal energy from warmer objects to cooler objects is called _____.

8. A form of energy that you can see is called _____.

friction F45
heat F42
light F58
reflect F60
refract F61
temperature F50
thermal energy F42
thermometer F50

Test Prep

Write the letter of the best answer choice.

9. A sweater looks blue if it _____.

   A. refracts blue light
   B. reflects blue light
   C. absorbs blue light
   D. reflects all light

10. When the thermal energy of an object increases, the particles in the object _____.

   A. stop moving
   B. start moving
   C. slow down
   D. speed up

11. Degrees Fahrenheit and degrees Celsius are used to measure _____.

   A. length
   B. volume
   C. temperature
   D. friction

12. Your body stays warm because it makes thermal energy from the stored _____ energy in food.

   A. chemical
   B. light
   C. mechanical
   D. electrical

13. **Observe** While playing outside in the afternoon, you notice that a long shadow seems to follow you everywhere. What causes the shadow?

14. **Predict** You take a metal spoon out of a drawer and put it in a cup of hot cocoa. Predict how the temperature of the spoon will change. Explain why you made your prediction.

15. **Compare** A wooden jewelry box sits on a dresser in front of a mirror. Compare what happens to light waves that bounce off the mirror and light waves that bounce off the jewelry box. How can you see this difference?

16. **Communicate** Write a paragraph describing three examples of how you use thermal energy. For each example, discuss what type of energy is changed into thermal energy.

17. **Synthesize** You get home after school and take a warm juice box out of your backpack. You place the juice box in the refrigerator. After an hour, will the particles of juice be moving more quickly or more slowly than they were when the box was in your backpack? Explain.

18. **Analyze** The brakes on a bicycle use friction to stop the wheels. If someone is riding downhill and uses the brakes often, how will the temperature of the brakes change? Explain.

19. **Apply** A flower stem in a glass vase filled with water looks broken. You take the flower out and see that it's not broken. Why did the stem look broken in the vase?

20. **Evaluate** Your friend tells you that the liquid in a thermometer rises when the temperature increases because heat rises. Evaluate this statement.

Map the Concept

Use the following terms to fill in the blanks:

refract   thermal energy   reflect
heat   light   flow

> **1. A light bulb produces both _____ and _____.**
>
> **2. When a light wave hits an object, it can _____ or _____.**
>
> **3. Heat is the _____ of _____ from warmer objects to cooler objects.**

Performance Assessment

Report a "Heat Wave"

A heat wave is a period of unusually hot weather. Write a newspaper article about a heat wave that occurs in an imaginary town. Use the terms *temperature*, *thermometer*, and *degrees* in your article. Include as many additional vocabulary terms from this chapter as you can. Draw a picture of a thermometer to illustrate your article.

Chapter 15

Force and Motion

LESSON 1

From the push of the wind on a sail to the pulls in a game of tug of war—what forces can cause a change in motion?

Read about it in Lesson 1.

LESSON 2

A soaring baseball, a racing car, and a running cheetah—how are distance, direction, and speed used to describe motion?

Read about it in Lesson 2.

LESSON 3

From a doorknob to a bicycle—how do machines make life easier?

Read about it in Lesson 3.

How Do Forces Affect Objects?

Why It Matters...

Have you ever played with magnets? Many toys, like the one shown here, use magnets. You may use magnets on your refrigerator door at home. Those magnets keep things in place. Other magnets make things move. Magnets can even be used to make electricity.

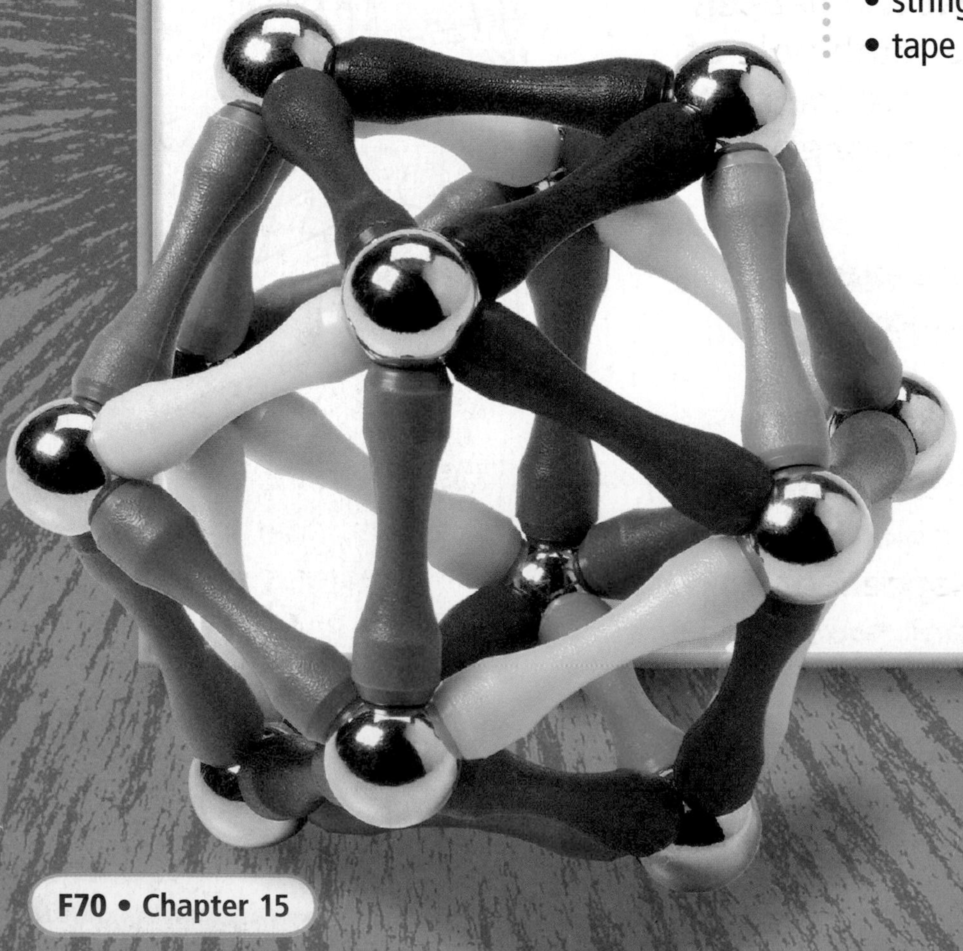

PREPARE TO INVESTIGATE

Inquiry Skill

Predict When you predict, you state what you think will happen based on your observations and experiences.

Materials

- 2 bar magnets
- string
- tape

Polar Opposites
Procedure

STEP 1

1. **Collaborate** Work with a partner. Tie one end of a string around the middle of a bar magnet. Tape the other end of the string to the edge of a table so the magnet hangs above the floor.

2. **Predict** Predict what will happen when you bring the north pole of a second magnet near the north pole of the hanging magnet. Record your prediction in your *Science Notebook*.

STEP 3

3. **Experiment** Test your prediction. Record your observations.

4. **Predict** Predict what will happen when you bring the south pole of the second magnet near the north pole of the hanging magnet. Record your prediction.

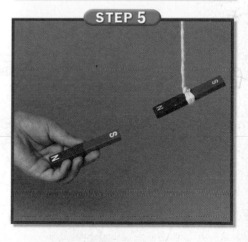

STEP 5

5. **Experiment** Test your prediction. Record your observations.

Conclusion

1. **Analyze Data** What happened when you brought the two north poles near each other? What happened when you brought the north and south poles near each other?

2. **Predict** What do you think would happen if you brought the two south poles of the magnets near each other?

Investigate More!

Research Do research in the library or on the Internet to find a way that magnets are used to create motion. Write a short paragraph describing what you learn.

Forces

MAIN IDEA Forces can change the motion of objects. Gravity, magnetism, and friction are forces.

Motion, Pushes, and Pulls

Suppose your chair is next to the wall, but you want the chair to be near your desk. How would you get it there? You would move it, of course. Moving it would change its position, or place. The change in position of an object is called **motion** (MOH shuhn). Motion occurs any time an object moves from one position to another. The furniture in the room shown is in motion. The children who are moving the furniture are also in motion.

These children are using forces to move the furniture in the room.

PUSH

PULL

How are the children using forces to arrange the books?

Think again about moving your chair. To change the chair's position, you would have to use a force on it. A **force** (fawrs) is a push or a pull. A push moves an object away from you. A pull moves an object toward you.

Any change in motion needs a force. You use a force to start a motion. You also use a force to speed up, slow down, or stop a motion. And you use a force to change the direction of a motion. Using a stronger force causes a bigger change in the motion.

▶ CAUSE AND EFFECT What is needed to change a motion?

Gravity

What force affects all matter on Earth, even air? What force keeps juice in your glass and your glass on the table? The force is gravity (GRAV ih tee). **Gravity** is a force that pulls objects toward each other. For example, Earth's gravity pulls objects toward the center of Earth. It causes objects to fall to the ground and water to flow downhill. Gravity exists between all objects, not just between Earth and other objects.

Gravity acts on objects without touching them. For example, Earth's gravity pulls on objects in space, such as the space shuttle or the Moon. The strength of gravity depends on the mass of each object. There is more gravity between objects that have greater masses. Earth has a large mass, so there is a strong pull between Earth and other objects on or near it.

An object's weight is a measure of how strongly Earth's gravity pulls on the object. Objects with greater mass are heavier than objects with less mass.

◄ Gravity pulls the glass toward Earth. The force of gravity is strong enough to break the glass as it strikes the floor.

Magnetism

Magnetism (MAG nih tihz uhm) is a force that pushes or pulls objects made of iron or nickel. It has little effect on objects made of other materials. All magnets have two poles: a north pole and a south pole.

Unlike poles pull toward each other. When the north pole of one magnet is brought near the south pole of another magnet, the magnets pull together. Like poles push away from each other. A magnet's force is strongest at the poles. Like gravity, magnetism can act on an object without touching it.

▶ **CAUSE AND EFFECT** **How does an object's mass affect its gravity?**

Like poles of magnets push away from each other.

Unlike poles of magnets pull toward each other.

The globe "floats" in the air because magnets in the globe push away from magnets in the stand.

F75

Friction

Friction is a force that slows down and stops motion between two surfaces that touch. There is more friction between rough or sticky surfaces than there is between smooth or slippery surfaces.

Friction can be useful. Without friction, your feet would slip and slide on the floor when you tried to walk. Sometimes friction is not useful. Friction can slow down machines and wear out their parts. Many machines use oil to make surfaces slippery and reduce friction.

▶ **CAUSE AND EFFECT** **What types of surfaces have less friction between them?**

▲ The smooth blade of the ice skate reduces friction between the blade and the ice. The rough tip increases friction. It helps the skater to start and stop on ice.

The soft cloth and smooth slide reduce friction, allowing a fast ride. ▶

Lesson Wrap-Up

Visual Summary

A force is needed to change a motion. Gravity pulls objects toward each other.

Magnetism is a force that pushes or pulls some materials.

Friction is a force that slows down and stops the motion of two surfaces that touch.

LINKS for Home and School

MATH **Order Numbers** The strengths of gravity of the six planets closest to the Sun are compared in the table. List the numbers in order, from least to greatest.

Mercury	Venus	Earth	Mars	Jupiter	Saturn
0.4	0.91	1.0	0.38	2.6	1.06

TECHNOLOGY **Build a Compass**
Rub a magnet 50 times along a needle in one direction. Float a cork in water and lay the needle on it. Earth's magnetic field will pull the needle toward the North Pole. Gently spin the cork. Which way does the needle point when the cork stops moving? Move the cup. Did the needle change direction?

Review

❶ **MAIN IDEA** What is a force?

❷ **VOCABULARY** Define the term *motion*.

❸ **READING SKILL: Cause and Effect** What effect does Earth's gravity have on objects on or near it?

❹ **CRITICAL THINKING: Apply** The brakes of a train grind against its wheels to stop the train. What force do the brakes use?

❺ **INQUIRY SKILL: Predict** You push a box across a rough concrete floor. Your friend pushes a box across a smooth tile floor. The boxes have equal masses. Predict which box will slide more easily.

✓ **TEST PREP**
A magnet pushes or pulls objects made of ___.

A. wood

B. plastic

C. copper

D. iron

Technology
Visit www.eduplace.com/scp/ to find out more about forces.

How Can Motion Be Described?

Why It Matters...

How would you describe the motion of the athlete in this picture? Fast? In a straight line? You can describe motion by saying how far, in what direction, and how fast an object moves.

PREPARE TO INVESTIGATE

Inquiry Skill

Communicate When you communicate, you share information using words, actions, sketches, graphs, tables, and diagrams.

Materials

- 2 marbles
- shallow bowl
- metric ruler

Science and Math Toolbox

For step 4, review **Using a Tape Measure or Ruler** on page H6.

Moving Marbles
Procedure

STEP 1

1. **Observe** Place one marble against the inside of a bowl. Push the marble so that it spins around the inside of the bowl. Observe the marble's motion as it moves inside the bowl.

2. **Communicate** In your *Science Notebook*, describe the motion of the marble. Describe its speed and its direction.

STEP 3

3. **Observe** Set two marbles next to each other on the floor. Gently push one of the marbles straight ahead. Then push the second marble straight ahead, but with more force. Describe how far each marble moved.

4. **Experiment** Set both marbles on the floor, about 10 cm apart. Gently roll the second marble so that it strikes the first marble. Describe the motions of the two marbles.

STEP 4

Conclusion

1. **Analyze Data** In step 1, how did the marble move inside the bowl?

2. **Analyze Data** In step 4, how did the first marble behave when the second marble struck it?

3. **Communicate** Draw diagrams to show the motions of the marbles in steps 1, 3, and 4.

Investigate More!

Be an Inventor Invent a device that uses marbles in a fun way. Your device should use different types of motion. Draw a sketch, and use arrows to show how the marbles move.

VOCABULARY

direction	p. F83
distance	p. F82
speed	p. F84

READING SKILL

Text Structure
Complete a word web. Write the term *motion* in a center circle. Write a main idea from each section of the lesson in outer circles.

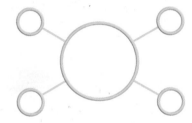

Moving Objects

MAIN IDEA You can describe the motion of an object by its distance, direction, and speed.

Position and Motion

Motion is a change in position. You can describe an object's position by comparing it to other objects around it. The athlete in the photo stands behind the foul line before he starts to run. As he moves, his position changes. He moves closer to the foul line, then leaps above it. Finally, he comes down in the landing pit.

Motion can change the potential and kinetic energy of objects. For example, the athlete has more potential energy when he is above the ground than when he is on the ground. He also has more kinetic energy when he runs than when he moves more slowly.

Every change in motion needs a force. A force is a push or pull that passes energy between two objects. Some forces, such as gravity and magnetism, can pass energy between objects even when the objects are not touching. Other forces, such as friction, can pass energy between objects only when the objects are touching.

What forces change the motion of the athlete? The athlete pushes against the ground to run. He also pushes against the ground to lift himself into the air. He uses friction between the sand in the landing pit and his feet to stop.

▶ TEXT STRUCTURE **What would be a good section title for the text on this page?**

The position of the long jumper changes from the time he leaves the ground to the time he lands.

Distance

Distance (DIHS tuhns) is a measure of length. You can describe the motion of an object by measuring the distance it travels. For example, a baseball player hits a ball at home plate. The ball travels to the center field wall. You can find the distance the ball traveled by measuring the distance from home plate to the center field wall.

How far must a baseball be hit in Wrigley Field to hit the center field wall?

When you apply a greater force, an object travels a longer distance. The distance a ball must travel to hit the center field wall varies for different ballparks. The distance from home plate to the center field wall at Fenway Park is greater than it is at Dodger Stadium. So, a player must hit the ball harder for it to reach the center field wall at Fenway Park than at Dodger Stadium.

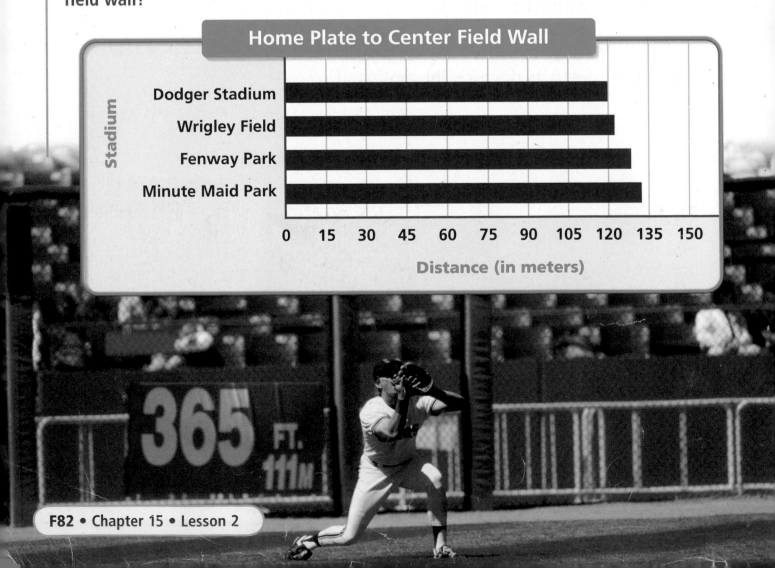

Home Plate to Center Field Wall

Stadium

- Dodger Stadium
- Wrigley Field
- Fenway Park
- Minute Maid Park

0 15 30 45 60 75 90 105 120 135 150

Distance (in meters)

Direction

Direction (di REHK shuhn) is the path an object follows. You can use direction to describe the motion of an object. Direction tells where the object is going. You can find the direction of an object by comparing its position now with its position at an earlier time.

Look at the photos. You can find the direction of the cars or planes by comparing their positions now with their earlier positions. You could describe the direction of a plane or car by saying that it is moving east or turning right. Like other changes in motion, a change in direction is caused by a force.

▲ You can describe the motion of the planes by describing the direction of their movement.

▶ **TEXT STRUCTURE** Based on the headings, identify two ways to describe the motion of an object.

◀ The cars entering and exiting this highway are traveling around curves. Their direction keeps changing as they turn.

▲ Sloths are known for their slow speed. A sloth travels only about 0.2 km (0.1 mi) in an hour.

Speed

Speed is a measure of how fast or slow an object is moving. Speed is another way to describe motion. Look at the animals shown. A cheetah is one of the fastest animals, and a sloth is one of the slowest. Some objects, such as a plant bending toward the light, move so slowly that you cannot see their motion. You know the object has moved only when you see that its position has changed over time. You can measure speed by finding the distance an object travels in a certain time. For example, a cheetah can run almost 30 m (98 ft) in one second.

 **TEXT STRUCTURE** How is speed related to motion?

A hummingbird's wings move so quickly that they look like a blur. ▼

◄ Cheetahs are the fastest animals on land. Some cheetahs can run almost 2 km (1 mi) in 1 minute.

Visual Summary

Motion is a change in position. The motion of an object can be described by the distance it travels.

The direction of an object is the path the object follows.

The speed of an object tells you how fast or slow the object is traveling

LINKS for Home and School

WRITING **Narrative** Write a paragraph that describes a trip you have taken in a car, bus, train, boat, or airplane. Use direction words such as *right, left, up, down, north, south, east,* and *west.* Use speed words such as *fast, slow, quickly,* and *slowly.* And use distance words such as *kilometers, near, far, long,* and *short.*

ART **Draw a Cartoon** Cartoonists often need to show objects in motion. Look through the comics pages of a newspaper. Observe the ways cartoonists show speed and direction. Draw a cartoon. Use what you observed, or your own ideas, to show motion.

Review

❶ MAIN IDEA What are three ways you can describe the motion of an object?

❷ VOCABULARY What does *distance* mean?

❸ READING SKILL: Text Structure Write a heading that could introduce the sections *Distance, Direction,* and *Speed.*

❹ CRITICAL THINKING: Analyze Use distance, speed, and direction to describe the motions of playing on a playground slide.

❺ INQUIRY SKILL: Communicate Make a simple map of your classroom. Draw a line that represents your motion as you travel from the door to your desk. Make sure the line shows distance and direction.

✔ TEST PREP
How fast or slow an object is moving is its ___.

A. distance.

B. direction.

C. speed.

D. force.

 Technology
Visit **www.eduplace.com/scp/** to find out more about describing motion.

Ups and Downs

Wheeeeee! In 1884, shouts of excitement rang through the air at Coney Island, New York. The first gravity-powered roller coaster raced up and down over tracks.

The *Gravity Switchback Railway*, as it was called, traveled at almost 10 km (about 6 mi) in an hour. The train had two flat steel tracks that were nailed to wooden planks. It used the force of gravity to move. The ride started up high, and the car picked up speed as the tracks dipped.

The riders had to do some work, too. To board the roller coaster, they had to climb stairs to a platform at the top of the first hill. At only five cents a ride, getting a thrill and some exercise was a bargain!

This painting shows what it was like to ride a roller coaster in the 1800s.

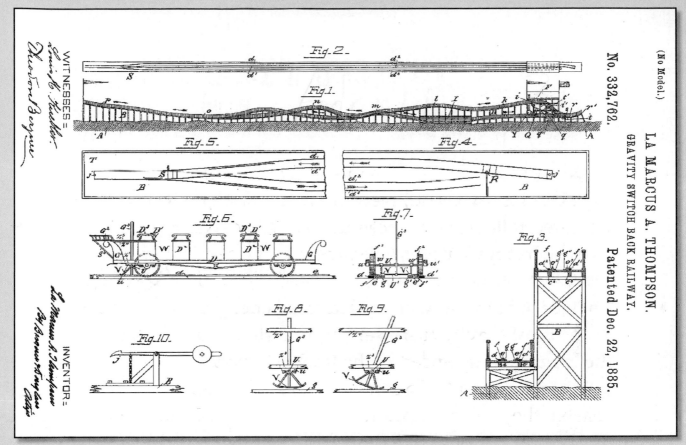

▲ LaMarcus Thompson's 1885 patent describes the materials and design of the *Gravity Switchback Railway.*

▲ Thompson designed many other coasters. This is a drawing from his patent for the *Pleasure Cable Railway.*

Sharing Ideas

1. **READING CHECK** Where was the *Gravity Switchback Railway* located?

2. **WRITE ABOUT IT** What force did Thompson's roller coaster use to move?

3. **TALK ABOUT IT** Discuss how it may have felt to ride on the first gravity-powered roller coaster.

What Are Simple Machines?

Why It Matters...

Is this girl using a machine? You might not think so, but the wheelbarrow she is using is a simple machine. The long handles make it easier for her to lift the heavy load. Simple machines make tasks easier by changing forces.

PREPARE TO INVESTIGATE

Inquiry Skill

Experiment When you experiment, you collect data that either supports a hypothesis or shows that it fails.

Materials

- large paper cup with holes at top
- rocks
- spool
- string
- pencil
- duct tape

Load Them Up
Procedure

STEP 1

1. **Collaborate** Work with a partner. Set a paper cup on the floor and fill it with rocks. Slide a spool onto a pencil. Tape one end of the pencil to the edge of a table. Drape a string over the spool.

2. **Hypothesize** In your *Science Notebook*, write a hypothesis about whether it will be easier to lift the cup of rocks by hand or by using the string and spool.

STEP 4

3. **Experiment** Using only your hands, lift the cup of rocks from the floor to the spool. Observe how much effort you use to lift the rocks. Record observations.

4. **Experiment** Attach one end of the string to the cup as shown. Set the cup on the floor again. Slowly pull on the other end of the string to lift the cup all the way up. Observe your effort. Record your observations.

STEP 4

Conclusion

1. **Analyze Data** In which direction did you pull when you lifted the rocks by hand? In which direction did you pull when you used the string and spool?

2. **Compare** Was it easier to lift the cup of rocks with your hands or with the string and spool?

Investigate More!

Be an Inventor Design a machine that makes lifting the cup of rocks even easier. What parts will the machine have? How will it move? How will you control it? Draw a picture of your machine.

Simple Machines

MAIN IDEA Simple machines make work easier by changing the strength or direction of a force.

READING SKILL

Classify Use a chart to classify simple machines by the way they change a force. They may change the strength of a force, the direction of a force, or both.

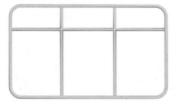

Machines and Work

What do you think of when you hear the word *machine*? Maybe you think of huge machines on farms or in factories. Perhaps you picture many gears and other moving parts. Did you know that some machines are very small and do not have any moving parts? A machine is any tool that makes work easier. In science, the word *work* has a special meaning. **Work** is the movement of an object by a force. A **simple machine** is a device that makes work easier. A simple machine changes the force that is needed to move an object. It changes the strength of the force or its direction.

This girl uses a hammer to do work. The force of the hammer moves the nail. ▶

upward force

downward force

fulcrum

A lever changes the strength and direction of a force.

Using the hammer as a lever makes it easier to pull the nail from the wood.

Lever

Do you think you could pull a nail out of wood using only your fingers? It would be hard to do. But it is easy to pull out a nail using a hammer. A hammer can be used as a simple machine called a lever (LEHV ur). A **lever** is a simple machine made up of a stiff arm that can move freely around a fixed point. The fixed point of a lever is called the fulcrum (FUL kruhm). You apply a weak force to the handle of the hammer. The lever changes the weak force on the handle to a strong force on the nail. It also changes the direction of the force. These changes in the strength and direction of the force make it easier to remove the nail.

▶ **CLASSIFY** What type of simple machine is a hammer when it is used to remove a nail?

Wheel and Axle

How do you open a door? You turn a doorknob, which moves the latch, and the door opens. The doorknob makes it easy to move the door latch.

A doorknob is a simple machine called a wheel and axle (AK suhl). A **wheel and axle** is a simple machine made up of a small cylinder, or axle, attached to the center of a larger wheel. On a doorknob, the knob is the wheel and the shaft is the axle. A wheel and axle makes work easier by increasing the strength of a force. When you apply a weak force to the wheel, it changes to a strong force on the axle. Other devices that contain wheels and axles include faucets and steering wheels.

weak force

strong force

A wheel and axle changes the strength of a force but not its direction.

A doorknob is a wheel and axle. Applying a weak force to the knob (wheel) creates a strong force on the shaft (axle). ▶

Pulley

The man is lifting a birdfeeder into the tree with another simple machine, a pulley (PUL ee). A **pulley** is a simple machine made up of a rope fitted around a fixed wheel. A pulley changes the direction of a force. You apply a force in one direction. Then the pulley changes it to an equal force in the opposite direction.

Pulleys and other simple machines can be combined to make complex (kuhm PLEHKS) machines. For example, a bicycle contains pulleys, wheels and axles, and levers.

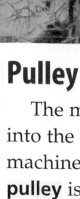 **CLASSIFY** What type of simple machine that contains a wheel would you use to change the direction of a force?

downward force

upward force

A pulley changes the direction of a force but not its strength.

The man pulls down on the rope of the pulley. In which direction does the birdfeeder move?

Inclined Plane

Movers often use a ramp to move heavy objects up to the level of a truck. A ramp is a type of simple machine called an inclined plane (ihn KLYND). An **inclined plane** is a simple machine made up of a slanted surface. Using an inclined plane makes it easier to move a heavy object to a higher position. Movers could use a stronger force to lift a heavy object straight up. By pushing the object up an inclined plane, they use a weaker force over a longer distance.

strong force

weak force

An inclined plane changes both the strength and the direction of a force.

Wedge

A **wedge** (wehj) is a simple machine made up of two inclined planes. Like the ax shown here, a wedge has a pointed end and a wide end. A wedge is used to cut or split objects. When you use a wedge, you apply a downward force to the wide end. The slanted sides change the downward force to sideward forces. This splits the object into two pieces.

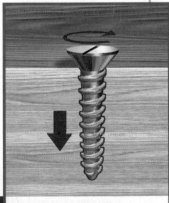

A wedge changes a downward force to an outward force.

Screw

A **screw** (skroo) is a simple machine made up of an inclined plane wrapped around a column. Screws are used to attach boards and other objects. When you turn a screw, the inclined plane moves the column up or down. You apply a weak circular (SUR kyuh luhr) force to the screw. The screw changes the force to a strong downward or upward force. This makes it easy to move the screw into a hard material, such as a wooden board.

▶ **CLASSIFY** What two simple machines are made up of one or more inclined planes?

A screw changes a weak circular force to a strong downward or upward force.

Visual Summary

Work is the movement of an object by a force. Simple machines change the needed force.

Simple machines include levers, wheels and axles, and pulleys.

Inclined planes, wedges, and screws are also simple machines.

LINKS for Home and School

WRITING **Narrative** Keep a log of your activities for one whole day. What machines did you use or encounter? Think about how machines work and how objects are held together. In your log, circle at least one example of each kind of simple machine.

SOCIAL STUDIES Make a Poster

Make a poster showing one real-life example of each simple machine (lever, wheel and axle, pulley, inclined plane, wedge, and screw). For each example, draw a simple diagram using one or more plane or solid figures. Label each diagram.

Review

① **MAIN IDEA** What do simple machines do?

② **VOCABULARY** Define the term *work* as scientists use it.

③ **READING SKILL:** **Classify** Which type of simple machine would you use to pry the lid off a can of paint?

④ **CRITICAL THINKING:** **Synthesize** Movers use ramps to move heavy objects. What simple machine are they using?

⑤ **INQUIRY SKILL: Experiment** Design an experiment in which you compare the effort needed to do work using a wheel and axle with the effort needed to do the same work without this simple machine.

✓ TEST PREP

A simple machine made up of an inclined place wrapped around a column is a _____.

A. pulley.

B. screw.

C. lever.

D. wedge.

 Technology
Visit **www.eduplace.com/scp/** to investigate more about simple machines.

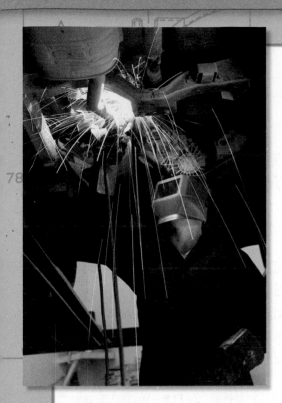

Automotive Mechanics

Even with regular service, most cars need repairs sooner or later. That's why automotive mechanics are always in demand. It is their job to keep cars running well. Automotive mechanics have to keep up with new technology.

What It Takes!
- A high-school diploma
- Courses in automotive repair
- On-the-job training

Mechanical Engineer

Mechanical engineers design, test, and improve all types of machines. They work on machines that produce power, such as engines and generators. They also work on machines that use power—from cake mixers to toys.

What It Takes!
- A degree in mechanical engineering
- Drafting, drawing, design, and problem-solving skills
- Knowledge of computer systems

Power Pitch

Strike one! Strike two! Could you hit a fast pitch coming at you at 70 miles an hour? You'd have to if you were playing against Jennie Finch. She was the star pitcher for the United States' gold medal Olympic women's softball team.

What makes Jennie's pitches come screaming across the plate so fast? It's the kinetic energy Jennie puts into throwing the ball. Her wrist, arm, shoulder, hips, and legs all move in just such a way to transfer as much kinetic energy to the ball as possible. You can see how much of her body she uses in the wind-up. **Strike three—you're out!**

Did You Know?

The softball leaves Jennie's hand at 70 mph. The speed limit on most highways is 65 mph. Believe it or not, Jeannie's softball would beat a speeding car to home plate.

Vocabulary

Complete each sentence with a term from the list.

1. A simple machine made up of a rope fitted around a fixed wheel is a/an _____.

2. How fast or slow an object is moving is its _____.

3. The measure of how far an object has traveled is _____.

4. A simple machine made up of two inclined planes is a/an

5. A device with few parts that makes work easier by changing the strength or direction of a force is a/an _____.

6. When you use a force to move an object, you do _____.

7. A change in an object's position is called _____.

8. The path a moving object follows is its _____.

9. A simple machine that is a slanted surface is a/an _____.

10. An inclined plane wrapped around a column is a/an _____.

direction F83
distance F82
force F73
gravity F74
inclined plane F94
lever F91
motion F72
pulley F93
screw F95
simple machine F90
speed F84
wedge F95
wheel and axle F92
work F90

✔ Test Prep

Write the letter of the best answer choice.

11. Gravity and friction are examples of _____.

    A. motions.
    B. simple machines.
    C. forces.
    D. distances.

12. A simple machine made up of a stiff bar and a fixed point is a _____.

    A. wheel and axle.   C. wedge.
    B. pulley.   D. lever.

13. The force that pulls objects toward each other is _____.

    A. friction.
    B. gravity.
    C. magnetism.
    D. motion.

14. A simple machine that changes a weak circular force to a strong circular force is a(n) _____.

    A. pulley.   C. screw.
    B. wheel and axle.   D. inclined plane.

15. Predict You have two bar magnets. The poles on the first magnet are labeled *A* and *B*. The poles on the second magnet are labeled *C* and *D*. You bring the *A* end close to the *C* end, and the two magnets pull toward each other. Predict what will happen if you try to bring the *A* end toward the *D* end.

16. Communicate The table below shows the speed of each of five toy cars. Make a bar graph using the data.

Color of Car	Speed (meters in 1 minute)
Red	7
Blue	9
Green	5
Yellow	8
Orange	11

Map the Concept

Use the words below to label the diagram.

distance   speed
motion   force
direction

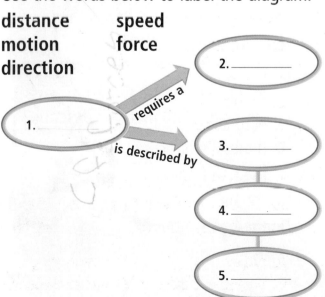

requires a

is described by

1. _____
2. _____
3. _____
4. _____
5. _____

17. Apply Your friend tells you how to get to her house from school. Her instructions tell you how far to go and which way to turn. Which description of motion is *not* included in her instructions?

18. Evaluate A friend says that a soccer ball stops rolling because the force of your kick stops acting on the ball. Is this statement correct? Why or why not?

19. Synthesize You have more potential energy after you climb to the top of a diving board than you have when you are on the ground. What force is acting on you to give you more potential energy at the top of the diving board?

20. Analyze The steering wheel of a car is part of a wheel and axle. The steering wheel is the wheel. Explain how turning the steering wheel a short distance affects the axle.

Performance Assessment

Show the Motion

Look in newspapers, in magazines, or on the Internet and find photographs of sporting events. Choose a photograph and make a poster. Label the forces, motions, and any simple machines that are used in that sporting event.

Write the letter of the best answer choice.

1. The Moon does not give off its own light. Why can you see the Moon?

   A. It bends light from the Sun.
   B. It reflects light from the Sun.
   C. It refracts light from the Sun.
   D. It absorbs light from the Sun.

2. A wheel and axle changes a weak force on the wheel to a strong force on the axle. Which shows a wheel and axle?

   A.

   B.

   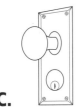
   C.

   D.

3. If you throw a ball straight up into the air, what sort of energy does it have at its HIGHEST point?

   A. potential energy
   B. chemical energy
   C. sound energy
   D. kinetic energy

4. When you turn on a lamp you change _____ .

   A. light energy to electrical energy.
   B. kinetic energy to potential energy.
   C. electrical energy to light energy.
   D. light energy to chemical energy.

5. Which force on the rough tip of an ice skate's blade makes a skater stop?

   A. energy
   B. friction
   C. gravity
   D. magnetism

6. A ball player hits a ball 120 meters. Which does "120 meters" describe?

   A. the ball's direction
   B. the ball's speed
   C. the ball's distance
   D. the ball's motion

7. You see a shadow because _____ .

    A. some objects reflect light.

    B. some objects refract light.

    C. some objects block light.

    D. some objects let light pass through them.

8. Matt has four samples of the same liquid. The temperature of each sample is different. Which shows the particles in the COOLEST sample?

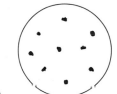

A.

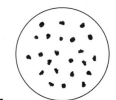

B.

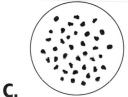

C.

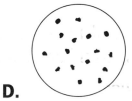

D.

Answer the following in complete sentences.

9. How does a plucked guitar string produce sound? Explain your answer.

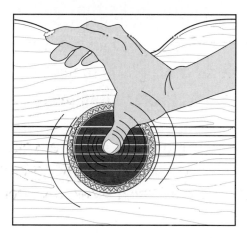

10. When sunlight passes through a prism, it forms a rainbow of colors. Explain why this happens.

Discover!

How a soccer ball moves is a result of the way the soccer player kicks that ball. Like all objects, a force must be applied for the soccer ball to move at all.

Kicking the ball provides the force that moves it. When a ball is kicked at its center, it moves forward in a straight line. When it is kicked to the left or right of its center, the ball's path curves to one side or the other. That's because kicking the ball left or right of its center causes the ball to spin. This spin causes the ball to move in a curved path.

Straight Path	**Curved Path**

Kicking the center of the soccer ball moves the ball forward in a straight line.	Kicking to the left or right of the soccer ball's center makes the path of the ball curve.

Kick a soccer ball that curves. Go to **www.eduplace.com/scp/** to learn to kick a ball in many directions.

Science and Math Toolbox

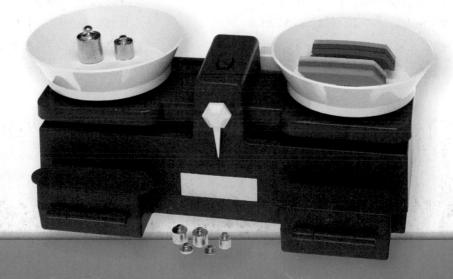

Using a Hand Lens

A hand lens is a tool that magnifies objects, or makes objects appear larger. This makes it possible for you to see details of an object that would be hard to see without the hand lens.

Look at a Coin or a Stamp

1. Place an object such as a coin or a stamp on a table or other flat surface.

STEP 1

2. Hold the hand lens just above the object. As you look through the lens, slowly move the lens away from the object. Notice that the object appears to get larger and a little blurry.

STEP 2

3. Move the hand lens a little closer to the object until the object is once again in sharp focus.

STEP 3

Making a Bar Graph

A bar graph helps you organize and compare data.

Make a Bar Graph of Animal Heights

Animals come in all different shapes and sizes. You can use the information in this table to make a bar graph of animal heights.

1 Draw the side and the bottom of the graph. Label the side of the graph as shown. The numbers will show the height of the animals in centimeters.

2 Label the bottom of the graph. Write the names of the animals at the bottom so that there is room to draw the bars.

3 Choose a title for your graph. Your title should describe the subject of the graph.

4 Draw bars to show the height of each animal. Some heights are between two numbers.

Heights of Animals

Animal	Height (cm)
Bear	240
Elephant	315
Cow	150
Giraffe	570
Camel	210
Horse	165

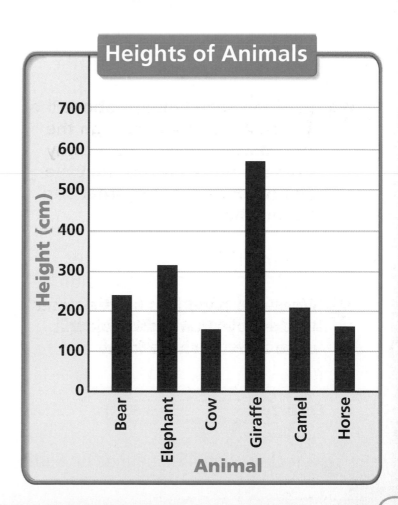

Heights of Animals

Using a Calculator

After you've made measurements, a calculator can help you analyze your data.

Add and Multiply Decimals

Suppose you're an astronaut. You may take 8 pounds of Moon rocks back to Earth. Can you take all the rocks in the table? Use a calculator to find out.

Weight of Moon Rocks	
Moon Rock	Weight of Rock on Moon (lb)
Rock 1	1.7
Rock 2	1.8
Rock 3	2.6
Rock 4	1.5

1. To add, press:

   [1] [.] [7] [+] [1] [.] [8] [+]
   [2] [.] [6] [+] [1] [.] [5] [=]

   Display: [7.6]

2. If you make a mistake, press the left arrow key and then the Clear key. Enter the number again. Then continue adding.

3. Your total is 7.6 pounds. You can take the four Moon rocks back to Earth.

4. How much do the Moon rocks weigh on Earth? Objects weigh six times as much on Earth as they do on the Moon. You can use a calculator to multiply.

   Press: [7] [.] [6] [×] [6] [=]

   Display: [45.6]

The rocks weigh 45.6 pounds on Earth.

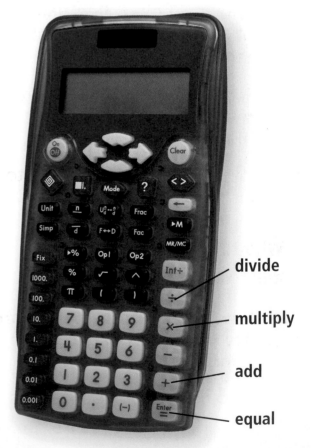

divide

multiply

add

equal

Making a Tally Chart

A tally chart can help you keep track of items you are counting. Sometimes you need to count many different items. It may be hard to count all of the items of the same type as a group. That's when a tally chart can be helpful.

Make a Tally Chart of Birds Seen

A group of bird watchers made a tally chart to record how many birds of each type they saw. Here are the tallies they have made so far.

- Every time you count one item, make one tally.

- When you reach five, draw the fifth tally as a line through the other four.

- To find the total number of robins, count by fives and then ones.

- You can use the tally chart to make a chart with numbers.

Birds Seen

Type of Bird	Tally
Cardinal	||
Blue jay	ⵌ ⵌ ⵌ
Mockingbird	||||
Hummingbird	ⵌ ||
House sparrow	ⵌ ⵌ ⵌ ⵌ |
Robin	ⵌ ⵌ ||

What kind of bird was seen most often?

- Now use a tally chart to record how many cars of different colors pass your school.

Birds Seen

Type of Bird	Number
Cardinal	2
Blue jay	15
Mockingbird	4
Hummingbird	7
House sparrow	21
Robin	12

Using a Tape Measure or Ruler

Tape measures and rulers are tools for measuring the length of objects and distances. Scientists most often use units such as meters, centimeters, and millimeters when making length measurements.

Use a Tape Measure

1. Measure the distance around a jar. Wrap the tape around the jar.

2. Find the line where the tape begins to wrap over itself.

3. Record the distance around the jar to the nearest centimeter.

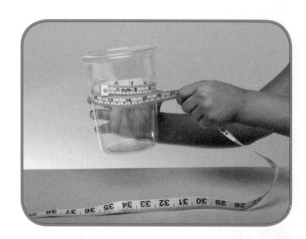

Use a Metric Ruler

1. Measure the length of your shoe. Place the ruler or the meterstick on the floor. Line up the end of the ruler with the heel of your shoe.

2. Notice where the other end of your shoe lines up with the ruler.

3. Look at the scale on the ruler. Record the length of your shoe to the nearest centimeter and to the nearest millimeter.

Measuring Volume

A beaker, a measuring cup, and a graduated cylinder are used to measure volume. Volume is the amount of space something takes up. Most of the containers that scientists use to measure volume have a scale marked in milliliters (mL).

Beaker
50 mL

Measuring cup
50 mL

Graduated cylinder
50 mL

Measure the Volume of a Liquid

1. **Measure the volume of juice.** Pour some juice into a measuring container.

2. Move your head so that your eyes are level with the top of the juice. Read the scale line that is closest to the surface of the juice. If the surface of the juice is curved up on the sides, look at the lowest point of the curve.

3. Read the measurement on the scale. You can estimate the value between two lines on the scale.

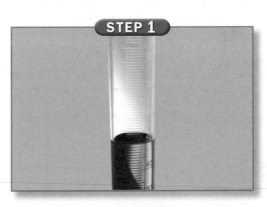

STEP 1

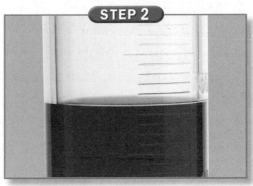

STEP 2

Using a Thermometer

A thermometer is used to measure temperature. When the liquid in the tube of a thermometer gets warmer, it expands and moves farther up the tube. Different scales can be used to measure temperature, but scientists usually use the Celsius scale.

Measure the Temperature of a Liquid

1. Half fill a cup with warm tap water.

2. Hold the thermometer so that the bulb is in the center of the liquid. Be sure that there are no bright lights or direct sunlight shining on the bulb.

3. Wait a few minutes until you see the liquid in the tube of the thermometer stop moving. Read the scale line that is closest to the top of the liquid in the tube. The thermometer shown reads 22°C (72°F).

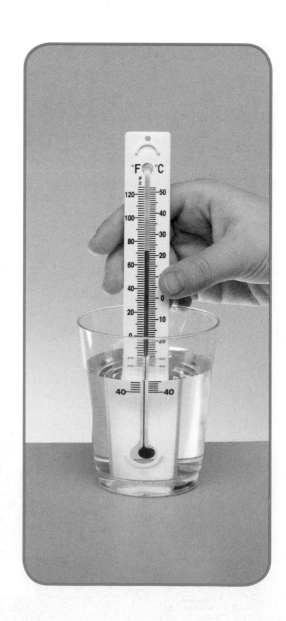

Using a Balance

A balance is used to measure mass. Mass is the amount of matter in an object. To find the mass of an object, place it in the left pan of the balance. Place standard masses in the right pan.

Measure the Mass of a Ball

1 Check that the empty pans are balanced, or level with each other. When balanced, the pointer on the base should be at the middle mark. If it needs to be adjusted, move the slider on the back of the balance a little to the left or right.

2 Place a ball on the left pan. Then add standard masses, one at a time, to the right pan. When the pointer is at the middle mark again, each pan holds the same amount of matter and has the same mass.

3 Add the numbers marked on the masses in the pan. The total is the mass of the ball in grams.

Making a Chart to Organize Data

A chart can help you keep track of information. When you organize information, or data, it is easier to read, compare, or classify it.

Classifying Animals

Suppose you want to organize this data about animal characteristics. You could base the chart on the two characteristics listed—the number of wings and the number of legs.

1 Give the chart a title that describes the data in it.

2 Name categories, or groups, that describe the data you have collected.

3 Make sure the information is recorded correctly in each column.

Next, you could make another chart to show animal classification based on number of legs only.

My Data

Fleas have no wings. Fleas have six legs.

Snakes have no wings or legs.

A bee has four wings. It has six legs.

Spiders never have wings. They have eight legs.

A dog has no wings. It has four legs.

Birds have two wings and two legs.

A cow has no wings. It has four legs.

A butterfly has four wings. It has six legs.

Animals–Number of Wings and Legs

Animal	Number of Wings	Number of Legs
Flea	0	6
Snake	0	0
Bee	4	6
Spider	0	8
Dog	0	4
Bird	2	2
Butterfly	4	6

Reading a Circle Graph

A circle graph shows a whole divided into parts. You can use a circle graph to compare the parts to each other. You can also use it to compare the parts to the whole.

A Circle Graph of Fuel Use

This circle graph shows fuel use in the United States. The graph has 10 equal parts, or sections. Each section equals $\frac{1}{10}$ of the whole. One whole equals $\frac{10}{10}$.

Oil Of all the fuel used in the United States, 4 out of 10 parts, or $\frac{4}{10}$, is oil.

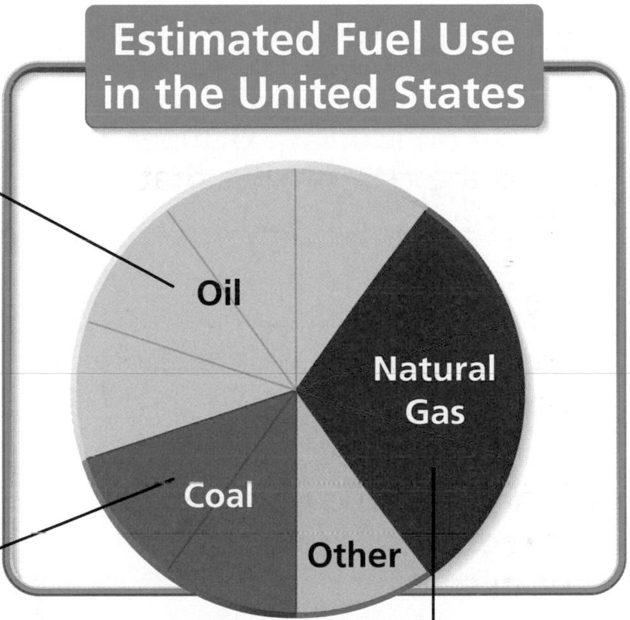

Estimated Fuel Use in the United States

Oil

Natural Gas

Coal

Other

Coal Of all the fuel used in the United States, 2 out of 10 parts, or $\frac{2}{10}$, is coal.

Natural Gas Of all the fuel used in the United States, 3 out of 10 parts, or $\frac{3}{10}$, is natural gas.

Measuring Elapsed Time

A calendar can help you find out how much time has passed, or elapsed, in days or weeks. A clock can help you see how much time has elapsed in hours and minutes. A clock with a second hand or a stopwatch can help you find out how many seconds have elapsed.

Using a Calendar to Find Elapsed Days

This is a calendar for the month of October. October has 31 days. Suppose it is October 22 and you begin an experiment. You need to check the experiment two days from the start date and one week from the start date. That means you would check it on Wednesday, October 24, and again on Monday, October 29. October 29 is 7 days after October 22.

Days of the Week

Monday, Tuesday, Wednesday, Thursday, and Friday are weekdays. Saturday and Sunday are weekends.

Last Month

Last month ended on Sunday, September 30.

October

Sunday	Monday	Tuesday	Wednesday	Thursday	Friday	Saturday
	1	2	3	4	5	6
7	8	9	10	11	12	13
14	15	16	17	18	19	20
21	22	23	24	25	26	27
28	29	30	31			

Next Month

Next month begins on Thursday, November 1.

Using a Clock or a Stopwatch to Find Elapsed Time

You need to time an experiment for 20 minutes.

It is 1:30 P.M.   **Stop at 1:50 P.M.**

You need to time an experiment for 15 seconds. You can use the second hand of a clock or watch.

Start the experiment when the second hand is on number 6.

Stop when 15 seconds have passed and the second hand is on the 9.

You can use a stopwatch to time 15 seconds.

Press the reset button on a stopwatch so that you see 0:00₀₀.

Press the start button. When you see 0:15₀₀, press the stop button.

Measurements

Volume

1 L of sports drink is a little more than 1 qt.

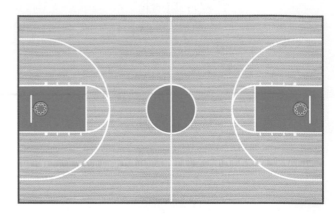

Area

A basketball court covers about 4,700 ft². It covers about 435 m².

Metric Measures

Temperature

- Ice melts at 0 degrees Celsius (°C)
- Water freezes at 0°C
- Water boils at 100°C

Length and Distance

- 1,000 meters (m) = 1 kilometer (km)
- 100 centimeters (cm) = 1 m
- 10 millimeters (mm) = 1 cm

Force

- 1 newton (N) =
  1 kilogram × 1(meter/second)
  per second

Volume

- 1 cubic meter (m³) = 1 m × 1 m × 1 m
- 1 cubic centimeter (cm³) =
  1 cm × 1 cm × 1 cm
- 1 liter (L) = 1,000 milliliters (mL)
- 1 cm³ = 1 mL

Area

- 1 square kilometer (km²) =
  1 km × 1 km
- 1 hectare = 10,000 m²

Mass

- 1,000 grams (g) = 1 kilogram (kg)
- 1,000 milligrams (mg) = 1 g

Temperature

The temperature at an indoor basketball game might be 27°C, which is 80°F.

Length and Distance

A basketball rim is about 10 ft high, or a little more than 3 m from the floor.

Customary Measures

Temperature

- Ice melts at 32 degrees Fahrenheit (°F)
- Water freezes at 32°F
- Water boils at 212°F

Length and Distance

- 12 inches (in.) = 1 foot (ft)
- 3 ft = 1 yard (yd)
- 5,280 ft = 1 mile (mi)

Weight

- 16 ounces (oz) = 1 pound (lb)
- 2,000 pounds = 1 ton (T)

Volume of Fluids

- 8 fluid ounces (fl oz) = 1 cup (c)
- 2 c = 1 pint (pt)
- 2 pt = 1 quart (qt)
- 4 qt = 1 gallon (gal)

Metric and Customary Rates

km/h = kilometers per hour

m/s = meters per second

mph = miles per hour

Health and Fitness Handbook

Health means more than just not being ill. There are many parts to health. Here are some questions you will be able to answer after reading this handbook.

- How do my body systems work?
- What nutrients does my body need?
- How does being active help my body?
- How can I be safe at home?
- How can I prevent food from making me ill?

The Digestive System

Your digestive system breaks down food into materials your body can use. These materials are called nutrients.

1 Digestion starts in your mouth.
- Your teeth break food into small pieces. Saliva mixes with the food. Saliva has chemicals that break down food more.
- Your tongue pushes the chewed food into your esophagus when you swallow.

2 Food travels through the esophagus to the stomach.
- Acid and other chemicals in the stomach break down the food even more.
- The food moves to the small intestine.

3 More chemicals flow into the small intestine. They come from the liver, pancreas, and other organs.
- These chemicals finish breaking down the food into nutrients.
- The nutrients are absorbed into the blood.
- The blood carries the nutrients to all parts of the body.

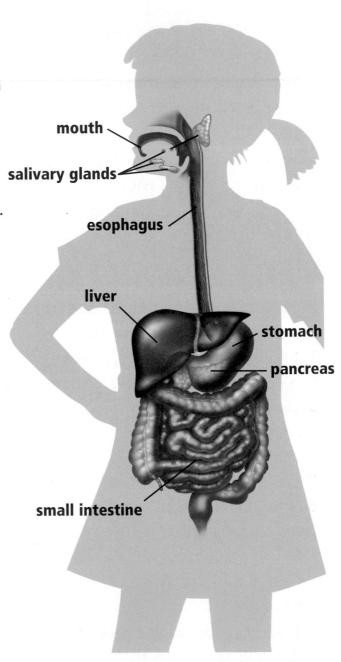

mouth

salivary glands

esophagus

liver

stomach

pancreas

small intestine

The Circulatory System

Your circulatory system moves blood through your body. There are three major parts to the circulatory system: the heart, blood vessels, and blood.

Heart Your heart has four chambers, or sections.

- The right two chambers take blood from the body and pump it to the lungs.
- There, the blood picks up oxygen and gets rid of waste.
- The left two chambers take blood from the lungs and pump it to the rest of the body.

Blood Vessels Two kinds of vessels carry blood through your body.

- **Arteries** carry blood from the heart to the body.
- **Veins** carry blood from the body to the heart.

Blood Your blood carries oxygen from your lungs to your body cells.

- Blood carries nutrients from your digestive system.
- Blood carries wastes away from the cells to organs that remove the wastes from the body.

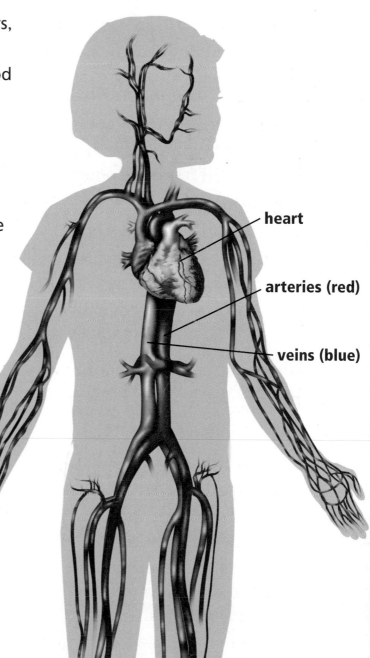

heart

arteries (red)

veins (blue)

Some Nutrients You Need

Nutrients are materials your body needs for energy and to grow. Three important nutrients are proteins, carbohydrates, and fats. Eating these nutrients in the right amount can help you stay at a healthful weight.

Proteins

Uses Your body uses proteins to build new cells and for cell activities. You need proteins to grow and develop.

Sources meat, chicken, fish, milk, cheese, nuts, beans, eggs

Fats

Uses Your body uses fat to store energy. You need to eat only a small amount of fat, because your body makes some on its own.

Sources oils and butter

Carbohydrates

Uses Carbohydrates are your body's main source of energy. Simple carbohydrates give quick energy. Complex carbohydrates give long-lasting energy. Complex carbohydrates should make up the largest part of your diet.

Sources simple carbohydrates: fruits and milk products

complex carbohydrates: whole-grain bread, cereal, pasta, potatoes

carbohydrate   fat   protein

Kinds of Physical Activity

Do you run, jump, and play every day? There are different kinds of physical activity. Each helps your body in a different way.

Endurance

Some activities help your body work hard for longer periods of time.

Activities That Build Endurance

- swimming
- jumping rope
- soccer
- in-line skating
- riding a bike
- walking fast
- basketball
- hockey

Do one of these activities for 20 to 60 minutes three to five times a week.

Flexibility

Stretching helps your muscles move smoothly.

Activities That Build Flexibility

- touching your toes
- stretching your arms
- sit and reach
- stretching your side

Do flexibility exercises two to three times a week.

Strength

These exercises make your muscles stronger. Ask an adult to show you how to do them safely.

Activities That Build Strength

- sit-ups
- push-ups
- pull-ups

Do strength training two to three days each week.

Home Safety Checklists

Most accidents happen at home. Here are some tips for staying safe.

Fire Safety

✔ Have smoke detectors. Check the batteries twice each year.

✔ Don't play with matches or candles.

✔ Only use the stove or oven if an adult is there.

✔ Have a family fire plan. Practice your plan.

Poison Safety

✔ Some chemicals and cleaners are poisons. So are some medicines. Keep them in high places away from small children.

✔ Post the phone number for Poison Control by the phone.

Kitchen Safety

✔ Never leave the kitchen while cooking.

✔ Store knives out of the reach of children.

✔ Wipe up spills immediately. Keep the floor clear of clutter.

Electrical Safety

✔ Keep electrical cords out of areas where someone could trip on them.

✔ Don't use electrical appliances near water.

✔ Unplug small appliances when you are not using them.

✔ Make sure electric cords are not damaged. They could start a fire.

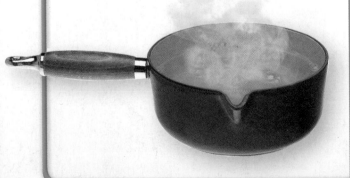

Food Safety

Foods and drinks can carry germs. These germs can cause disease. Remember these four steps to keep food safe.

Clean

✔ Wash your hands before and after you cook. Wash them again if you handle raw meat, poultry, or fish.

✔ Wash all the dishes and utensils you use.

✔ Wash your hands before you eat.

Separate

✔ Keep raw meat, poultry, and fish away from other foods.

✔ Keep cooked food away from raw food.

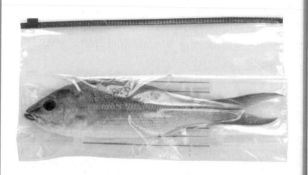

Chill

✔ Some foods need to be kept cold. Put leftovers in the refrigerator as soon as possible. This slows down the growth of germs.

✔ If you are having a picnic, keep foods in an icechest until you are ready to cook or serve them

Cook

✔ Cook food thoroughly. Cooking kills many germs.

✔ Use a thermometer to make sure foods are hot enough.

Glossary

A

adaptation (ad ap TAY shuhn) A behavior or a body part that helps a living thing survive in its environment. (B22)

alloy (AL oy) A solid solution made of at least one metal. (E55)

alternate energy resource (AWL tur niht EHN ur jee REE sawrs) An energy resource other than a fossil fuel. (C52)

amphibian (am FIHB ee uhn) A vertebrate that starts life in the water and then lives on land as an adult. (A40)

analyze data (AN uh lyz DAY tuh) To look for patterns in collected information that lead to making logical inferences, predictions, and hypotheses.

aquatic habitat (uh KWAT ihk HAB ih tat) A place where organisms live in or on water. (B60)

arthropod (AHR thruh pahd) An invertebrate that has jointed legs, a body with two or more sections, and a hard outer covering. (A48)

ask questions (ask KWEHS chuhz) To state orally or in writing questions to find out how or why something happens, which can lead to scientific investigations or research.

asteroid (AS tuh royd) A piece of rock that orbits the Sun. (D48)

atmosphere (AT muh sfihr) The layers of air that cover Earth's surface. (D14)

axis (AK sihs) An imaginary line through the center of an object. (D68)

B

backbone (BAK bohn) A series of bones that runs down the back of a vertebrate animal. (A36)

behavior (bih HAYV yur) The way that an organism typically acts in a certain situation. (B22)

bird (burd) A vertebrate that has feathers, lungs, wings, and two legs and lays eggs that have hard shells. (A38)

C

carnivore (KAHR nuh vawr) An animal that eats only other animals. (B51)

cell (sehl) The smallest and most basic unit of a living thing. (A8, B45)

chemical change (KEHM ih kuhl chaynj) A change in matter in which one or more new kinds of matter form. (E23)

chemical property (KEHM ih kuhl PRAHP ur tee) A property that describes how matter can react with other kinds of matter. (E22)

chrysalis (KRIHS uh lihs) The hard case an insect forms to protect itself during the pupa stage. (A76)

classify (KLAS uh fy) To sort objects into groups according to their properties or order objects according to a pattern.

climate (KLY miht) The average weather conditions in an area over a long period of time. (D25)

collaborate (kuh LAB uh rayt) To work as a team with others to collect and share data, observations, findings, and ideas.

communicate (kah MYOO nuh kayt) To explain procedures or share information, data, or findings with others through written or spoken words, actions, graphs, charts, tables, diagrams, or sketches.

community (kuh MYOO nih tee) A group of plants and animals that live in the same area and interact with each other. (B15)

compare (kuhm PAIR) To observe and tell how objects or events are alike or different.

condensation (kahn dehn SAY shuhn) The change of state from gas to liquid. (D7)

condense (kuhn DEHNS) To change state from gas to liquid. (E15)

conifer (KAHN uh fur) A plant that makes seeds inside cones. (A72)

conservation (kahn suhr VAY shuhn) The safe-keeping and wise use of natural resources. (C62)

constellation (kahn stuh LAY shuhn) A group of stars that forms a pattern shaped like an animal, person, or object. (D86)

consumer (kuhn SOO mur) An organism that gets energy by eating other living things. (B51)

core (kohr) The innermost layer of Earth. (C14)

crater (KRAY tur) A bowl-shaped dent caused when an object from space strikes the surface of a planet or a moon. (D78)

crest (krehst) The highest point of a wave. (F15)

crust (kruhst) The thin, outermost layer of Earth. (C14)

data (DAY tuh) Information collected and analyzed in scientific investigations. (S3)

direction (di REHK shuhn) The path an object follows. (F83)

dissolve (dih ZAHLV) To mix completely with another substance to form a solution. (E52)

distance (DIHS tuhns) A measure of length. (F82)

earthquake (URTH kwayk) A sudden movement of large sections of Earth's crust. (C21)

ecosystem (EE koh SIHS tuhm) All of the living and nonliving things that exist and interact in one place. (B10)

electric circuit (ih LEHK trihk SUR kiht) A path around which electric current can flow. (F29)

electric current (ih LEHK trihk KUR uhnt) The flow of charged particles. (F28)

endangered species (ehn DAYN jurd SPEE sheez) A species that has so few members that it may soon become extinct. (A60)

energy (EHN ur jee) The ability to cause change. (B7)

environment (ehn VY ruhn muhnt) All the living and nonliving things that surround and affect an organism. (A24, B10)

equator (ih KWAY tuhr) An imaginary line around the Earth, halfway between the North Pole and the South Pole. (D26)

erosion (ih ROH zhuhn) The process of carrying weathered rock from one place to another. (C31)

evaporate (ih VAP uh rayt) To change state slowly from liquid to gas. (E15)

evaporation (ih vap uh RAY shuhn) The change of state from liquid to gas. (D7)

experiment (ihks SPEHR uh muhnt) To investigate and collect data that either supports a hypothesis or shows that it is false while controlling variables and changing only one part of an experimental setup at a time.

extinct species (ihk STIHNGKT SPEE sheez) A species that has disappeared. (A57)

filter (FIHL tur) A device or material that traps some substances and allows others to pass through. (E44)

fish (fihsh) A vertebrate that lives in water and uses gills to take oxygen from water. (A39)

food chain (food chayn) The path that energy takes through a community as one living thing eats another. (B50)

force (fawrs) A push or a pull. (F73)

fossil (FAHS uhl) The very old remains of a plant or animal. (A56, C22)

fossil fuel (FAHS uhl FYOO uhl) A fuel that forms over a very long time from the remains of plants and animals. (C50)

freeze (freez) To change state from liquid to solid. (E15)

friction (FRIHK shuhn) A force that occurs when one object rubs against another object. (F45)

fruit (froot) The part of a plant that contains the seeds. (A70)

full moon (ful moon) The phase of the Moon when all of the Moon's sunlit side faces Earth. (D75)

gas (gas) Matter that has no definite shape and does not take up a definite amount of space. (E7)

geothermal energy (jee oh THUR muhl EHN ur jee) Heat from inside Earth. (C52)

gravity (GRAV ih tee) A force that pulls objects toward each other. (F74)

habitat (HAB ih tat) The place where an organism lives. (A57, B32)

heat (heet) The flow of thermal energy from warmer objects to cooler objects. (F42)

herbivore (HUR buh vawr) An animal that eats only plants. (B51)

humus (HYOO muhs) The decayed remains of plants and animals. (C32)

hydroelectric energy (hy droh ih LEHK trihk EHN ur jee) Electricity made from the force of moving water. (C52)

hypothesize (hy PAHTH uh syz) To make an educated guess about why something happens.

igneous rock (IHG nee uhs rahk) Rock that forms when melted rock from inside Earth cools and hardens. (C18)

inclined plane (ihn KLYND playn) A simple machine made up of a slanted surface. (F94)

individual (ihn duh VIHJ oo uhl) A single member of a species. (A86)

infer (ihn FUR) To use facts and data you know and observations you have made to draw a conclusion about a specific event based on observations and data. To construct a reasonable explanation.

inner planets (IHN ur PLAN ihts) The four planets closest to the Sun: Mercury, Venus, Earth, and Mars. (D46)

invertebrate (ihn VUR tuh briht) An animal that does not have a backbone. (A46)

kinetic energy (kuh NET ihk EHN ur jee) Energy of motion. (F8)

landform (LAND fawrm) A part of Earth's surface that has a certain shape and is formed naturally. (C8)

larva (LAHR vuh) The second, worm-like stage in an insect's life cycle. (A76)

latitude (LAT ih tood) The distance north or south of the equator. (D26)

leaf (leef) The part of a plant that collects sunlight and gases from the air and uses them to make food for the plant. (A8)

lever (LEHV ur) A simple machine made up of a stiff arm that can move freely around a fixed point. (F91)

life cycle (lyf SY kuhl) The series of changes that a living thing goes through during its lifetime. (A70)

light (lyt) A form of energy that you can see. (F58)

liquid (LIHK wihd) Matter that takes the shape of its container and takes up a definite amount of space. (E7)

magnify (MAG nuh fy) To make an object appear larger. (D38)

mammal (MAM uhl) A vertebrate that has hair or fur, produces milk for its young, and breathes air with its lungs. (A37)

mantle (MAN tl) The thick, middle layer of Earth. (C14)

mass (mas) The amount of matter in an object. (E9)

matter (MAT ur) Anything that has mass and takes up space. (E6)

measure (MEHZ uhr) To use a variety of measuring instruments and tools to find the length, distance, volume, mass, or temperature using appropriate units of measurement.

melt (mehlt) To change state from solid to liquid. (E15)

metamorphic rock (meht uh MAWR fihk rahk) Rock that forms when other rock is changed by heat and pressure. (C18)

mineral (MIHN ur uhl) A material that is found in nature and that has never been alive. (C16)

mixture (MIHKS chur) Matter that is made up of two or more substances or materials that are physically combined. (E35)

moon (moon) A small, rounded body that orbits a planet. (D45)

motion (MOH shuhn) A change in the position of an object. (F72)

natural resource (NACH ur uhl REE sawrs) A material from Earth that is useful to people. (C42)

netted veins (NEHT tihd vaynz) Veins that branch out from main veins. (A16)

new moon (noo moon) The phase of the Moon when the Moon is not visible from Earth because none of its sunlit side faces Earth. (D75)

nonrenewable resource (nahn rih NOO uh buhl REE sawrs) A natural resource that is in limited supply and that cannot be replaced or takes thousands of years to be replaced. (C44)

nutrient (NOO tree uhnt) A substance that living things need in order to survive and grow. (A7)

observe (UHB zuhrv) To use the senses and tools to gather or collect information and determine the properties of objects or events.

offspring (AWF sprihng) The living thing made when an animal reproduces. (A78)

omnivore (AHM nuh vawr) An animal that eats both plants and animals. (B51)

orbit (AWR biht) To move in a path, usually around a planet or a star. (D44)

ore (AWR) Rock that contains metal or other useful minerals. (C42)

organism (AWR guh nihz uhm) Any living thing. (B8)

outer planets (OW tur PLAN ihts) The five planets farthest from the Sun: Jupiter, Saturn, Uranus, Neptune, and Pluto. (D47)

parallel veins (PAR uh lehl vaynz) Veins that run in straight lines next to each other. (A16)

phases of the Moon (FAYZ ihz uhv thuh moon) The different ways the Moon looks throughout the month. (D76)

physical change (FIHZ ih kuhl chaynj) A change in the size, shape, or state of matter. (E14)

physical property (FIHZ ih kuhl PRAHP ur tee) A characteristic of matter that can be measured or observed with the senses. (E7)

pitch (pihch) How high or low a sound seems. (F18)

planet (PLAN iht) A large body in space that orbits a star. (D44)

plant (plant) A living thing that grows on land or in the water, cannot move from place to place, and usually has green leaves. (A6)

polar climate (POH lur KLY miht) A climate with long, cold winters and short, cool summers. (D27)

pollution (puh LOO shuhn) 1. Any harmful material in the environment. (B34); 2. The addition of harmful materials to the environment. (C60)

population (pahp yuh LAY shuhn) All the organisms of the same kind that live together in an ecosystem. (B14)

potential energy (puh TEHN shuhl EHN ur jee) Stored energy. (F8)

precipitation (prih sihp ih TAY shuhn) Any form of water that falls from clouds to Earth's surface. (D8)

predict (prih DIHKT) To state what you think will happen based on past experience, observations, patterns, and cause-and-effect relationships.

producer (pruh DOO sur) An organism that uses energy from the Sun to make its own food. (B51)

pulley (PUL ee) A simple machine made up of a rope fitted around a fixed wheel. (F93)

pupa (PYOO puh) The third stage of an insect's life cycle, during which it changes into an adult. (A76)

record data (rih KAWRD DAY tuh) To write (in tables, charts, journals), draw, audio record, video record, or photograph, to show observations.

recycle (ree SY kuhl) To collect old materials, process them, and use them to make new items. (C62)

reflect (rih FLEHKT) To bounce off. (F60)

refract (rih FRAKT) To bend. (F61)

renewable resource (rih NOO uh buhl REE sawrs) A natural resource that can be replaced by nature. (C44)

reproduce (ree proh DOOS) To make new living things of the same kind. (A26)

reptile (REHP tyl) A vertebrate that has dry, scaly skin and lays eggs on land. (A41)

research (rih SURCH) To learn more about a subject by looking in books, newspapers, magazines, CD-ROMs, searching the Internet, or asking science experts.

resource (REE sawrs) A material found in nature that is useful to organisms. (B15)

revolve (rih VAHLV) To move in a path around an object. (D68)

root (root) The part of a plant that takes in water and nutrients and provides support for the plant. (A8)

rotate (ROH tayt) To turn on an axis. (D68)

satellite (SAT l yt) Any object that revolves around a planet or other larger object. (D74)

scientific inquiry (sy uhn TIHF uhk ihn - KWIHR ee) The ways scientists ask and answer questions about the world, including investigating and experimenting. (S4)

screw (skroo) A simple machine made up of an inclined plane wrapped around a column. (F95)

sedimentary rock (sehd uh MEHN tuh ree rahk) Rock that forms when sediment is pressed together and hardens. (C18)

seed (seed) The first stage in the life cycle of most plants. (A70)

simple machine (SIHM puhl muh SHEEN) A tool with few parts that makes work easier. (F90)

soil (soyl) The loose material that covers much of Earth's surface. (C30)

solar energy (SOH lur EHN ur jee) The energy that comes from the Sun and provides Earth with light and heat. (B44)

solar system (SOH lur SIHS tuhm) The Sun and the planets, moons, and other objects that orbit the Sun. (D45)

solid (SAHL ihd) Matter that has a definite shape and takes up a definite amount of space. (E7)

solution (suh LOO shuhn) A special kind of mixture in which two or more substances are so evenly mixed that the separate parts cannot be seen. (E52)

space probe (spays prohb) A craft that explores outer space carrying instruments, but not people. (D58)

speed (speed) A measure of how fast or slow an object is moving. (F84)

star (stahr) A ball of hot gases that gives off light and other forms of energy. (D84)

stem (stehm) The part of a plant that holds up the leaves and carries water and nutrients through the plant. (A8)

substance (SUHB stuhns) A single kind of matter that has certain properties. (E34)

Sun (suhn) The nearest star to Earth. (D44)

tadpole (TAD pohl) The stage in a frog's life cycle when it hatches from the egg and has a long tail, gills, and no legs. (A77)

technology (tek NAHL uh jee) The tools people make and use and the things they build with tools. (S11)

telescope (TEHL ih skohp) A tool that makes distant objects appear larger and sharper. (D38)

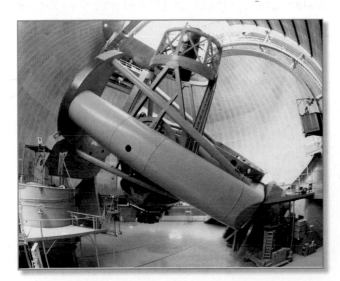

temperate climate (TEHM pur iht KLY miht) A climate with warm or hot summers and cool or cold winters. (D26)

temperature (TEHM pur uh chur) The measure of how hot or cold something is. (D16, F50)

terrestrial habitat (tuh REHS tree uhl HAB ih tat) A place where organisms live on land. (B62)

thermal energy (THUR muhl EHN ur jee) The energy of moving particles in matter. (F42)

thermometer (thur MAHM ih tur) A tool that is used to measure temperature. (F50)

tropical climate (TRAHP ih kuhl KLY miht) A climate that is very warm and wet for most of or all of the year. (D26)

trough (trawf) The lowest point of a wave. (F15)

use models (yooz MAHD lz) To use sketches, diagrams or other physical representations of an object, process, or idea to better understand or describe how it works.

use numbers (yooz NUHM burz) To use numerical data to count, measure, estimate, order, and record data to compare objects and events.

use variables (yooz VAIR ee uh buhlz) To keep all conditions in an experiment the same except for the variable, or the condition that is being tested in the experiment.

vein (vayn) A tube that carries food, water, and nutrients throughout a leaf. (A16)

vertebrate (VUR tuh briht) An animal that has a backbone. (A36)

vibrate (VY brayt) To move back and forth quickly. (F16)

volume (VAHL yoom) 1. The amount of space that matter takes up. (E9); 2. How loud or soft a sound seems. (F19)

water cycle (WAH tur SY kuhl) The movement of water between the air and Earth as it changes state. (D8)

water vapor (WAH tur VAY pur) Water in the form of an invisible gas. (D6)

wave (wayv) A movement that carries energy from one place to another. (F14)

weather (WEHTH ur) The condition of the atmosphere at a certain place and time. (D16)

weathering (WEHTH ur ihng) The breaking up or wearing away of rock. (C30)

wedge (wehj) A simple machine made up of two inclined planes. (F95)

wheel and axle (hweel and AK suhl) A simple machine made up of a small cylinder, or axle, attached to the center of a larger wheel. (F92)

work (work) The movement of an object by a force. (F90)

Credits

Permission Acknowledgements

Excerpt from Deer, Moose, Elk, and Caribou, by Deborah Hodge, illustrated by Pat Stevens. Text Copyright © 1998 by Deborah Hodge. Illustrations copyright © 1998 by Pat Stevens. Reprinted by permission of Kids Can Press, Ltd., Toronto. Excerpt from The Wump World, by Bill Peet. Copyright © 1970 by Bill Peet. Reprinted by permission of Houghton Mifflin Company. Excerpt from Thunder and Lightning from How & Why Stories: World Tales Kids Can Read & Tell, by Martha Hamilton and Mitch Weiss. Copyright © 1999 Martha Hamilton and Mitch Weiss. Reprinted by permission of Marian Reiner on behalf of August House Publishers, Inc. Excerpt from Thunderstorms What is a Thunderstorm? from Hurricanes Have Eyes But Can't See, by Melvin and Gilda Berger. Copyright © 2003, 2004 by Melvin and Gilda Berger. Reprinted by permission of Scholastic Inc. Excerpt from Freckle Juice, by Judy Blume. Text copyright © 1971 by Judy Blume. Reprinted with the permission of Harold Ober Associates Incorporated and Simon & Schuster Books for Young Readers, an imprint of Simon & Schuster Children's Publishing Division. Excerpt from Freckle Juice, by Judy Blume. Text copyright © 1971 by Judy Blume. Reprinted with the permission of Simon & Schuster Books for Young Readers, an imprint of Simon & Schuster Children's Publishing Division and Harold Ober Associates Incorporated.

Cover

(Toucan) © Steve Bloom/steve-bloom.com. (Rainforest bkgd) © Bill Brooks/Masterfile. (Back cover toucan) Masterfile Royalty Free (Spine) Natural Visions/Alamy.

Photography

Unit A Opener: Doug Perrine/Innerspace Visions/Seapics.com. A1 Michael S. Nolan/AGE Fotostock. A3 (tr) Burke/Triolo/Brand X/Picturequest. (br) Karl & Kay Amman/Bruce Coleman Inc. (lc) Grant Heilman Photography. A2–A3 (bkgd) Photo 24/Brand X. A6–A7 (b) Charles O'Rear/Corbis. (t) Terry W. Eggers/Corbis. A8 (r) © Phil Degginger/Color Pic, Inc. (c) © Dwight Kuhn. A9 (r) © Dwight Kuhn. (bc) Microfield Scientific LTD/Science Photo Library/Photo Researchers, Inc. A10 Melanie Acevedo/Botanica/Getty Images. A11 (tr) Peter Chadwick/DK Images. (br) Dave King/DK Images. A10–A11 (b) David M. Schleser/Nature's Images, Inc./Photo Researchers, Inc. A13 (t) Charles O'Rear/Corbis. (c) © Phil Degginger/Color Pic, Inc. A14 (bl) Judy White/Garden Photos. A14–A15 (bkgd) Roger Ressmeyer/Corbis. A16 (r) Neil Fletcher & Matthew Ward/DK Images. (l) Matthew Ward/DK Images. A17 (bl) Andrew McRobb/DK Images. (br) Nigel Cattlin/Holt Studios Int./Photo Researchers, Inc. (tl) Norman Owen Tomalin/Bruce Coleman, Inc. (tc) Neil Fletcher & Matthew Ward/DK Images. (tr) Ian O'Leary/DK Images. A18 (br) © Dwight Kuhn. (tl) ChromaZone Images/Index Stock Imagery. (tr) © E.R. Degginger/Color Pic, Inc. (bl) John Kaprielian/Photo Researchers, Inc. A19 (t) Matthew Ward/DK Images. (c) ChromaZone Images/Index Stock Imagery. (b) © Dwight Kuhn. A21 (cr) Dave King/DK Images. A20–A21 (bkgd) Bruce Dale/National Geographic/Getty Images. A22 (bl) © E.R. Degginger/Color Pic, Inc. A22–A23 (bkgd) Natural Selection Stock Photography. A24 (bl) Francois Gohier/Francois Gohier Nature Photography. (r) Michael & Patricia Fogden/Corbis. A25 (r) Michael Fogden/DRK Photo. (l) © E.R. Degginger/Color Pic, Inc. A26 (br) Angelo Cavalli/Superstock. (tl) © Dwight Kuhn. (bl) © Dave Kuhn/Dwight Kuhn Photography. A27 (c) Michael Fogden/DRK Photo. (t) Michael & Patricia Fogden/Corbis. (b) Angelo Cavalli/Superstock. A33 (t) A. & S. Carey/Masterfile. (c) Geoff Dann/DK Images. (b) Chip Clark/Smithsonian Museum of Natural History. A32–A33 (bkgd) Bios/Peter Arnold. A34 (bl) George Shelley/Masterfile. A35 (picture card, snake) GK Hart/Vikki Hart/Photodisc/Getty Images. (picture card, bird) GK Hart/Vikki Hart/Photodisc/Getty Images. A34–A35 (bkgd) Miep Van Damm/Masterfile. A36 Ernest Janes/Bruce Coleman, Inc. A37 (t) Tom & Dee Ann McCarthy/Corbis. (b) © E.R. Degginger/Color Pic, Inc. A38 (c) Mervyn Rees/Alamy Images. (b) Tom Tietz/Stone/Getty Images. (tl) Photri. A39 (bkgd) Jeff Greenberg/Photo Edit, Inc. A39 (tr) Jeff Hunter/The Image Bank/Getty Images. (t) Brandon Cole Marine Photography/Alamy Images. (c) Franklin Viola/Animals Animals. A40 (b) Frank Krahmer/Bruce Coleman, Inc. (tr) Gregory G. Dimijian/Photo Researchers, Inc. A41 (t) C.K. Lorenz/Photo Researchers, Inc. (b) Sidney Bahrt/Photo Researchers, Inc. (c) Gerry Ellis/Minden Pictures. A42 (tc) Daniel Zupanc/Bruce Coleman, Inc. (b) Art Wolfe/Getty Images. (c) Jeff Rotman/Photo Researchers, Inc. (t) Art Wolfe/Photo Researchers, Inc. (bc) Corbis. A44 (bl) Larry West/Bruce Coleman, Inc. A44–A45 (bkgd) Gary Meszaros/Dembinsky Photo Associates. A46 (c) I & K Stewart/Bruce Coleman, Inc. (bl) Christy Gavitt/DRK Photo. (br) Jett Britnell/DRK Photo. A47 (c) Carl Roessler/Bruce Coleman, Inc. (t) Grant

H41